T0354626

SUBMARINE OPERATIONAL
EFFECTIVENESS IN THE 20TH CENTURY

SUBMARINE OPERATIONAL EFFECTIVENESS

IN THE 20TH CENTURY

PART ONE (1900 – 1939)

CAPTAIN JOHN F. O'CONNELL, USN (RET.)

iUniverse, Inc.
New York Bloomington

Submarine Operational Effectiveness in the 20th Century Part One (1900 - 1939)

iUniverse books may be ordered through booksellers or by contacting:

iUniverse
1663 Liberty Drive
Bloomington, IN 47403
www.iuniverse.com
1-800-Authors (1-800-288-4677)

Because of the dynamic nature of the Internet, any Web addresses or links contained in this book may have changed since publication and may no longer be valid. The views expressed in this work are solely those of the author and do not necessarily reflect the views of the publisher, and the publisher hereby disclaims any responsibility for them.

ISBN: 978-1-4502-3689-8 (sc)
ISBN: 978-1-4502-3690-4 (ebk)

Printed in the United States of America

iUniverse rev. date: 06/14/2010

Dedicated to
the officers and men
of the U.S. Submarine Service
with whom I served from 1954 through 1976,
and particularly to the officers and men of
U. S. S. Spinax (SS-489)
which it was my privilege to command from
March 1966 to November 1967

Preface

The author served in the U.S. Submarine Service from 1954 through 1976, after graduation from the United States Naval Academy in 1952 and subsequent assignments in an aircraft carrier and a heavy cruiser. He served in five submarines, commanded USS Spinax (SS-489), Submarine Division Forty-One, and Submarine Group Hawaiian Area, the latter command coincident with primary duty as Assistant Chief of Staff for Operations, Plans and Intelligence (N 3) on Commander Submarine Force Pacific staff.

He went on to serve as Defense Attaché and Naval Attaché Tokyo before he retired from active service in 1982 after 30 years. His active duty period included eight deployments in surface ships and submarines to the Seventh Fleet in the Western Pacific during the period 1952 through 1967 as part of Cold War operations.

Hopefully the facts presented are correct, but the opinions and conclusions of the author are his alone, and therefore open to discussion and argument. One *caveat*:

the book is not encyclopedic in nature and will not touch on all or every class of submarine, however interesting because of its technical nature. The primary focus is on the demonstrated effectiveness of submarines in warfare.

The author has provided some maps of the various submarine/U-boat operating areas to assist the reader in following the story of submarine operations. Since he is not a cartographer by trade, the maps are merely rough approximations of the actual geography. No claims for damage by anyone attempting to use his maps for marine navigation will be entertained.

He previously authored three books on airpower in the 20th century. They are: *The Effectiveness of Airpower in the 20th Century, Part One (1914 – 1939); Part Two (1939 – 1945); and Part Three (1945 – 2000)*. All may be found on *Amazon.com* under the author's name.

CONTENTS

Introduction

Submarine Operational Effectiveness in the 20th Century is about the development of the submarine weapons system and focuses on its effective employment in warfare. This volume, Part One, deals with the period from 1900 to 1939 when World War Two began. It deals with early theory and practice of submarine warfare, and the demonstrated effectiveness of submarine operations during WW I and the Spanish Civil War. The description of submarine warfare includes antisubmarine measures adopted and used by the opposing side.

The discussion of submarine warfare theory in literature is fairly thin, although there are many books about submarines. Lacking accomplished snake-oil salesmen of the stature of General Gulio Douhet of Italy, Air Chief Marshall of the Royal Air Force HughTrenchard of Great Britain, or Brigadier General Billy Mitchell of the United States Army Air Service, naval submarine warfare theorists initially limited their dreams to breaking close-in naval blockades of ports.

Early exercises and maneuvers demonstrated that the first crude, limited range, submarines of the 20th century could "sink" major warships if they operated close to a port. Theorists did not envision the major threat to battle fleets at sea they would become, nor the antisubmarine warfare measures that their presence would require.

There is no clear record of anyone laying out, prior to WW I, the idea of a major anti-shipping campaign to be conducted by submarines. Submarines lacked the range and endurance to conduct "cruiser warfare". Cruiser warfare is the interdiction of enemy merchant ships, stopping them to check for contraband, and then either capturing them and sending them into a neutral port for adjudication, or sinking them after taking the crew and passengers aboard the capturing vessel.

The economic hardships imposed upon Germany in WW I by the British North Sea blockade directed German naval attention to the submarine as a way to retaliate. It soon became clear that a "restricted" submarine campaign could not promise the victory that had been denied German ground forces in France. However, if German U-boats were to abandon their observance of the Laws of War, and sink without warning all merchant ships entering a declared War Zone around Great Britain, the outcome might be different. It appeared that enough merchant ship tonnage could be sunk that the government of Great Britain would be forced to negotiate an end to its participation in the war.

With Great Britain thus disposed of, Germany could deal with the French.

Perhaps only Admiral Sir John "Jackie" Fisher, RN had the insight to realize the economic-military box the Germans were in as a result of the British blockade and to predict the means they would use to extricate themselves from it. He clearly foresaw the resumption of the unrestricted submarine campaign that Germany first used intermittently in 1915.

In late 1916, when the Kaiser realized that there was little hope of breaking the Western Front deadlock, he finally agreed to a German Navy proposal to reopen an unrestricted submarine campaign against all shipping. The German government was well aware of the threat of American intervention but calculated that it would be too late to be effective. Thus the first submarine strategic campaign of the 20th century began. Like the ineffective air strategic bombing campaigns of WW I it was focused upon forcing the defeat of the enemy. Unlike WWI strategic bombing campaigns, it was nearly successful in changing the course of the war.

Submarines were openly employed in hostilities during World War I (1914 – 1918). They also were employed although covertly, by Germany and Italy, during the Spanish Civil War (1936 – 1939). In 1940 Italy, although at peace with Greece, also covertly employed a submarine to sink a Greek cruiser that was anchored just offshore a Greek Aegean island, in an apparent attempt to provoke Greece into war.

During World War I Germany was nearly successful in forcing Great Britain to the negotiating table in late 1917 through an unrestricted campaign of sinking any ship found near the United Kingdom. German U-boats sank 6,196 allied and neutral ships during the war, totaling just over twelve million tons of shipping. The belated widespread introduction of merchant convoys by the British Admiralty in mid-1917, the ability to efficiently use neutral shipping to supplant lost UK merchant ships, and the addition of U.S. - built merchant ships successfully defended against the German submarine threat.

Antisubmarine warfare measures were developed from scratch and pursued energetically during WW I but had little effect on the unrestricted submarine campaign Germany was waging. The widespread introduction of convoys was the key to defeating German U-boats during WW I.[1]

The submarine story begins with the independent development of what became the primary submarine weapon, the automotive or self-propelled torpedo. Without the torpedo the submarine, a ship that could operate underwater, would have been a mere technical curiosity in military terms.

---

1   Defeat of the U-boats did not necessarily mean their destruction. It referred to the ability of threatened merchant ships to avoid attack and deliver their cargos successfully.

PART ONE

THE TORPEDO AND THE SUBMARINE

(1866 – 1900)

CHAPTER ONE –
THE WHITEHEAD TORPEDO[2]

The Whitehead torpedo was developed in 1866, well in advance of a practical machinery propelled submarine. It was a very significant weapon for use against the unprotected lower hull of large warships. Large caliber guns had been in place in warships for some years. As a result attention was paid to installing deck armor and side armor at or above the waterline to defeat their projectiles. Armor-piercing shells were then developed to pierce armor plate. However the below-water hull was not usually protected to the same degree.

Prior efforts to exploit this potential weakness included underwater rams, sticking out below the bow of the attacking ship, designed to make a large hole in the target which would then flood and sink. Rams were even employed in ancient times by relatively speedy row galleys.

---

2   The automotive (self-propelled) torpedo was absolutely key to the development of the submarine as a weapons system, hence is discussed first.

Later, after the introduction of gunpowder to Europe, spar torpedoes were developed to deliver a standoff explosive charge against the target's underwater hull.

Small fast torpedo boats were rapidly developed to deliver the Whitehead torpedo at close range, usually under cover of darkness or a smoke screen. In turn, batteries of rapid fire small caliber cannon and searchlights were installed on large warships to defend against torpedo boat attacks. By 1890 over nine hundred torpedo boats were in service in the five leading navies of the world. The torpedo had become a major threat.[3]

In 1891 during the Chilean Civil War, Chilean warship *Almirante Lynch* torpedoed and sank a rebel armored vessel, *Blanco Encalaba*, with a 14-inch diameter Whitehead torpedo delivered at the very close range of one hundred yards. Torpedo tubes were installed on large warships as well as in small fast torpedo boats. At the time maximum torpedo range was no more than one thousand yards. Both U.S. and Spanish warships in the Spanish-American War (1898) were equipped with torpedoes, and the Spanish naval torpedo boat arm was feared. USS Oregon and USS Olympia both had installed torpedo tubes. However the only damage inflicted by a torpedo during the Spanish-American War occurred when an American shell hit a loaded torpedo tube in the bow of

---

3   The United States Navy established a Torpedo Facility at Newport, R.I. in 1870

the Spanish cruiser *Vizcaya*, which exploded putting the ship out of action at the battle of Santiago in Cuba.

Robert Whitehead was an English engineer employed as manager of a metal foundry in Rjecka (Fiume) in Croatia, then part of Austria. A local engineer, Giovanni Luppis invented a self-propelled "torpedo". Luppis had recently retired from the Austrian Navy and moved to Trieste. In the early 1860s Luppis contracted with Whitehead to further develop Luppis' invention. Luppis' device was not an underwater shape as we know the torpedo today. Rather it was a small surface craft, containing an explosive charge, propelled by a clockwork motor. It was steered by an observer on shore, using tiller lines. Whitehead was impressed by the possibilities, but finally decided that the engineering problems were too difficult to solve. Whitehead and Luppis ended their partnership.

However Luppis' concept stuck in Whitehead's mind and several years later he set about to apply the general idea to a submerged body. Over several years he struggled to develop a submerged torpedo that could be powered by compressed air. In 1866 he submitted a design for testing by the Austrian Navy. The trials revealed shortcomings. Whitehead returned to the drawing board and continued his development work.[4]

By 1870 Whitehead had boosted the torpedo speed to 7 knots (13 km/hr) and its range to 700 yards (640 m). He developed a mechanism to allow the torpedo to maintain a

---

4   Gray, The Devil's Device, pp. 53 - 89

constant depth during its travel. Later, in 1898, Whitehead purchased a newly invented gyroscope mechanism from its inventor, Ludwig Obry, also an Austrian naval officer. The gyro enabled the torpedo to travel a very stable path along its line of launch.

The Whitehead firm produced torpedoes at Fiume, and later near Portland, England, and St. Tropez, France. Sales and production soared. By 1881 nearly 1,500 torpedoes had been produced. Initially Whitehead torpedoes were propelled by a compressed air engine, and consequently had very short ranges. Later, internal combustion engines were developed to increase the torpedo's speed and range. In 1900 the union of the existing Whitehead torpedo and the new submarine torpedo boat provided an even deadlier threat to the world's navies and merchant fleets.

Chapter Two –
John Holland and
the Modern Submarine
Torpedo Boat
"An Irish Invention"[5]

Although a number of people in various countries over the years thought about, drew sketches of, even attempted to build submarines, and sometimes experimented with their strange devices, one man stands out as the father of the modern submarine torpedo boat. His design and arrangements proved eminently practical and were adopted by a number of nations. He was John Philip Holland, an Irishman born in 1841 who immigrated to the United States in 1873 and became an American citizen. He was motivated by Irish nationalism to free Ireland from English domination. Recognizing that the powerful Royal Navy was the key to England's

---

5   Richard Compton-Hall's marvelous book *Submarine Boats* uses that phase as the sub-title for his Chapter Three

domination of subject lands, he sought a way to destroy its surface warships.

Landing in Boston with his first submarine design in his luggage, he broke his leg after slipping on some ice. However he recovered, and was able to find a teaching position in Paterson, New Jersey in a school run by the Teaching Order of the Irish Christian Brothers. He had been a member of that order in Ireland but obtained a dispensation to leave the order so he could go to America. In the United States he found financial support for his desires to build a submarine from the Fenian Brotherhood, an Irish-American organization whose aims were to free Ireland.

In 1876 he demonstrated the principles of the submarine he hoped to build with a 30 inch scale model at Coney Island, New York to interested Fenian Brotherhood supporters. He called it a "wrecking boat". They were definitely interested and provided funds that had been raised from fellow immigrants.

In 1878 John Holland completed his first working submarine. There were a few problems of the sort not unknown to any submariner who has participated in sea trials after a shipyard repair period. The submarine went unbidden to the bottom, unmanned, in shallow water because John had calculated the water density as sea water when at that location it was mostly fresh water. There is a significant difference. In any case the submarine was raised and was not damaged. The gasoline engine he had procured didn't work so he substituted a steam engine. He also had placed the diving planes amidships at the center of buoyancy, as had other inventors, only to find out that the best location was well aft. They were later moved aft.

The Fenian Brotherhood provided funding for his efforts and on 3 May 1879 work began on the "Fenian Ram" at Delamater Iron Works at West 13th Street, New York City. Holland had left his teaching position in 1878 to devote full time to the submarine venture. The estimated cost was $20,000.00 and two years to build. The final cost was slightly less at $18,000.00 but still a considerable sum in those days. The submarine was launched in May 1881. It was 31 feet long, and was equipped with a petrol engine but no battery. The petrol engine was also used when the vessel was submerged as long as it didn't go too deep, that is a depth at which the engine exhaust pressure could not overcome sea pressure.[6]

There were a steady stream of visitors to the Iron Works, from Sweden, Russia, Germany and Italy, all nations that had an interest in the new fangled submarine. The Turkish Sultan even sent a pair of representatives. British visitors were not encouraged since the weapon was intended to discomfort the Royal Navy. The British government attempted to have the United States government shut down the construction, but was told that it was a private enterprise and the government could not interfere.

---

6   Not a very satisfactory design in that the petrol engine would have soon consumed the available air in the submarine hull, asphyxiating the crew.

In 1883 the vessel made its first dive, successfully. It was equipped with a 9 inch diameter pneumatic gun, about 11 feet in length, and fired 6-foot Ericson projectiles. This was the same Ericson who built the Union ironclad "Monitor" of Civil War fame. The Fenians and John Holland got into an argument and the Fenians seized the submarine. It never sailed against England, but was exhibited much later at Madison Square Garden in 1916, spent some time at the New York State Marine School, and finally found its way to Paterson, New Jersey where it rests today.

With Fenian money no longer available, Holland got a job at the Pneumatic Gun Company to pay the rent and buy food while he kept going on his quest to build a submarine that the U.S. Navy would adopt. In 1886 he published a newspaper article titled "Can New York be Bombarded?" seeking to draw attention to the mischief that a submarine (of his design), equipped with a pneumatic gun firing dynamite projectiles could do.

In 1888 the U.S. Navy announced an open competition for a submarine torpedo boat. The requirements were for a craft that could do 15 kts on the surface, and 8 kts submerged for two hours. It would be a very long while before the second requirement could be met. There were four competitors including Thorston Nordenfelt of Sweden, a large scale arms manufacturer. Holland won the design competition. A two million dollar appropriation was provided to Cramps Ship Building Company of Philadelphia to build the selected design.[7] The project ended without result when Cramps was not able to provide appropriate assurances about the end result.

In 1889 another completion was held. Holland's design won again, but the national administration changed as the result of a presidential election and the new administration moved the appropriated funds to surface ship procurement. In 1890 Holland moved employment again to the Morris and Cummings Dredging Company at the princely wage of four dollars a day.[8]

In 1894 Grover Cleveland won a second election as President. In his earlier administration his Secretary of the Navy had tried to adopt the submarine. The Navy now formally decided to adopt the submarine as a defense weapons system. The French were procuring submarines at a great rate at this time and other European nations were showing interest. On 3 March 1894 the Congress

7   This was probably the first interaction between Cramps and the Submarine Service but not the last. Cramps built several submarines of WW II design, and in every case their designers seemed to look for the most awkward location in a compartment to place a valve and then did their best to install it backwards to make it even more difficult for the operators. In 1971 the author, then Commander Submarine Division 41, was inspecting the control room of USS Trumpetfish (SS-425), and after several puzzling minutes turned to the commanding officer and asked "Is this a Cramps' boat?". Shamefacedly the CO admitted that it was - which explained why things seemed so out of place.

8   That would be $80 a month, which compared with the normal $30 and "found" a month as the wages of a working cowhand was not too bad.

approved $20,000 for a submarine design competition.[9] On 1 April Holland completed his design drawings, and that same day founded the John P. Holland Torpedo Boat Company. On 13 March 1895 a contract was signed to build the "Plunger" at William T. Malster Company in Baltimore, Maryland. The same company was busy building a submarine designed by Simon Lake, as a private venture.

To meet Navy requirements Plunger had a steam engineering plant. She was 85 feet in length with a 11.5' beam, and displaced 154/168 tons. Holland was not satisfied with the steam plant requirement and persuaded his company board and backers to fund another submarine to his specification. The company secretary/treasurer was obviously well connected politically because he managed to get an amendment to the appropriation authorizing a second submarine "similar to the submarine boat Holland". In 1897 Plunger was launched but she never completed trials successfully.

John Holland then turned to Holland VI, which was built at Nixon's Crescent Shipyard in Elizabethport, New Jersey from 1896 to 1897. Holland VI was 53'10" in length, had a 10'3" beam, and displaced 63.3/74 tons. She was equipped with an Otto gasoline (petrol) engine capable of driving her at 8 knots maximum on the surface. Submerged she was driven by a 50 hp. motor using

---

9   If he had lived long enough John Holland would probably have enjoyed the movie "Ground Hog Day".

batteries for electrical power. There were two clutches that permitted direct engine drive or driving the motor – generator unit to recharge the battery. She was equipped with a single, bow, 18" torpedo tube for the Whitehead automotive torpedo, and carried two reloads. Finally there were two pneumatic guns, one forward and one aft. There was neither deck gun nor space to mount one.

John Holland's run of bad luck wasn't totally over. A workman left a hull valve open and at high tide Holland VI flooded and remained so for 18 hours before she could be pumped out. A young engineer named Frank T. Cable applied electrical power to the electrical machinery with the current reversed and that generated enough heat to dry out all the wiring that had been submerged. His action saved the submarine.

On 25 February 1898 she made her first surface run. On 17 March (appropriately St. Patrick's Day) she made her first successful underway dive off Staten Island. Formal trials began 27 March. The Navy provided a crew of officers and men, who didn't understand Holland VI nearly as well as John Holland, to conduct the trials which were a bit shaky. She conducted her final trials in Little Peconic Bay on 6 November 1899.

On 11 April 1900 Holland VI was commissioned in the United States Navy as USS Holland (SS-1). She would serve as a model of what a modern submarine ought to include: a dual propulsion plant, streamlined hull and internal torpedo tubes. The Holland submarine design would be procured by a number of other nations, including Russia, Great Britain and Japan. Her length/breadth ratio was well suited to submerged control, and many years later would be replicated in modern nuclear powered submarines. John Philip Holland was not the only submarine designer of his day but he was arguably the most influential.

In the United States, USS Holland (SS-1) was followed by a series of submarines of various classes, almost all Holland designs. In November 1900 Great Britain contracted with Electric Boat Company to build submarines of Holland design. Five were built with the first commissioned in 1903. Fourteen submarines of the British "A" class followed. They were based on the Holland design.

In 1901 the Bubnov Committee in Imperial Russia started work on a submarine based on the Holland design. It was *Delfin*, commissioned in 1903. Later seven more of Holland design were completed. In 1904 Japan purchased five Holland boats. At that time Japan was engaged in a war with Russia. None of these craft saw combat.

The Austro-Hungarian Empire also acquired a pair of Holland boats, U V and U VI, in 1910 and 1911 respectively. Among the major maritime powers, only France, Germany and Italy did not adopt the basic Holland design.

PART TWO

SUBMARINE DEVELOPMENT
IN MAJOR NATIONS

(1900 – 1914)

CHAPTER THREE –
SUBMARINE FORCES
PRIOR TO WWI

Austro-Hungarian Empire

The Austro-Hungarian Navy had a very small submarine service, boasting only six boats. The U I class of two boats (U I and U II) were built by Simon Lake's firm in the United States. They were a typical Lake design with wheels for rolling along the sea bottom and a diver lockout arrangement. They were completed in 1909 and were only used for training. They were 230/250 tons, with speeds of 10/6 knots, with three 45 cm. (17.7 inch) torpedo tubes, and a crew of 17. [10] In 1915 their gasoline engines were replaced with diesel engines.

The U III class of two boats was German designed and built. They were also launched in 1909. They displaced 240/300 tons, with speeds of 12/8 knots, with equipped with two 45 cm. torpedo tubes and a crew of 21.

---

10   Displacements are shown as surfaced/submerged as are speeds.

The final class of pre-war A-H submarines was the U-V class of three boats. Only two, U V and U VI, were completed before the war started. They were Holland Boat designs built by Electric Boat Company in New York. They were 240/275 tons, with speeds of 8/6 knots, with two 45 cm. bow torpedo tubes and a crew of 19. They were completed in 1910 and 1911.

The third boat, an improved Holland type, was built "on spec" by the Whitehead firm but the A-H Navy showed little interest and Whitehead was unable to find another buyer. However, when the war started, the A-H Navy bought her and commissioned her as U XII.

All the A-H boats were gasoline engine powered on the surface, and the torpedoes were compressed air powered (consequently with very short ranges).

Another class of five boats, U VII through U XI, was under construction for the A-H Navy in Germany before the war started. It appeared that the British blockade would prevent them from transiting from Germany into the Mediterranean and Adriatic Seas to reach their new home port at Pola. Therefore in November 1914 Germany purchased them from A-H. They were subsequently commissioned in the German Navy as U 66-70.

France

The 1901 French naval budgetary estimates called for the construction of 23 new submarines to add to the existing stock of about 14. All were of the *sousmarin* type.[11] During 1901 maneuvers *Gustav Zede* attacked the French Mediterranean Fleet as it departed Ajaccio, and successfully "torpedoed" battleship *Charles Martel*. The *Zede* had transited from Toulon to the target area on its own, a distance of 149 nautical miles (nm).[12]

In 1903 the French Navy conducted extensive competitive trials of the two different types of submarines. Submersible *Aigrette's* performance was compared to that of *sousmarin* "Z'". The submersible type won the trials and the French Navy decided to build only submersibles in the future.[13] The submersible used steam, petrol, kerosene or diesel power for propulsion on the surface. When the submarine dove, the engines were shut down and the submarine switched to battery propulsion for submerged operations.

In 1906 during fleet exercises French submersibles "torpedoed" 21 opposing blockading ships at Toulon, Marseilles and Bizerta. Submarine flotillas were subsequently established at Rochefort, Dunkirk, Toulon and Cherbourg. Several submersibles were forward deployed to Bizerta in North Africa, and to Saigon in Indochina.[14]

---

11 *Sousmarin* type submarines had only electric motor propulsion, powered by a large battery. They had to return to port to be recharged.

12 Hezlet, The Submarine and Sea Power, pp. 16-17. Formal exercise usually called for umpires to rule on successful attacks and to declare that certain forces were "out of action" after such attacks.

13 Submersibles had dual propulsion, while *sousmarins* had only battery propulsion.

14 Hezlet, Op cit., p. 17

By 1914 France had a total of 75 submarines in commission. A number were one-off designs. One design, *Aloise*, with 20 in the class, was only 67 tons submerged displacement. The *Pluviose* class, with 33 boats, displaced 391 tons surfaced and 550 tons submerged. They had 6 or 7 non-watertight torpedo launchers, or drop collars, located on their decks where the torpedoes were exposed to sea water and other influences. One of the class was *Marie Curie*. She was sunk in the Adriatic in December 1914 when she attempted to penetrate the defenses of the A-H harbor of Pola, and eventually was put into service by the Austro-Hungarian Navy as submarine U XIV.[15] During A-H service she was depth charged and escaped, but had all her topside torpedoes damaged by the underwater explosions.

Germany

Germany lagged France and Great Britain in bringing submarines into its fleet. Admiral von Tirpitz was intent on building a fleet of "Dreadnought" class battleships capable of challenging the British fleet, and saw no reason to give opponents in the *Reichstag* (German Parliament) an opportunity to focus on cheaper alternatives. In addition there were a number of technical problems with early submarines and their power plants. He was content to allow time for those to be worked out before committing the German Navy to submarine construction.

---

15   In 1918 U XIV, former *Marie Curie*, was returned to France.

In 1905 - 1906 Germany built its first U-boat (*Untersee boot*) (U 1), somewhat smaller than the British "C" class submarine, at 238 tons with a crew of 12 men. It had a single bow torpedo tube, 18 inches in diameter, two Korting heavy oil (paraffin) engines and twin shafts.[16] U 1 was used for training all through WW I and survived the war. Today she sits in a museum in Munich.

The next U-boat (U 2) was completed in 1908. U 2 displaced 341 tons and had a crew of 22. U 2 and her two sisters still had heavy oil engines but carried two TT forward and two aft, providing flexibility in torpedo shooting. From 1908 on, diesel engines replaced the very smoky heavy oil engines in the German U-boat service. In 1912 secret trials were conducted in the Baltic Sea. Results indicated that U-boats had the endurance to conduct patrols off the east coast of England.

Between 1908 and 1912 the German Navy ordered a total of 42 "overseas" type U-boats. Twenty-nine had been completed before World War I began in August 1914. German diesel engines and periscopes were first-rate. German "overseas" U-boats were the equivalent of the British "E" class submarines. Germany had about twice the number of "overseas" U-boats as the British had "E" class submarines.

---

16 The Korting heavy oil engine burned paraffin, or kerosene as it is commonly known in the United States. The combustion resulted in heavy smoke requiring long ventilation pipes that had to be rigged for diving thus slowing submergence. The smoke also could be easily seen by enemy lookouts.

Great Britain

As the 19th Century rolled over into the new 20th Century the Royal Navy began to view France's plans for an extensive submarine force with alarm.[17] It realized that, lacking English submarine builders, it needed more information about submarine operations and capabilities if the Royal Navy was to combat them successfully. Therefore it approached the United States to request that Holland boat plans be provided. The Admiralty contracted with Electric Boat Company in New York in November 1900 for their construction in Great Britain. Subsequently five Holland boats were laid down in Vickers Shipyard at Barrow-in-Furness using the American patents and with American engineering assistance. The first was launched in November 1902 and commissioned in 1903. They were 104/122 tons, had one 14" TT forward, one 4-cylinder petrol engine, and one main motor. Their speeds were 8/7 knots, and they had a complement of 7 men. They had a range of 500 miles at 7 knots. All the original "Hollands" were out of service by 1913.

The Admiralty appointed a very capable RN Captain as Inspecting Captain of Submarine Boats and gave him a relatively free hand in developing and modifying this new

---

17   England and France had a long history of warfare going back centuries, the most recent having been during the Napoleonic Wars in the early 1800s. England recognized that French submarines could break close blockades and thus let French corsairs loose for a *guerre de course* against British seaborne trade.

weapons system. He devised a periscope for the Holland boats whose plans did not include one, and in general set about successfully to improve the new submarine weapons system.

The British "A" submarine class (14 boats), based on the Holland design, followed in 1903-1905. They were 165/180 tons, had two 18-inch bow TT , one 12-cylinder petrol engine, and made 11/7 knots, with a crew of 11-14 men. Their surface range was 310 miles at 10 knots. A-5 through -14 had somewhat larger surfaced/dived displacements and equivalent dimensions. A-13 was fitted with a heavy oil (paraffin) engine in place of the then standard petrol engine. They were intended for local defense of ports and harbors.[18]

In 1904 Admiral Sir John (Jackie) Fisher, First Sea Lord, concluded that submarines could replace controlled mine fields at naval ports since they could reach greater ranges than existing shore batteries.[19] He set a new defense plan into place. It relied on motor torpedo boats at night and submarine torpedo boats during daytime.[20]

---

18   Two A class were soon lost; A-1 rammed by SS Berwick Castle in 1904 with 11 lives lost, and A-5 by explosion the following year with identical loss of life.

19   Important ports were protected with controlled mine fields and shore gun batteries. The mines could be exploded by signals from a shore station when an enemy ship steamed near it. Gun batteries could sink enemy ships including any minesweepers sent in to clear the mine field. In the United States the army had responsibility for coast defense and the Coast Artillery Branch laid and maintained controlled mine fields and manned coast defense artillery batteries.

20   Hezlet, Op cit., pp. 18 - 19

The "B" class (11 boats) followed in 1905-1906: 280/313 tons, petrol-electric propulsion plants, 2 TT forward (18"), and a range of 1,000 miles at 8.7 knots - to be used for coast defense. They had speeds of 13/8 knots and a complement of 16 men. They were the first British submarines to be fitted with fore-hydroplanes (bow planes). One of the 1907 war plans called for a British battle fleet to operate in the Baltic Sea, with B class submarines using bases in Danish islands against the German port of Kiel.

38 "C" class boats followed in 1906-1908. They were also classified as coastal submarines. They were 290/320 tons, and had 2 forward 18" TT, They were equipped with petrol-electric drive, made 13/8 knots, with a range of 1,000 miles at 8.7 knots. Some of the later "C" class boats were fitted with wireless/telegraph (W/T) equipment enabling them to communicate at a distance using Morse code.

1907 war plans called for Holland and "A" class submarines to defend home ports; and "B" class to defend Dover Strait. Subs were being built at a rate of ten per year, and submarine flotillas were established at Devonport, Harwich, and Dundee as well as Portsmouth. The entire English East Coast was now to be defended by submarines. This represented a major change from the previous scheme that used submarines solely for indoctrination and training of surface forces in response to the French "submarine threat".

In 1908 the "D" class (8 boats) were put into service: 550/595 tons, twin diesel-electric propulsion plants, 2 TT forward (18"), intended for overseas or offensive patrols, with a range of 2,500 miles, and speeds of 16/9 knots. D-1 capabilities were clearly demonstrated in 1910 maneuvers. She was attached to the "offensive" side. D-1 transited from Portsmouth on the Southeast English coast to the west coast of Scotland and "torpedoed" two cruisers. As a result the Royal Navy changed its focus to "overseas" or offensive type submarines vice smaller "coastal" types. D-4 was the first British submarine to be fitted with a deck gun.

In 1912 the "E" class (57 boats): four TT (1 forward, 1 aft, and two transverse amidships, all 18") followed with an increase in displacement to 680/800 tons.[21] They had a range of 3,000 miles at speeds of 16/10 knots, and a complement of 30 men.[22]

That year four submarines attached to one fleet in maneuvers successfully "torpedoed" a battleship of the opposing forces. However it was noticed that the fleet speed had to be reduced to allow the submarines to keep up. As a result emphasis was placed on greater surface speed for submarines. Two new submarines of greater speed were authorized: the Nautilus class

---

21   At this point it may be useful to reflect on the fact that Germany nearly won the Battle of the Atlantic in 1943 with the Type VII U-boat that displaced only about 750 tons submerged and had twin diesel propulsion.

22   E 9 and subsequent had an additional internal tube forward, for a total of five TT.

Nautilus was the final class laid down before the beginning of WW I: 1270 tons, twin diesel/electric drive, five TT (one 21" TT forward, and four 18' beam TT), with a range of 5,000 miles. They also had a 12-pounder (3 inch) deck gun, and were intended to operate with the fleet. They had speeds of 17/10 knots. The first of the class was completed just before the end of the war but none saw action.

Italy

Prior to 1900 Italy had experimented with submarines as had other nations. [23] Between 1900 and 1915 when she entered the war, Italy constructed 18 coastal submarines. Five were *Glauco* class boats, displacing 215 tons submerged, with 2 bow TT, a petrol engine and one shaft. They could make 14 kts surfaced and 7 kts submerged. They were built during the period 1906 – 1910. The next class was built in 1911 – 1912, the *Medusa* class. There were 8 of these, with twin diesel engines and two shafts. They displaced 345 tons submerged and had a crew of 14. Two *Nautilus* class submarines were built about the same time as the *Medusa* class. Three more submarines were built before the war: *Atropo* a one-off German design with a paraffin engine, and two *Pullino* class diesel submarines,

---

23   Italy launched its first submarine, *Delfino* in 1892. It was stricken in 1918.

slightly larger than the *Medusa*.[24] In addition Italy built two midget submarines, Alfa and Bravo, in 1913.

The Italian submarine service mirrored the British in starting out with a petrol-electric propulsion combination and then switching to diesel-electric as soon as possible. While diesel fuel was smelly it was not usually dangerous, but gasoline (petrol) fumes were much more volatile and explosions of gasoline vapors were not uncommon.[25] In addition gasoline vapors produced a kind of intoxication of the crew exposed to them. An example of this occurred in A-H submarine U-V during combat operations in the Adriatic Sea in 1915.

Japan

In 1904 Japan purchased five Holland boats from the Electric Boat Company of New York, Japan then being at war with Russia. None saw action in that war or during WW I.

Russia

Russian interest in submersibles can be traced well back into the 18th Century under Peter the Great. In 1718

---

24 It was fairly common before WWI for a navy to order a submarine from a foreign building yard and design in order to compare its merits with their own design and building practices.

25 The author's wife never allowed him to hang his seagoing uniforms in a closet where her clothes hung because of the lasting diesel smell they introduced.

a Russian inventor named Yetim Nikonov proposed an oar-driven underwater craft. The project was approved by the Tsar in 1719 and the craft was completed and tested successfully in June 1720. Its proposed armament consisted of copper tubes to fire rockets.

During the 1800s interest continued. In November 1855 the Russian Admiralty accepted Wilhelm Bauer's submersible *le Diable Marin* built at St. Petersburg. Its propulsion system involved crew operated treadmills driving a single propeller. Between May and October 1856 it completed 156 dives successfully.

The Russo-Turkish War of 1877 provided more impetus for development of submersibles and other underwater weapons including mines. A leading Russian submarine designer of that era was Stefan Karloviy Dzhevetskiy. He designed several submersibles during the period 1877-onward. In addition he developed a torpedo launch system, called a Dzhevetskiy drop collar. It was a set of two collars, holding the torpedo external to the hull. The torpedo rear end was held on a pivot that could rotate up to 90 degrees, allowing the early torpedo, driven by a compressed air engine, to be angled just prior to launch. In some ways it was ahead of its time. Early torpedoes did not have a settable gyro but rather traveled on a straight course with the gyro holding it on that course. The drop collar arrangement allowed a submarine commanding officer to select the proper torpedo firing angle to intercept its target. The weakness in this system, compared to an internal torpedo tube, was that the torpedo was exposed to sea pressure and corrosion continuously when the submarine was submerged, rather than resting safely and dryly in the submarine torpedo tube until just before launch when the tube was flooded and the muzzle door opened. It also exposed the torpedoes in drop collars to the full force of depth charges (that had yet to be developed). Russian submarine designs from 1900 to 1917 all basically called for drop collar torpedo installations. The drop collars were also installed in a number of French submarines of that period.

The development of Russian submarines in the early 20th century involved several different paths: native Russian design, the introduction of two American submarine designs (Holland and Lake), and German-built submarines which were based upon French submarine designs. Submarine development was also influenced by the Russo-Japanese war (1904-1905).

In 1901 the first Russian submarine of the 20th Century was built at Kronshtadt. It displaced 20 tons, was 50 feet long and had a 4 foot beam. It carried two torpedoes in Dzhevetskiy drop collars.[26] The operational concept called for the submarine to be transported aboard a surface ship, and launched when within submerged attack range. It had nine water tight compartments and was driven by electric

---

26   Dzhevetskiy was a Polish citizen of Russia and a submarine designer. His torpedo "drop collars were used in torpedo boats and some surface ships in lieu of torpedo tubes. Some U.S. WW II motor torpedo boats used drop collars.

motors and accumulators (batteries). It was completed in 1902 and named *Petr Koshka*. It moved to Sevastopol for trials.[27]

On 19 December 1900 a special submarine committee of the Navy Technical Committee was established in order to evaluate foreign submarine designs, and to prepare proposals for a submarine design for the Russian Navy. One member, Lt. Mikhail Nikolaevich, visited the United States in 1901 where he looked at Holland and Lake submarine designs. The chairman of the committee was Naval Architect Senior Assistant (later Mayor-General of the Naval Architect Corps) Ivan Gregor'evich Bubnov, the leading Russian submarine designer of the pre-war period.[28]

In May 1901 the Bubnov Committee proposed a submarine based on a Holland design. The Committee recommended some changes to the ballast tanks, and substituted torpedo drop collars topside for internal torpedo tubes. On 5 July 1901 such a submarine was ordered from the Baltic Works in St. Petersburg. It was named *Delfin*. Its sea trials were held in June 1903. After war broke out with Japan in 1904 it was used as a training unit.

In 1904 Russia ordered three submarines from Germany's Krupp-Germania firm. They were based on a French design. Russia also ordered seven Holland and six Lake-type submarines from the United States, plus an additional four boats from Germany because of the

---

27   Polmar, Russian submarines, pp. 10-11
28   Ibid, p. 10

Russo-Japanese War.[29] The Holland Company shipped *Fulton*, later renamed *Som* to Russia. Six more of the Holland design were ordered from the Nevskiy Works in St. Petersburg to be complete by 1 September 1904.

The lead Lake-design submarine was named *Protector* It displaced 135/175 tons, had two petrol engines, electric motors powered by batteries, and two shafts. It carried three torpedo tubes, a diver lock-out chamber, and had wheels for movement along the sea bottom. *Protector* was shipped to Russia after purchase, and five more of the same design were produced by the Newport News Shipbuilding and Dry Dock Company in the United States for Russia.

A number of submarines were shipped by rail to the Far East and operated from Vladivostok. None of them saw action in the Russo-Japanese War which ended in September 1905.

By late 1906 Russia had a total of 19 submarines in commission: one in the Black Sea Fleet; five in the Baltic Fleet; 12 in the Far East Squadron; and one in the Amur River Flotilla. Russia's immense geographic expanse was both an asset and a liability. The maritime areas were too distant for easy or rapid movement of naval units between them.

In early 1906 the Russian Navy ordered submarine *Minoga*, with the first internal combustion engine (diesel)

---

29   Japan declared war on Russia on 8 February 1904 but conducted a surprise naval attack on the Russian Pacific Fleet in its harbor at Port Arthur several hours before the formal declaration..

built in Russia. It also possessed variable pitch propellers, an innovation that would take many years to find more widespread use. *Minoga* displaced 117/142 tons, was 105 feet in length, had two diesel engines and could make 11 kts/5 kts. It had a crew of 20 and in addition to two bow torpedo tubes, carried a 37 mm gun and one machine gun.

Pochtovy, another one-off design of 134/146 tons was built in 1908. It was a Dzhevetskiy design, with a unique feature. Compressed oxygen was stored in 45 cylinders, permitting the use of her gasoline engines while submerged.[30] The exhaust was led overboard by a compressor to a perforated pipe under her keel. However there was a problem with steam collecting inside the boat while running submerged. She was stricken in 1913 after brief trials.

Plans for expansion of the Russian fleets went through a number of iterations, usually coming to grief upon the rocks of fiscal realities. Finally a significant submarine building program was begun in 1912. It called for 12 Bars-class submarines for the Baltic Fleet, and six submarines for the Black Sea Fleet (three Morzh-class and three Holland type 31A), and six more Bars-class for the Siberian Flotilla.

Morzh-class submarines displaced 630 tons submerged, and were 220 feet in length. They had four internal torpedo tubes (two forward and two aft) plus eight external torpedo drop collars, four to a side. The torpedo

30   Much later such devices would be categorized as "Air Independent Propulsion (AIP)"

armament, twelve torpedoes, was unusually large for that period. They also carried small deck guns. The pressure hull had no internal watertight bulkheads. Their diving time (3-4 minutes) was slow because of poor tank venting capability. Their test depth was 164 feet (50 meters).

Bars-class submarines were a modification of the Morzh-class with an additional 3-foot section inserted amidships. They displaced 650 tons, and also had four internal torpedo tubes (two forward and two aft) plus eight external drop collars. Like Morzh-class submarines they had no internal bulkheads. Two of the class, *Ersh* and *Forel*, were completed as mine laying submarines. These two had two mine laying tunnels aft outside the hull and could carry up to 42 mines. Their after torpedo tubes and drop collars were removed in favor of the mine capability.

Holland 31A-type submarines had internal water tight bulkheads and a much faster diving time – one minute. They were double-hull construction and carried ballast water in saddle tanks. They featured four internal torpedo tubes (two forward and two aft) plus either four or eight external drop collars. They were 230 feet in length and displaced 621 tons. They were generally considered the most successful Russian submarines of the period.[31]

When World War I began in August 1914 the total Russian submarine fleet consisted of 23 submarines in commission, distributed as follows: Baltic Fleet – 11 submarines, Black Sea Fleet - 4, Pacific Fleet- 8.

---

31   Ibid, p. 29

United States

USS Holland (SS-1), John Holland's latest experimental submarine, was commissioned in the Navy in April 1900. It displaced 74 tons, was equipped with a petrol-electric propulsion plant, with speeds of 8 kts. /5 kts. It carried 1050 gals. of gasoline, had one torpedo tube (TT) forward and carried three torpedoes.

The United States public had been spooked by fears of Spanish warships raiding east coast ports in 1898 during the Spanish-American War. In response the Congress authorized six new Holland type submarines. These were to be a first installment of a total of 20 intended to provide local defenses for New York, Long Island Sound, and the Delaware and Chesapeake Bays. Some seven boats of an improved Holland design, the Adder class (later A 1- A 7), were commissioned. They were 120 tons, equipped with one TT forward and five torpedoes (18 inch). They had a 160 hp petrol engine and battery electrical propulsion plants. They could make 9 kts /7 kts. They had a crew of 7, carried 850 gals. of gasoline, and had a surfaced range of 800 miles@ 9 kts.

More Holland type boats followed. Three Cuttlefish class (later B1- B3): 170 tons, 1 TT forward, petrol-electric propulsion, 10 /8 kts, two periscopes, and surfaced range 500 miles @ 9 kts.

The next class was the Octopus class (later C1- C5): 238 tons /275 tons, 2 TT forward, petrol (500 hp.)/electric propulsion plants, 11 kts/10 kts, crew – 10, range 900 miles @ 9 kts/80 miles at 5 kts. They were commissioned 1907 – 1909.

Finally three more Narwhal class boats (later D1- D3) were commissioned in 1909. They were 280/345 tons, 2 TT forward, petrol (600 hp)/electric propulsion, 13 kts/9 kts, crew 15, commissioned in 1909.

A series of "letter class" submarines followed, each usually slightly bigger and marginally more capable than the preceding class. They were "E" (2), "F" (4), "G" (4), "H"(9), "K" (8) and "L" (11) between 1909 and 1914 with numbers built in each class shown in parentheses.

The "E" class was the first U.S. submarine class to have diesel engines instead of the previous unsatisfactory petrol (gasoline) engines installed, thus eliminating possible gasoline explosions and crew intoxication from breathing gasoline-laden air. The "E" and "F" classes were the first Electric Boat submarines to have bow planes. They also had a single shaft. The various classes are displayed in the table with key parameters:

Submarine Class	Displace-ment (tons)	Length (feet)	Speed (Kts.)	Range (nm.)	Armament	Crew Size
E	350/435	135'3"	14/9	2500/100	4x18", 4 torpedoes	20
F	350/435	142'6"	14/9	2500/110	4x18"	22
G	366/406	157'	14/9.5	NA	4x18"	24
H	363/434	150'3"	13/10	2300/100	4x18"	22
K	392/591	153'7"	14/10	4500/120	4x18"	28
L	463/532	169'	14/10.5	4500/150	4x18"	28

Although the United States considered itself the home of the "modern" submarine, having commissioned the sixth experimental Holland-designed boat as USS Holland in April 1900, the United States Navy Submarine Service had fallen behind in both numbers and technical development by 1914. France, Germany and Great Britain had forged ahead. Both Germany and Great Britain had invested in "overseas" type submarines, capable of carrying out offensive patrols off an enemy coastline while in the U.S. Navy, the lack of a close "enemy" relegated submarines to coast defense roles.

Part Three

Submarine Operations of the Allied and Associated Nations

World War One

CHAPTER FOUR –
WORLD WAR I
(1914 – 1918)

O n the eve of WW I most informed naval opinion about the usefulness of the new submarine weapons system was that the submarine torpedo boat was a technical curiosity, of very limited range and endurance, which conceivably might be useful in the event of a close-in blockade of a port with blockading warships just offshore. After all, back in 1863 during the American Civil War a Union warship had been sunk by a Confederate semi-submerged craft equipped with a spar torpedo just off Charleston harbor.

The 1914 edition of Jane's Fighting Ships had nothing to say about submarine warfare prospects. It merely listed the number of submarines by class for each of the major powers, but after their torpedo boat flotillas, an indicator of submarines' lesser importance.[32] Brassey's

---

32   Jane's Fighting Ships, 1914.

Naval Annual for 1914 lists submarines of the major nations much as Jane's. Its index has no submarine listing, although torpedo boats have a number of entries. Among the feature articles in the 1914 edition of Brassey's is one of five pages on Air Ship Sheds of the major nations, apparently a topic of some naval interest at the time, but nothing on submarines.[33]

The idea that submarines could present a serious threat to warships in the open ocean would have been rejected as ludicrous. Similarly the idea that submarines might be used to enforce a blockade would have been rejected. Civilized nations were agreed on a code of naval warfare that required placing the crew and passengers of a seized ship in a place of safety before it might be destroyed.[34] That meant either aboard the capturing ship or in lifeboats within sight of land. Submarines had tiny crews and thus could not spare a prize crew, and had no room for passengers, or life boats of their own. The idea that they might sink ships without warning was rejected by almost all, including firebrand Winston Churchill. Only one somewhat "bloody minded" individual, Sir Jackie Fisher, First Sea Lord of Great Britain's Royal Navy, accurately predicted that logic would drive submarines to sink their prey without warning or regard for diplomatic niceties.

---

33 Brassey's Naval Annual 1914
34 The 1909 Declaration of London's intent was incorporated into various navies' Prize Regulations which set down the rules of naval warfare. See Messimer, Dwight R., *Find and Destroy*, p 4

In 1914 Europe was a bit of a banked fire waiting for a blast of air to start a fresh blaze. Two groups of empires had banded together to offset each other. The first, the Triple Alliance involved Germany, the Dual Monarchy of Austria-Hungary, and Italy. The combination would later, less Italy, be called the "Central Powers". The second combination consisted of Great Britain, France and Russia, called the Triple Entente. It would later be called the Allied Powers. Russia and France, the primary members, had allied themselves for mutual protection against Germany, threatening her with a two-front war if she attacked one or the other.

World War I began somewhat accidentally in late July 1914 as a result of the assassination of Grand Duke Franz Ferdinand, heir to the throne of the Austro-Hungarian Empire, during a ceremonial visit to Sarajevo in the province of Bosnia.[35] The captured assassin was a Bosnian nationalist supported and funded by Serbia. The Austro-Hungarian Empire pressured Serbia, which looked to its Orthodox-Christian/Slav-ethnic mentor Russia, for assistance.

Europe was bound by a conflicting web of treaties, some published and some not. Russia indicated to Austria-Hungary that it did not look kindly on threatened Austria-

---

35   On 23 July Austria-Hungary sent an ultimatum to Serbia, and then declared war on Serbia on 28 July. Meanwhile Russia began mobilization and Germany declared war on Russia on 1 August. France, allied to Russia, declared war on Germany on 3 August. Germany invaded neutral Belgium on 4 August, and Great Britain declared war on Germany that same day in response.

Hungarian moves against Serbia. Germany somewhat casually gave the Austro-Hungarian Empire a promise of support against Russia. When Russia began mobilization it triggered German mobilization that in turn triggered mobilization by France.

Today most of us have little understanding of the threatening implications of the term "mobilization" at that time. All major European nations' armies employed conscription. A relatively small regular army cadre brought a new class of physically qualified male conscripts into mandatory service each year after graduation from high school. After two to three years of training the class was released into the Reserve, with an annual training obligation until ages 30 – 40. The system provided a means of greatly and instantly enlarging the size of the standing army through mobilization. In a time of need the most recently trained classes were mobilized first, their relatively young age, fitness and recent active training making them instantly useful in warfare. General mobilization had a significant impact upon a nation's economy and was not ordered lightly.[36]

Contingency plans existed for warfare against traditional enemies, e.g. Germany and France, and the first nation to mobilize could jump the gun and begin to execute its

---

36   In 1936 Germany reoccupied the Rhineland, territory which was supposed to remain neutral under the Versailles Treaty. France dithered, not having a relatively small ground force it could send into the Rhineland to push the single German battalion out. Faced with having to order general mobilization during the Depression, the French government did nothing.

contingency war plans. Therefore a general mobilization order was effectively an informal declaration of war that the rival could not ignore. General mobilization by a rival meant war and every major nation understood it.

Russia's mobilization triggered Germany's; that in turn triggered France's and thus World War I started. The interested reader is referred to Barbara Tuchman's *Guns of August*, a splendid description of that summer and events that changed the world.

German war plans called for an immediate army sweep through neutral Belgium into northern France in an attempt to capture Paris and repeat their decisive 1870 victory.[37] But Belgian borders had been guaranteed by Great Britain. The German invasion of Belgium brought Great Britain into the war on the French side. The Central Powers: Germany and the Austro-Hungarian Empire were opposed by the Allied Powers: France, Great Britain, Belgium, Russia and Serbia.

Japan, invoking an article of a naval treaty with Great Britain, and focusing on coveted nearby German-controlled colonies in the Far East and western Pacific islands, entered the war as an Allied Power on 23 August. Italy did not enter the war at this time.

At the outset the German Army executed the *Schlieffen* Plan, a dash through neutral Belgium and a fast paced wheeling movement intended to quickly take

---

37   At that time army movement was largely at an infantryman's pace, although cavalry was used for scouting and horse-drawn wagons brought guns, ammunition and supplies forward.

Paris and knock the French out of the war. It failed at the Battle of the Marne in September, and the opposing forces then rapidly moved north to outflank each other. When the race was over, the two sides faced each other from opposing trench lines that stretched from the Swiss border to the North Sea shore, and four years of brutal and costly trench warfare began.

This book deals principally with submarine operations by the Allied and Associated Powers (France, Great Britain, Italy, Russia and the United States), and the Central Powers (Germany and the Austro-Hungarian Empire).[38] Japan did not operate any submarines in combat during WW I. Information about significant land and naval operations, and international diplomatic pressures, are included to provide the appropriate context for submarine operations.

By late 1916 it was clear that German submarine operations had the potential of strangling England economically, forcing her to negotiate an end to her participation in the war. A cessation of Great Britain's blockade of Germany and the loss of British support to France would probably have brought the war to a conclusion on terms favorable to Germany. Therefore the German unrestricted submarine campaign is the principal

---

38 . The United States steered clear of formal alliances, fearful of being drawn into European conflicts that had little or nothing to do with U.S. interests. Therefore the U.S. did not formally ally herself with the Allied Powers but rather "associated" herself with them. For practical purposes it was an alliance.

focus in discussions of Central Powers' submarine operations during WW I.[39] Other submarine operations could be significant tactically and even operationally within a theater, however they did not have the potential to seriously affect the outcome of the war.

On the eve of World War I the submarine, like the airplane, was a very new military development. USS Holland, the first "modern" submarine, was commissioned in 1900. Submarines appeared to be potentially useful for harbor defense and perhaps even for coast defense. Sea mines were already used for both purposes but they were fixed in place.[40] The submarine offered some mobility in addition to stealth. Submarines could carry and fire the relatively new automotive (self-propelled) torpedo like torpedo boats but they had the additional ability to make undetected approaches and attacks which made them particularly dangerous to blockading ships. Although Jules Verne had written engagingly in 1870 about a futuristic submarine named *Nautilus* sinking surface ships, reality was much more restricted in 1914. However, during the course of WW I the submarine would develop into a devastating weapon against warships and merchant ships.

---

39   The German submarine campaign against British commerce and that of neutral shipping supporting Great Britain took place both in the sea areas around the United Kingdom and in the Mediterranean Sea .

40   Sea mines were sometimes called "torpedoes". During the American Civil War when Commodore Farragut famously shouted "Damn the torpedoes, full speed ahead", he was referring to Confederate States' sea mines that had just sunk one of his flotilla.

CHAPTER FIVE –
FRENCH SUBMARINE
OPERATIONS

In 1914 the nations of the world operated a total of about 400 submarines.[41] Many were older with either gasoline or steam engines for surface propulsion and electric batteries for submerged operations. Only about 25% of existing submarines were advanced diesel-electric models with 4 – 5 torpedo tubes (TT).

Normally a submarine would surface after dark to recharge batteries. Both gasoline and steam types of surface propulsion had serious disadvantages. Volatile gasoline

---

41   Although the term submarine is used the reader should be aware that the submarines of WW I were really submersibles. They transited to their patrol area on the surface, diving as necessary to avoid enemy contacts or to conduct a submerged attack. On patrol they usually operated on the surface during the day because of better visibility. At night they were on the surface to charge their electric storage batteries. The nuclear attack submarine (SSN) today usually dives after leaving port and remains submerged throughout its operations, surfacing only to reenter port.

fumes frequently disabled the crew. Steam plants of the day allowed high speed on the surface but generated a terrific amount of heat that could not be readily dissipated when submerged. Steam-powered submarines also took an inordinately long time to prepare to dive, about 5 to 10 minutes or more.

France's rather large number of submarines in the early 1900s stemmed from French concerns over rival Great Britain's command of the sea with a large battle fleet. France had to have a large army to deal with next door neighbor Germany. Therefore she could not afford a large enough surface navy to stand a chance against the Royal Navy of Great Britain. She looked to submarines to preclude a close blockade of French ports such as had occurred during the Napoleonic Wars, and to carry out a *"guerre de course"* against British merchant shipping if the need arose. However her Navy technical branch had problems with the relatively new diesel engine. The French Navy relied on tried and true steam propulsion which had some serious disadvantages in a submarine application.

When war came it was against Germany, and Great Britain was her ally and therefore France had no need for operations against British shipping. The Royal Navy's distant blockade of Germany in the North Sea precluded any significant French involvement against German merchant shipping. The French submarine service was left to focus on ASW operations in and around the English

Channel in close coordination with the Royal Navy, and Adriatic and Mediterranean Sea operations against Austria-Hungary forces.

French surface forces immediately established a blockade of the Otranto Strait to keep A-H warships and merchant shipping inside the Adriatic. The French Navy and submarine service later joined coordinated operations with the British against the Turks in 1915.

On 21 November 1914 the Anglo-French channel defenses against German U-boats were reorganized into eight zones. Each zone was patrolled twenty-four hours a day, seven days a week, by destroyers in relays. There was always an RN destroyer in each zone. However the destroyers had no hydrophones or any other sensors except lookouts to detect submarines. Other destroyers, supported by French submarines, operated along lines from Cape Griz Nez to the Vorne, and from Calais to Goodwin Sands.[42] This was mostly wasted effort. No U-boats were sunk by French submarines involved in this activity.

In December 1914 French submarine *Marie Curie*, operating in the Adriatic Sea against the Austro-Hungarian Empire, made a daring attempt to penetrate the harbor defenses of Pola, Austria. She became entangled in antisubmarine nets, tried to work her way free, could not and was hit repeatedly with gunfire when she surfaced. Some of her crew got off and were captured. She sank,

---

42   Messimer, Find and Destroy, pp. 23 - 24

and was later salvaged by the Austrians, dewatered and refitted and placed into service as the U-XIV.[43] As U-XIV she performed very creditably for her new owners, survived the war, and was returned to France as part of the surrender terms.

About 15 January 1915 French submarine *Saphir* was the first Allied submarine to attempt to break into the Sea of Marmara to attack Turkish resupply shipping to the Gallipoli Peninsula She ran aground and was destroyed trying to get by the minefields and shore battery defenses at Nagara Point.

On 1 May 1915 French submarine *Joule* struck a mine in the Dardanelles and was lost with all hands.[44] She was part of the Anglo-French Flotilla that was attempting to force the Dardanelles and take the Ottoman Empire out of the war. If successful it would have opened a sea route to Russia through the Dardanelles and the Black Sea. On 26 July 1915 French submarine *Mariotte* became entangled in a Turkish-laid antisubmarine net in the Dardanelles. She was forced to surface in an attempt to get clear but was immediately taken under fire by Turkish shore batteries and sank. Most of her crew got off and were captured.[45]

Later that year on 30 October French submarine *Turquoise* ran aground in the Dardanelles near Nagara

---

43 The Austro-Hungarian Empire used Roman numerals to distinguish between its submarines, while Germany used Arabic numbers

44 Messimer, Op cit., p. 247

45 Ibid, p. 248

Point and was captured. Her crew failed to scuttle her and the Turks recovered sensitive material on board relating to the planned rendezvous of *Turquoise* and British submarine E-20 in the Sea of Marmara on 6 November. The Turks promptly passed that information to their German allies, and UB-14 waited submerged at the rendezvous point. When E-20 showed up on the surface she was torpedoed and sunk by UB-14. There were nine survivors.[46] *Turquoise* was refloated and taken into the Turkish Navy as *Mustadieh Ombashi* but never recommissioned.

December 1915 was a bad month for the French submarine service. On 5 December *Fresnel* ran aground in the southern Adriatic and was destroyed by Austro-Hungarian forces. On 29 December while operating off the enemy port of Cattaro, *Monge* was rammed and sunk.

During 1916 two Austrian seaplanes claimed the honor of sinking a French submarine, *Foucalt,* in the Adriatic Sea, a first for air ASW.[47] That was on 15 September. The airmen were thoughtful enough to land on the sea and rescue some survivors and turn them over to a patrol boat. The previous month *Gustave Zede* was destroyed in the Adriatic by a battery explosion. Most of her crew survived.

On 24 May 1917 French submarine *Circe* sank UC-24 off Cattaro.[48] On 16 June *Ariane* was lost in the central

---

46   Ibid, p. 251
47   Evans and Peattie, Kaigun, p. 168
48   Messimer, Op cit., p. 202

Mediterranean near the Gulf of Bizerta, torpedoed by UC-22 while on sea trials after repairs. UC-22 was a German coastal minelayer and was probably in the area on a mine laying mission when she happened upon *Ariane*.

1918 saw the loss of five French submarines in action or to operational accidents. On 11 February *Diane* was lost off La Pallice, France due to an internal explosion while escorting a vessel. On 13 February *Bernoulli* was mined and sunk off Durazzo in the Adriatic. On 28 April, in the English Channel, *Prairal* was lost in a collision with a British ship off the port of Le Harve. On 2 August *Floreal* was lost in the northern Aegean Sea in a collision with an armed British steamer. Finally, *Circe* was torpedoed and sunk on 20 September off Cattaro by U-XLVII while on ASW patrol.

From start to finish the French submarine service lost 15 submarines: eleven to enemy action; two in collisions; and two more due to internal explosions. Seven were lost in the Adriatic; four in the Dardanelles; two in the English Channel; and one each in the Mediterranean and the Aegean seas. France began the war with 55 submarines and added 19 during the war for a total of 74 boats. The fifteen lost equated to an attrition rate of about 20%. It can be seen that the French Submarine Service was very active during the war but not very effective.

CHAPTER SIX – BRITISH SUBMARINE OPERATIONS

Great Britain had 74 submarines in commission when the war started. Nine were stationed overseas: three "C" class at Gibraltar, three "B" class at Malta and three more at Hong Kong. The remaining 65 were at home, organized in nine flotillas. 8th Flotilla, the 'Overseas Flotilla' under command of Commander Keyes, consisted of 8 "D" class and 9 "E" class submarines, based at Harwich. Their principal targets were major warships of the German High Seas Fleet. They were supported by two depot ships (submarine tenders). Five other flotillas, consisting of "B" and "C" class submarines, guarded the East Coast and the Dover Strait. They were based at Dover, Chatham, Humber, Tyne and Forth. The three remaining flotillas, all "A" class submarines, belonged to local defense commands. Their role was strictly in-shore. The Royal Australian Navy (RAN) possessed two "E" class submarines, AE 1 and AE 2, both in Australian waters.[49]

Thirty-two submarines were under construction at the start of the war. The November 1914 Emergency War Program called for another 65 submarines including 20 to be built in Canada and the United States.[50] Seven new submarines entered service in 1914 and three were lost.[51]

During the war British submarines operated in these areas:

- in the Baltic Sea in support of the Russians;
- in the Mediterranean Sea including the Dardanelles;
- on offensive patrols in the North Sea against German warships;
- on antisubmarine warfare patrols in the North Sea and the sea areas around the British Isles[52]

When the war began 17 British "overseas" submarines, based at Harwich, were intended as a strike force for use against the German High Seas Fleet. The British Grand Fleet outnumbered the German High Seas Fleet by the ratio of 3:2. Germany decided to avoid a general fleet engagement until such time it could reduce the odds

---

49   Gray, Edwyn, *British Submarines in the Great War*, p. 25.
50   The submarines built in the U.S. and Canada would constitute the "H" class and will be discussed later.
51   Hezlet, Op cit., p. 32
52   British submarines were very active throughout the war and sank 18 U-boats although they were not specifically designed for ASW activities

by inflicting significant attrition on the Grand Fleet.[53] German U-boats were attached to the Scouting Force, and were stationed at Heligoland, an island in the North Sea just off the German coast. The attrition campaign involved mines, motor torpedo boats and U-boats, and an occasional surface warship excursion designed to lure a portion of the Grand Fleet into action.[54]

Sorties by the German High Seas Fleet were designed to try to trap smaller units of the British Home Fleet and destroy them, thus reducing Home Fleet's numerical superiority. Such sorties usually involved strategic reconnaissance by Zeppelins, and "submarine traps", that is lines of U-boats positioned to attack and sink major Royal Navy surface warships.

By the end of 1914 British subs had sunk German light cruiser *Helas* and a destroyer in the North Sea.[55] A second German cruiser had escaped due to a torpedo malfunction. The German Navy was starting to realize the significance of the submarine threat to their own capital ships. The *Helas* loss caused the German fleet to shift its training operations from the North Sea to the

---

53 The British Grand Fleet will also be referred to as the Home Fleet from time to time.
54 Ibid, p. 24
55 The term "light cruiser" refers to a cruiser with 6" or lesser caliber guns. A "heavy cruiser" carries 8" guns. This distinction came into play after WWI when various attempts to limit a naval arms race took place. Usually a light cruiser will have lesser displacement than a heavy cruiser.

Baltic Sea.[56] The Kiel Canal provided a ready route to shift units between the two bodies of water.

Baltic Sea Operations

The Baltic Sea was basically off limits to the British Grand Fleet. German mines and a lack of bases made it impractical for surface warships to operate there against German units. Furthermore the Kiel Canal allowed the German High Seas Fleet to operate freely in the North Sea in the event the Grand Fleet tried to enter the Baltic.

The German Baltic Fleet had control of much of the Baltic in the face of an inferior Russian Baltic Fleet. The High Seas Fleet used the safe western Baltic waters for fleet exercises and new ship trials. The Russian Navy requested assistance, and the Royal Navy attempted to send three E class submarines into the Baltic. In 1914 E 1 and E 9 got in safely, but E 11 had to turn back. E 11 had an encounter with a supposed U-boat during its attempt to enter the Baltic, and fired but missed, fortunately. Its target was a misidentified Danish submarine. E-11's CO, Martin Nasmith, went on to establish a glorious submarine record during the Dardanelles campaign for which he was awarded the Victoria Cross.

E 1 and E 9 didn't come across any High Seas Fleet units but did have some encounters with German Baltic Fleet units. They continued on to Russia and there operated under Russian operational control against

---

56   Ibid, pp. 26 - 27

German warships on the flank of the Russian Army.[57] They sank old battleship *Pommern* and a destroyer and three naval auxiliary ships.[58]

On 18 October 1914 E 1 began its first Baltic Sea patrol. It fired at cruiser *Victoria Luise* but the torpedo ran too deep and missed. An alert lookout spotted the wake and the ship turned causing the second torpedo to miss ahead. It turned out that the warhead was about 40 pounds heavier than the exercise head used in practice firings. The weight difference caused the war shot to run deeper than set.[59] It took the Admiralty a while to acknowledge and fix the problem, although their response was like lightning in its relative speed compared to that of the U.S. Navy Bureau of Ordnance during WWII when serious torpedo problems were reported by the operating forces.

In June 1915 E 9 was on patrol and sighted a submariner's dream target; a light cruiser and four destroyers with a collier. The collier was an underway fuel replenishment ship of the era and carried coal. The collier had stopped to transfer coal to the destroyers while the cruiser circled. Max Horton, E 9's CO, bided his time. When things were lined up properly he fired his port beam tube at the cruiser and two bow tubes at the

---

57   Messimer, Op cit., pp, 230 – 231. Admiral Nicholas von Essen, Commander Russian Baltic Fleet, directed them to operate against German warships rather than against the Swedish iron ore trade. However, the German Navy was most concerned about the safety of the iron ore trade.

58   Hezlet, Op cit., pp. 33 - 34

59   Gray, Op cite, p. 67

collier.[60] He missed the cruiser but hit the collier and an alongside destroyer and both sank.[61] In these early days of submarine warfare the only sensors available to surface forces were lookouts' eyes. If the submarine CO was judicious in his use of the periscope, there would be no warning of danger until a torpedo wake appeared.

Baltic Sea Map

---

60   The E class submarine had two bow torpedo tubes, one stern tube, and two beam tubes, one firing to starboard and one to port. At that time most torpedoes did not have settable gyros and so the torpedoes had to be fired at the correct offset angle to hit a ship that was underway. Having beam tubes afforded some flexibility to the CO during an attack.

61   Ibid, pp. 78 - 79

On 2 July after fog had cleared E 9 sighted two large warships escorted by a destroyer and Horton fired two tubes at 400 yards and severely damaged cruiser *Prinz Adalbert* putting her into dock for several months. The torpedoes of that day were 18 inch diameter and did not carry a large warhead. Lcdr. Horton was decorated with the Order of St. George, Russia's highest military medal.[62]

On 25 July 1915 Germany unleashed a new ground offensive on its Eastern Front and brought in several High Seas Fleet battle cruisers for naval support of ground operations. The Russian government again requested British assistance. In reply the Admiralty reinforced its Baltic Flotilla. E 8, E 13, E 18 and E 19 were ordered in via the Kattegat passage from the North Sea, while C 26, 27, 32 and 35 were towed to Archangel and then barged via inland waterways to St. Petersburg (later Petrograd). The C-class submarine batteries were shipped separately and lost to a U-boat attack in the North Sea. It took several months to get replacement batteries to St. Petersburg so the small C-class submarines could operate.

On 14 August E 8 and E 13 departed Harwich. E 8 got into the Baltic with some difficulty, wiping her starboard propeller blades in the process. E 13 had compass problems and ran aground on Saltholm Flats in Danish territorial waters. By international law she could only remain there for 24 hours before being interned. A Danish guard ship, an old gunboat, was standing by

---

62   Ibid, pp. 79-80

observing as E 13 tried to get free. Two German torpedo boats came on the scene and violated international law by attacking E 13 inside Danish territorial waters. E 13 was lost along with 15 of her crew. Danish ships rescued 16 survivors. Presumably the Danish official diplomatic protest wound up in the circular file in the Berlin Foreign Ministry. E 18 and E 19 were more successful and got into the Baltic without incident.

On 19 August E 1 sighted four German battle cruisers in the Gulf of Riga. Her CO fired two torpedoes and hit battle cruiser *Moltke,* damaging it. As a result Admiral von Hipper called off the operations in progress, an attack on the Russian submarine base in the Gulf and naval gunfire support for German Army operations ashore.

The arrival of additional E-class submarines and the reduction of German naval support operations allowed the British Baltic Flotilla to go after the Swedish iron ore trade with Germany. Sweden was neutral, as she would be later during WW II. Trading legally, she supplied Germany with vital iron ore for munitions manufacture.

British submarines operated under international law. They could stop a ship, inspect its papers and either seize or sink it if contraband was being carried. Iron ore fell into that category. If no contraband was found the ship was allowed to proceed. If the ship was to be sunk, the crew were put into their boats and given directions to nearest land. In the Baltic where distances are short that situation presented no particular problems.

On 5 October E 8 captured SS *Margarette* departing Konigsberg and sank her with gunfire. On 23 October, off Libau E 8 sighted a cruiser with two escorting destroyers. She fired and sank recently repaired cruiser *Prinz Adalbert* whose magazine exploded.

On 11 October E 19 intercepted and sank ore-carrier *Walter Leonhardt* with explosive charges. The same day she chased *Germania* which ran aground and sank. She also sank *Gutruse*, another ore ship bound for Hamburg from Lulea. *Direktor Rippenhagan*, an ore carrier, was also stopped and sunk. Finally *Nicomedia* was stopped and sunk. E 19's activities on that one day resulted in a complete stoppage of the iron ore trade between Sweden and Germany. Fifteen ore ships were held in Lulea, Sweden until convoy could be arranged. The High Seas Fleet released two cruisers and two destroyer flotillas for trade protection in the Baltic, rendering the High Seas Fleet incapable of carrying out "sweeps" in the North Sea to lure Grand Fleet units into combat. Rarely have the activities of one submarine had such clearly related and significant reaction.

Not to be outdone, E 9 sank four large steamers on 18 and 19 October. On 7 November E 19 sank light cruiser *Undine* with two torpedo hits despite her destroyer escort. One of the torpedoes struck a magazine and *Undine* went up in a fiery blast. By the end of November all the E boats were back in Revel and submarine operations stopped because of ice formation in the Baltic. The Baltic Flotilla's debut was spectacular but it would not continue - given the professionalism of the German Navy.

In spring 1916 when ice receded and submarine operations could resume, the Baltic Flotilla found that the German Navy had instituted strict convoy procedures for all iron ore ships from Swedish ports. In addition, they had a total of 70 torpedo boats and armed trawlers available to escort the convoys. As a result the iron ore supply from Sweden went through without any particular problems.

C 27 sank a transport in the Gulf of Riga, while E 18 blew off the bow of destroyer V 100, which was able to limp back to its base. One day later E 18 vanished without a trace, presumably a victim of a mine in late May or early June 1916.[63] The Russians were masters at mine warfare, and the Germans also employed mines freely. E 13 was lost on passage that year and C 32 was lost due to grounding.[64]

During 1917 German convoy methods continued to block British submarine operations against iron ore shipping. Not only were professional prospects poor, but the stirrings of revolution were being felt in the Russian Fleet. In October 1917 C 26 attacked German naval forces supporting ground operations in the Gulf of Riga area. C 26 came under attack with depth charges, a first in Baltic waters. She barely got away, having been trapped in 20

---

63   The wreckage of E 18 was finally discovered close to the Estonian island of Hiiumaa in October 2009 by a Swedish Marine Survey Company, MMT.

64   Ibid, pp. 89-90

feet of water. On 24 October C 32 grounded on a mud bank and had to be blown up by her crew.

During 1917 the Russian Revolution seriously interfered with British submarine operations in the Baltic. Eventually the British subs were withdrawn to Helsingfors (present day Helsinki) and scuttled in early April 1918 lest they fall into the hands of the Germans as was required at the signing of the Treaty of Brest-Livosk between Russia and Germany on March 3, 1918.[65]

British submarines had a serious impact on German naval operations in the Baltic, damaging and sinking a number of large warships. They also stopped the important iron ore trade between Sweden and Germany in 1915. However, the introduction of a convoy system in 1916 countered their operations. During 1916 and 1917 they were unable to interfere with iron ore shipping. It was a lesson for the British Admiralty that went begging. Convoy was equally useful against a submarine campaign that observed international law (stop, search, and capture or sink ships carrying contraband) or one that ignored international law and sank ships without warning.

Dardanelles Operations

In October 1914 the Royal Navy established a naval force base at Tenedos and a larger base at Mudros on the island of Lemnos in the Aegean Sea. From there submarines B-9, B-10 and B-11 operated throughout October in a

---

65   Messimer, Op cit., p. 240

close blockade of the Dardanelles, the waterway between the Mediterranean Sea and the Black Sea, to prevent German warships SMS *Goeben* and *Breslau* from exiting the Sea of Marmara where they had taken refuge. At the time Turkey was neutral.[66] The German government transferred "ownership "of the two warships to Turkey, and their German crews then continued to operate their ships while wearing Turkish fez headgear. The German admiral commanding the small squadron was appointed Commander in Chief of the Turkish Navy.

On 28 October 1914 *Goeben, Breslau* and Turkish ship *Hamidich* sortied into the Black Sea and bombarded the Russian ports of Sebastopol, Novorossik and Odessa, thus bringing Turkey into the war as an ally of Germany. Somewhat belatedly the Ottoman Empire (Turkey) declared war on 1 November. In reaction, on 3 November HMS Indomitable and HMS Indefatigable bombarded the Turkish fortresses at the Dardanelles. French warships operated in support.[67] Finally, Great Britain and France formally declared war on Turkey on 5 November 1914.

The Russian government requested assistance from Great Britain and France. Lord Kitchener, head of the British Imperial General Staff, requested that the Admiralty make a demonstration against the straits' fortresses but emphasized that he had no troops to spare for a ground campaign.

---

66   Turkey's neutrality was highly suspect since warships of
      belligerent powers were only entitled to a 24 hour grace
      period in neutral territorial waters before being interned.
67   Gray, Op cit., pp. 95-96

Winston Churchill embraced the idea wholeheartedly although First Sea Lord Admiral Jackie Fisher did not, having had personal experience in opposing shore fortress guns from the sea during a bombardment of Alexandria, Egypt in the 1880s. On 28 January 1915 a decision to proceed with a naval bombardment was made, and it began 19 February. Along with the bombardment decision was a move to send seven E class British submarines plus Australian AE 2 to Mudros.[68]

From December 1914 through January 1916, when the last British and ANZAC ground forces were withdrawn from the Gallipoli Peninsula, Great Britain and France engaged initially in a naval and later an amphibious campaign to seize Constantinople (now Istanbul), the capital of the Ottoman Empire, and knock Turkey out of the war.

Turkey and the Dardanelles

CIA World Factbook

---

68   Ibid, pp. 102-103

The scheme was pushed by Winston Churchill, First Lord of the Admiralty, and civilian head of the Royal Navy.[69] The campaign bogged down and Allied forces took heavy casualties and ultimately had to withdraw. As a result Churchill was forced out of office. The plan was somewhat grandiose but had possibilities of opening a sea route through the Dardanelles and the Sea of Marmara into the Black Sea and on to Sevastopol, a major Russian naval base. Success would have allowed the movement of Russian grain to its western allies, and arms and ammunition to Russia.[70] Such events might have forestalled the Russian revolution that tore that country apart in late 1917 and led to the formation of the USSR.

The Royal Navy moved a group of "coast defense" subs from the island of Malta to the Dardanelles vicinity. B 9, B 10 and B 11, built in 1906 were the British contributions to an Allied submarine flotilla. Three French submarines also joined the flotilla, which was under the command of Lcdr. Pownall, RN. They were supported by a depot ship, *Hindu Kush*, which served as headquarters ship and provided accommodations for submarine crews in port. Another pair of B class subs, B 6 and B 7 was transferred from Gibraltar to join the flotilla.

---

69   The First Lord of the Admiralty was civilian head of the Royal Navy. The First Sea Lord, an admiral, was the military head of the Royal Navy and served under the First Lord.

70   The Baltic was closed to Allied shipping, and northern Russian ports were icebound for part of the year. A Black Sea route would have been open year round.

Lcdr. Pownall proposed submarine activity in the Dardanelles Strait if anti-mine guards could be fitted to the British B class submarines. The Strait was known to be heavily mined. The submerged endurance of B class was far too short to permit long enough submerged operations to allow them to penetrate into the Sea of Marmara. His plan was approved in December 1914.

With both British and French subs available, Lcdr. Pownall had to decide which submarine would make the first attempt to operate in the Dardanelles. British submarines had greater submerged endurance (greater battery capacity) than did French submarines so the choice was obvious. B 11 had a brand new battery so it was chosen for the first mission. At 0415 on 13 December 1914 B 11 was on the surface about three miles off the straits' entrance. She crept in to one mile off Cape Helles and submerged. About half way up the Strait she came to periscope depth and sighted armored Turkish warship *Messoudieh*. B 11 fired her torpedoes and sank her.

The Dardanelles, a narrow passage from the eastern Mediterranean Sea into the Sea of Marmara, would seem an unlikely venue for submarines since it was heavily mined, defended by steel wire underwater nets and covered by shore batteries. The currents were contradictory and there was an outflow of fresh water which made diving officers' task of keeping their submarines in trim very difficult.[71]

However it became a very active route for allied submarines, all attempting to penetrate into the Sea of Marmara to interdict Turkish shipping providing resupply to their ground forces on the Gallipoli Peninsula. Two routes were used by the Turks to resupply their troops; the first was overland by camel or pack mules or oxen cart and took about seven days. The second, faster route was by sea through the Sea of Marmara. Powered ships and sailing vessels were used for resupply.

On 17 April 1915, E 15 made the first attempt to penetrate the Dardanelles to get into the Sea of Marmara. She ran aground at Kaphez Point and was lost. Her CO was killed by Turkish gunfire while trying to evacuate his crew. B 6 was then sent in to attempt to torpedo E 15 in order to destroy her. Both her torpedoes missed. Royal Naval Air Service seaplanes attempted to bomb E 15 but were similarly unsuccessful. A pair of destroyers were sent in next but had to withdraw under heavy and accurate gunfire from Turkish shore batteries. Submarine B 11 was then dispatched but mist kept her from torpedoing E 15. Battleships HMS Majestic and Triumph were

---

71   Salt water and fresh water have different densities. A submarine properly trimmed for salt water operations will start to sink if it goes into an area of fresh water such as a river estuary, and the diving officer must re-compensate the boat by pumping water out of variable ballast tanks into the sea until the submarine is back in "trim", that is properly trimmed for neutral buoyancy at slow speed..

employed but could not get closer than 12,000 yards due to heavy Turkish gunfire. At that range their guns were not accurate enough to hit E 11. Finally, as a last ditch attempt, a pair of British picket boats, jury-rigged with two fourteen inch torpedoes apiece made a desperate try. They were successful. Two torpedoes fired at a range of 200 yards struck and destroyed E 15.[72]

Australian submarine AE 2 set out on 25 April, the date of the first Gallipoli landings. She was the second submarine to try and the first to reach the Sea of Marmara. However she experienced trim problems after reaching the Sea of Marmara.. She was sighted by a Turkish torpedo boat while inadvertently surfacing. It opened fire and hit her three times in the engine room. Unable to dive with her pressure hull ruptured, she was scuttled by her crew. The torpedo boat, *Yar Hissar*, rescued her crew.[73]

E 14, on the third attempt, got through successfully and inflicted serious damage to Turkish resupply shipping. Her CO had his own ideas about how to penetrate the Straits successfully. He ran in on the surface at night using his diesel engines with his submarine trimmed down so that the main deck was awash and only the conning tower was above water. He passed Chanak Kale and then submerged to avoid numerous Turkish gunboats. In the Sea of Marmara he torpedoed and damaged a transport, and then rendezvoused with AE 2. AE 2 had

72   Ibid, pp. 105-106
73   Messimer, Op cit., p. 250

missed several targets including a Turkish battleship – with torpedoes that ran too deep. The following day AE 2 was lost.

On 1 May French submarine *Joule* struck a mine while attempting to penetrate the Straits and was lost with all hands. Several weeks earlier another French submarine, *Saphir*, had run aground off Nagara Point and was lost.[74]

E 14 was replaced by E 11. During the campaign from April to December 1915 there was always a British sub in the Sea of Marmara, and sometimes two.[75] In October 1915 a total of four Allied subs were there.

E 14 found very few targets in the Sea of Marmara while she patrolled there. Turkish naval authorities had taken note of the submarine threat and were sending replacement troops and supplies by road rather than risk them to submarine attack. On 3 May E 14 spotted a transport, escorted by a destroyer. She hit the transport but the torpedo was a dud. She stopped and searched several ships but found that they were evacuating refugees and so allowed them to continue. On 10 May she spotted two transports plus one destroyer. She missed the lead ship but hit 5,000 ton transport *Gul Djemal*, which sank, taking down 6,000 troops and an artillery battery. That was her last torpedo. On 17 May she was ordered out, and followed a Turkish patrol vessel through the Chanak

74   Gray, Op cit., pp. 115-116
75   Hezlet, Op cit., pp. 35 - 38

minefield and then dove deep to get under the other minefields. Her CO, Boyle, was promoted to Commander and awarded the Victoria Cross for his success.[76]

On 19 May E 11 under Martin Nasmith set out. About 0350 abeam of *Aichi Baba*, a prominent height on the Gallipoli Peninsula, she went down to 80 feet to run the minefields, successfully. On 23 May she approached the Turkish capital of Constantinople and sank a Turkish gunboat with a torpedo, but a very accurate Turkish round struck one of her periscopes and put it out of commission. On 28 May she sank a large steamer. Air reconnaissance reports from RNAS seaplanes were relayed to E 11 by HMS Jed, a destroyer serving as a communications relay ship. That information reported shipping traffic at the eastern end of the Dardanelles. Subsequently E 11 sank a large liner off Ponderma.

Nasmith decided that losing a torpedo that missed a target for any reason and then sank was unacceptable. He had his torpedo men trim the remaining torpedoes so that they would float at the end of their run – if they had not hit anything and exploded. His idea was to disarm the warhead while the torpedo was floating in the water, then take the torpedo aboard and strike it below, refurbish it and use it again. E 11 proceeded to carry out this evolution

76   Gray, Op cit., pp. 118-120

with Nasmith going into the water himself to disarm the first torpedo before it was brought aboard.[77]

On leaving the Sea of Marmara, E 11 snagged a moored mine while submerged. Nasmith could see the mine cable and the mine through the conning tower scuttles but chose not to inform his crew. The cable had broken and E 11 was dragging the mine along. The mine was designed for use against surface ships and had contact horns only on the upper part of the sphere. Several hours later, after E 11 got through the Straits, Nasmith backed E 11 down and the mine cable slipped free.[78]

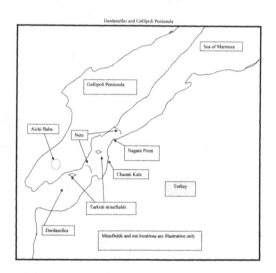

Dardanelles and Gallipoli Peninsula

---

[77] You will not find a better example of leadership than Nasmith's behavior. He didn't ask or tell his crew to do something he was unwilling to do himself. Incidentally he also violated International Law by directing his torpedo men to adjust the valve that would ordinarily cause the torpedo to sink at the end of its run if it had not exploded - a requirement for torpedoes.

[78] Ibid, pp. 148-149

The British-French Dardanelles Flotilla's submarine campaign lasted from April through December 1915. Nine British and four French submarines took part, carrying out 15 patrols in the Sea of Marmara. In August E 11 made a 29 day patrol and sank a Turkish battleship, a gunboat, seven transports and 23 sailing vessels.

Several allied submarines were lost attempting to go up the strait into the Sea of Marmara and one was lost coming out. *Joule* was mined, while *Mariotte* and E 7 were caught in steel antisubmarine nets. On 25 July 1915 *Mariotte* headed for the Sea of Marmara, but was caught in a net and forced to surface near Chanak where she was shelled, and scuttled by her crew who surrendered.

Turquoise and E 15 both ran aground within range of Turkish shore batteries. E 20 was lost in the Sea of Marmara, torpedoed by UB-14.

E 11 left harbor on 5 August for her second patrol. The Royal Navy had decided to maintain two submarines in the Sea of Marmara. E 11 torpedoed *Beri-i-Satvet,* a torpedo gunboat of 775 tons mounting two four-inch guns. The torpedo boat ran aground to keep from sinking. On 8 August E 11 torpedoed battleship *Hairredin Barbarossa.* Fire reached her magazine and she blew up. She displaced 10,000 tons and was equipped with four 11-inch guns.[79]

E 14 sank a 5,000 ton transport and then returned home. On 21 August E 2 sank a 1,500 ton armed steamer. On 22 August she sank a large steamer, and then a

79   Ibid, pp. 148-149

transport several days later. On 3 September both E 11 and E 2 departed the Sea of Marmara.

On 15 September E 12, equipped with a 4-inch gun, shelled the gun powder mills at Mudania, and sank a large steamer. She fought a surface gun action with a torpedo boat, and sank a 3,000 ton supply ship. On 4 October she rendezvoused with submarine H 1. On 2 October H 1 had sunk two steamships, one of 3,000 tons and the other of 1,500 tons. Two days later French submarine *Turquoise* penetrated into the Sea of Marmara. On 23 October E 20 joined, making four Allied submarines, three British and one French, conducting offensive operations in the Sea of Marmara.[80]

By mid-September 1915 British forces had sealed off the eastern entrance to the Dardanelles against U-boats, using nets and mines. On 13 September von Heimburg in U-21 found his way blocked when he attempted to enter the Dardanelles to reach Constantinople.[81]

On 7 November the Germans announced the destruction of two allied submarines, *Turquoise* and E 20. *Turquoise* was captured intact on 30 October in the Straits with a chart showing a planned rendezvous with E 20. German submarine UB-14 kept the rendezvous instead of *Turquoise*, torpedoing E 20. There were nine survivors.[82]

Communications between allied submarines in the Sea of Marmara and the headquarters ship were somewhat

---

80   Ibid, p. 169
81   Messimer, Op cit., p. 202
82   Gray, Edwyn, Op cit., pp. 171-172

tenuous. At night the submarines would surface to conduct a battery charge and rig their antennas for communications. A British destroyer operated west of the Gallipoli Peninsula to act as a relay ship.

On 2 January 1916 E 2 departed the Sea of Marmara, the last British submarine there on patrol. A week later allied forces at Cape Helles were evacuated, ending the Gallipoli Campaign. Four E class subs, five B class subs, and six H class subs remained in the Mediterranean Sea.

The Dardanelles Submarine Flotilla had inflicted a great deal of damage, sinking one battleship, one destroyer, five gunboats, 11 transports, 44 supply ships and 148 sailing vessels, thus seriously interfering with the resupply of Turkish troops on the Gallipoli Peninsula.[83] However, overall the Gallipoli Campaign was a costly failure.

Mediterranean Sea Operations

The Royal Navy had three problems in the Mediterranean Sea now that Dardanelles operations were over:

- Battle cruiser *Goeben* and cruiser *Breslau* might break out and attack the allied forces at Salonika, Greece;
- the Austro-Hungarian fleet had to be contained within the Adriatic Sea; and
- U-boat sinking's in the Mediterranean Sea were increasing sharply.

---

83   Hezlet, Op cit., pp. 35-36

American diplomatic pressure had been brought to bear on Germany to stop torpedoing ships without warning in the Atlantic where U.S. flag ships mostly sailed. However, the U.S. seemed to ignore the same practice when carried out in the Mediterranean Sea where few U.S. ships sailed. The German Navy and government discerned that subtle difference and took advantage of it. During the first six months of 1916, 256 ships (662,131 tons) were sunk in the Med, many without warning. Whether a ship carrying supplies or raw materials to the United Kingdom was sunk in the Atlantic or the Med made little difference. It was a loss of vital supplies and merchant ship capacity in either case.

British submarines were redeployed to help deal with the problems. E 2 stayed off the Dardanelles in case of a sortie by the two major enemy warships. Six subs were sent to reinforce the Otranto Barrage, designed to keep the Austro-Hungarian fleet and its U-boats bottled up in the Adriatic Sea; and eight subs were redirected to conduct antisubmarine patrols in the Med.

Adriatic operations cost the Royal Navy two submarines: H 3 was lost at the Otranto Barrage, and B 10 was sunk during an air raid on Venice.

Finally in January 1918 battle cruiser *Goeben* and cruiser *Breslau* broke out of the Dardanelles to attack allied forces in the Aegean Sea. Both ships struck mines. *Breslau* sank but *Goeben* managed to get back inside the Dardanelles. E 14 was sent in to finish *Goeben*, but was distracted by an auxiliary ship and commenced an attack. She was detected, and depth charged to the surface. Her crew was killed by gunfire as they attempted to abandon ship, and E 14 sank.

On 23 May 1918 British H 4 sank UB-52 in the Otranto area with two torpedoes. Another British H boat spotted and sank another submarine, but the four rescued survivors indicated the victim was an allied Italian H-class submarine instead of an enemy submarine.

North Sea Operations

On 13 September 1914 E 9 under Max Horton sank German cruiser *Hela* with two torpedoes and one hit. That same month on the other side of the globe, Australian submarine AE 1 was on patrol off German New Guinea looking for German cruiser *Geier*. AE 1 went missing and no trace of her has ever been located.

During 1914 British submarine D 5 was on patrol in the Heligoland Bight when she sighted and attacked German cruiser *Rostok*. D 5 fired two torpedoes, which unfortunately ran deep and went under her hull. The explosive warheads were forty pounds heavier than the exercise heads used in peacetime practices, and they ran deeper - unbeknownst to the Admiralty technical personnel.[84] Late that year E 9 was on patrol near Kiel Bay. The CO, Horton, attacked a German destroyer, S.120, and fired at a range of 600 yards with a depth setting of 8

---

84   Gray, Op cit., pp. 30-31

feet. The heavier warhead caused the torpedo to run deep, under the intended target, and then to explode against a mud bank. S.120 was shaken but otherwise undamaged.

Later in September 1914 Horton set his torpedoes to run shallow and sank German destroyer S.116 with one torpedo. On the following day German naval authorities stopped all merchant ship movement from Lubeck for 24 hours. The German Navy Commander-in-Chief noted that enemy submarine activity had seriously altered operational conditions in the Heligoland Bight. On 17 October 1914 E 3 was operating off the River Ems and was torpedoed and sunk by U-27

French steam-powered submarine *Archimede* was on patrol in the North Sea on 17 December 1914 when heavy seas damaged her funnel which precluded her from diving, thus pointing out one of the vulnerabilities of steam powered submarines at the time. She made it back to a British port safely on the surface.

British submarine S 1, an Italian design by Laurenti, was also on patrol in the North Sea. She suffered a major engine casualty, such that she could not recharge her battery. Her CO put her on the bottom in daytime to conserve the remaining battery capacity. That evening he came to periscope depth and closed and captured a German trawler, which he put to use to tow S 1 back to Harwich and safety.[85]

A German surface naval attack on England's East Coast drew a retaliatory response from offensive-minded

---

85   Ibid, pp. 59-61

Winston Churchill. He laid on a planned coordinated air-surface-submarine attack. The air attack was to destroy the German airship sheds at Cuxhaven, using RNAS seaplanes. The German High Seas Fleet was expected to sortie in response and to be met by the waiting British Grand Fleet. Eleven submarines of the 8th Flotilla were to support the seaplane raid and to cover all lines of approach to the area where seaplane carriers were located, to ambush any responding German surface warships, and to conduct air-sea rescue for seaplanes in trouble. Submarines S 1 and nine others deployed on 23 December. E 7 was already on patrol off Heligoland.

In the event, nine seaplanes were placed on the sea by their carriers. Only seven could get off the water. Two were unable to locate the target and dropped their bombs willy-nilly. Three returning seaplanes reached their mother ships and were recovered. One came down in Dutch territorial waters. The other three could not locate their mother ships.

E 11 was submerged on patrol off Norderny. Seeing a RNAS seaplane on the surface he surfaced his submarine, picked up the pilot and took the seaplane in tow. E 11 then spotted a German Zeppelin and two other RNAS seaplanes. E 11 rescued the two RNAS pilots and used her gun to destroy the planes. The Zeppelin commander saw E 11 take the planes under fire and understandably thought that E 11 was a U-boat so did not attack.[86]

---

86   Ibid, p. 50

In the North Sea and the area around the British Isles, German U-boats were taking a toll. British ASW measures included putting in a large mine field north of the Dover strait, equipping some 500 trawlers with guns and explosive sweeps, and bombarding the U-boat port of Zeebrugge in occupied Belgium. Indicator nets were still under development.

A major element in the British ASW system was minefields. However, the British mine mooring system was defective. The moorings were weak and mines frequently broke loose. Some mines were laid too near the surface so that they were visible at low water. The mine case was supposed to float about 5-10 feet below the surface, anchored to the bottom weight by a cable less than 100 feet in length. In spite of these limitations on 9 December U-14 was sunk, and on 18 December U-5 was sunk, both by mine explosions.[87]

Arrangements were also made to tow small submerged C-class submarines behind trawlers. A telephone connection kept the sub CO advised of any U-boat contacts. If one was made, the tow would be slipped and a submerged attack made on the surfaced U-boat. Two U-boats were sunk in this fashion during 1915.[88]

British submarines continued offensive patrols in the North Sea off German naval ports. They suffered the loss of three submarines during 1914.

---

87   Messimer, Op cit., pp. 25-26
88   Hezlet, Op cit., p. 30

On 1 January 1915 the German U-Boat Service celebrated the New Year by sinking HMS Formidable, a battleship, with two torpedoes.

After the Dogger Bank surface engagement in the North Sea in January 1915, UK subs routinely patrolled in the Heligoland Bight, the Skagerrak, and sometimes off the Norwegian coast. The patrols were not continuous but rather thrusts or sorties paralleling surface warship operations, or keyed to suspected enemy operations.

Most of British "overseas submarines" (D and later classes) in the United Kingdom were kept in port in readiness to respond to news that the German High Seas Fleet had sortied.[89] The High Seas Fleet came out seven times after the Dogger Bank action, but UK subs were on patrol only twice. E 6 fired a torpedo at battle cruiser *Moltke* in May and missed, and again attacked a light cruiser, *Rostok*, in October but missed again. This was the 7th sortie of the High Seas Fleet into the North Sea since the start of the war.

In September 1915 British submarines had attempted, unsuccessfully, to shoot down German Zeppelins.[90] They were singularly ill-equipped for the job, and the tasking probably represented the political state of panic in the United Kingdom over German Zeppelin raids.[91]

---

89   Ibid, pp. 31 33
90   Ibid, p. 31
91   O'Connell, The Effectiveness of Airpower in the 20th Century, Part One (1914 – 1939), p. 13

During 1915 six British submarines were lost and 31 new boats were commissioned. In the New Year January 1916 was not a good month for British submarines. On 6 January E 17 was wrecked off the Dutch coast. On 18 January H 6 followed suit. She was salvaged by the Dutch and interned. Later the Dutch purchased her from the UK and recommissioned her as the Dutch submarine O-8. However that was not the end of her story. She was scuttled at Dan Helder in 1940 during the German WW II invasion of Holland. The Germans salvaged her and she sailed under the Nazi flag as UD-1. She was finally paid off at Kiel in March 1943 and scuttled in 1945.[92]

British patrol submarines were fitted with a new 3 kilowatt radio transmitter during 1916. This equipment gave them the capability to report important German surface warship sightings directly to the Admiralty. Three British submarines were in the path of the German High Seas Fleet at the time of the Battle of Jutland but they had been instructed to lie doggo on the sea bed until June 21st. While resting on the bottom they could not receive radio messages hence were unable to enter into the action.[93]

---

92   Gray, Op cit., p. 190
93   Hezlet, Submarines and Sea Power, p. 133

North Sea Area Map

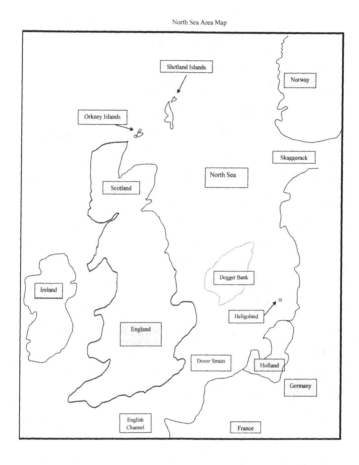

On 4 May 1916 a British seaplane raid against the German airship sheds at Tondern took place. In connection with the seaplane raid, two minefields were scheduled to be emplaced. The raid was a failure. Of nine seaplanes, only two got off the water. One of the two that took off caught a destroyer radio aerial in its float and crashed. The remaining seaplane dropped a few bombs

at Tondern without causing any significant damage. The initial launch was at 0300 and the single seaplane to make it to the target got back at 0500. Once she was recovered the force headed home.

About 0700 Zeppelin L 7 showed up. HMS Galatea and HMS Phaeton fired at L 7, hit her and she started to lose altitude. E 31, one of the nine submarines involved, surfaced and found L 7 almost overhead at a low altitude. Fearing aerial attack, E 31 immediately went deep. When she returned to periscope depth, no bombs having been dropped, she observed L 7 at a low altitude and realized the zeppelin was in trouble. E 31 then surfaced and opened fire with her deck gun. L 7 was only at an altitude of several hundred feet and E 31's shells set her hydrogen gas bags afire, destroying her.

The climactic Battle of Jutland was fought on 31 May 1916. The German High Seas Fleet inflicted a tactical defeat upon the British Grand Fleet, but suffered a strategic defeat in turn. The German High Seas Fleet never again attempted to challenge the British Grand Fleet in a major naval battle. The High Seas Fleet essentially remained in port until the end of the war, leaving the battle to the U-boat arm. There were a few more limited sorties against England's east coast ports, intended to isolate and destroy Grand Fleet units that might respond.

In August 1916 German Admiral Scheer planned operations by the High Seas Fleet to bombard the port of Sunderland, in an attempt to bring Grand Fleet units out. Scheer's plan was to draw the responding Grand Fleet into a U-boat trap. Admiral Jellicoe was aware of the possibility and determined that he could not take the Grand Fleet south of the Dogger Bank without adequate destroyer screens. The hitch was that he didn't have enough destroyers, thereby limiting Grand Fleet movements in the North Sea. Whether U-boats were actually there or not was immaterial, the threat was there.

On the other side of the equation, High Seas units were unable to depart their ports without encountering British subs on patrol station. These reported contacts and attacked if the opportunity presented itself. After June 1916 there were enough submarines in the Home Fleet of the United Kingdom to establish fairly permanent submarine patrol stations or areas in the North Sea to monitor German ports and operating areas. There were 38 "overseas" submarines at Harwich by mid-1916. Submarines based at Harwich were out operating north of Terschelling watching the exits from the Bight; while boats based at Blyth and Tyne covered Horn's Reef and Jutland Bank.[94]

On 14 July H-5 torpedoed U-51 off Borkum. Ordinarily such a success brought the immediate award of a Distinguished Service Order (DSO) to the commanding officer. In this instance the CO had to wait a year to receive it because he had violated patrol orders and left his assigned operating area to "poach" in another area.[95] He

94   Hezlet, Op cit, pp. 67 – 68. Also see Hezlet, Electronics and Sea Power, p. 40.
95   Gray, Op cit., p. 200.

was fortunate to receive an award, albeit belated, instead of a general court martial since "friendly fire" cost several submarines sunk by their own side during the war.

During 1916 the Royal Navy began to copy the U-boat mining capability to lay minefields off enemy ports. Some "E" class boats were modified to provide the capability to carry and plant mines. Each could carry a total of twenty mines. Their beam torpedo tubes were removed to allow installation of mine handling equipment.[96]

In August 1916 units of the High Seas Fleet sortied. At 0919 on 19 August, Room 40 intercepted and broke German radio traffic indicating a High Seas Fleet sortie scheduled for 2100. At 1830 the British Grand Fleet, forewarned, sortied from its bases. On 20 August at 0400 British submarine E 23 torpedoed German battleship *Westfalen*, and reported the action at 0916. Of course radio intelligence had already alerted Admiral Jellicoe several hours earlier.[97] On 19 August two light cruisers, HMS Nottingham and HMS Falmouth were sunk by U-boats.[98]

In October 1916 E 38 torpedoed and damaged light cruiser *Munchen*. In November 1916 battleships *Grosser Kurfurst* and *Kronprinz* were damaged by J 1's torpedoes. These offensive patrols were not without cost. During 1916 eight British submarines failed to return from patrol in the North Sea.[99]

---

96   Ibid, pp. 190-192.
97   Hezlet, Electronics and Sea Power, p. 131
98   Hoehling, The Great War at Sea, p. 181
99   Hezlet, The Submarine and Sea Power, pp. 72 - 73

Unrestricted U-boat attacks starting 1 February 1917 drew British submarines into an important ASW role.[100] Most submarines of the day did not have hydrophones (passive listening sonar) so had no means of detecting and tracking another submerged submarine. What they had was stealth through submergence and a watchful eye through a periscope. Stationed in areas frequented by U-boats and operating submerged in daylight, they might get a glimpse of a surfaced U-boat conducting an anti-shipping patrol.[101] If the lurking ASW sub could get into a firing position, a salvo of two torpedoes was likely to claim a U-boat victim. Seven U-boats were sunk during 1917, and six in 1918, for a total of eighteen sunk by British submarines during the war. Six of the U-boats were sunk off their bases, four more on passage to or from their patrol areas, and eight while patrolling trade routes.[102]

Overall Admiralty statistics indicated that most submarine ASW patrols were a waste of time, according to

---

100   Messimer, Op cit., pp. 27 – 28. Room 40 had an excellent idea from radio intelligence of the location of most U-boats, either at home or on patrol. They could not fix the exact position but did have a good idea about the U-boat operating area.

101   Submarines normally operated on the surface in daylight, using their lookouts to spot ships' masts or funnel smoke. Then the patrolling U-boat would close in on the surface using its relatively higher speed to get into a position to either make a submerged attack, or to use its deck gun to halt the ship and check its cargo for contraband. Daytime surface operations by submarines were only feasible in areas that were not under heavy aircraft surveillance. When an aircraft or airship was spotted by a U-boat lookout, the watch officer usually submerged immediately.

102   Hezlet, The Submarine and Sea Power, p. 77

one historian.[103] There were 56 enemy submarines sighted, from which six attacks were developed, and five U-boats sunk. That gives percentages of 10.7% chance of sighting an enemy submarine, and 8.92% chance of sinking an enemy submarine. However, the question must be asked whether there was an alternate employment for British submarines that would have contributed more to the overall war effort. Since the Royal Navy's distant blockade of Germany had eliminated German merchant ship trade, there was no necessity for a submarine blockade. Convoy was the correct strategic riposte to German U-boat operations of course, but sinking 18 U-boats was a very useful contribution. The author's conclusion is that their employment in the combined ASW campaign was justified.

January 1918 was a black month for British submarines, with five sunk. On 6 January H-5 was lost in a collision in the Irish Sea. On 14 January G-8 failed to return from a North Sea Patrol. On 19 January H -10 was lost. On 28 January E-14 was sunk by Turkish forces in the Dardanelles, and on 30 January E-50 was lost.[104]March 1918 was not much better. During the infamous "Battle of May Island", a major RN fleet exercise involving K-class steam-powered submarines, K-4 and K-17 were lost to collisions. On 15 March D-3 was sunk by a French airship off the Flanders coast, another victim of "friendly fire". Her identification rockets were mistaken for an attack against the airship.

---

103   Gray, Op cit., p. 211.
104   Ibid, p. 228.

April was a little better. During the last sortie of High Seas Fleet units, E-42 torpedoed *Molkte* and badly damaged her. May was even better: G-2 sank U-78, L-12 sank UB-90, E-35 sank U-154 and L-10 sank destroyer S.20.

In July E-34 was mined, and on 15 October J-6 was sunk by an enemy Q-ship. Finally on 1 November 1918, G-7 was reported overdue and presumed lost, the last British submarine lost during WW I.

"H" class submarines

Early in the war British authorities arranged for the construction of a number of Holland design submarines (Electric Boat Company) to be built in the United States and Canada. The American built H class boats, H-11 through H-20, were completed but neutrality concerns prevented delivery of any of them to Great Britain until 1917 when the United States entered the war. H-11 and H-12 were delivered to the Royal Navy, while H-14 and H-15 went to the Royal Canadian Navy. The remaining six were delivered to the Chilean Navy in compensation for the seizure of warships under contract to Chile which the Royal Navy had appropriated at the start of WW I.

The Canadian built boats, H-1 through H-10, were delivered to the United Kingdom. In addition to these destinations, Italy received six H class submarines, and Russia received eight. The Russian H class were designated *Americanski Golland (AG)*, meaning "American Holland" to distinguish them from other Russian submarines. Some of the AG submarines saw action in the Baltic Sea.

The H class was single hull construction with internal ballast tanks, carried 16 tons of fuel and had an operating depth of 100 feet. They were 171 feet long, and had four internal TT forward.[105] The crew size was 22. They could make speeds of 13/10.5 kts. They were simple and reliable and were well liked by their crews in various navies. Several British H class boats served in WWI and WW II.

Fleet Submarines

The Admiralty entertained the hopeful idea that submarines might be integrated directly into fleet operations, if only a submarine engineering plant could produce enough horsepower to propel the submarine at speeds equal to major warships (about 20-21 kts.) The Admiralty had realized that the new J class submarines' top diesel engine speed (18 – 19 knots) would still be inadequate for them to operate at fleet speeds. Therefore a requirement for a high surface speed steam powered submarine was established. The K class would be three times the size and 7 - 8 times the horsepower of any existing RN submarine. Fourteen were ordered in 1915. The first one completed, K 3, was built in 18 months. It had a surface speed of 24 knots, adequate to keep up

---

105   British-built H-class submarines were 21 feet longer and had slightly greater displacements than the American/Canadian-built H-class boats..

with the fleet. Two flotillas were formed in 1917 and became part of the Grand Fleet. Their operational scheme involved being stationed close astern of the advanced light cruiser screen, with a light cruiser as Submarine Flotilla Leader. When the enemy fleet approached they would spread out in pairs, five miles apart, and try to pass the enemy and get between the enemy force and its base. After the classic surface gunnery engagement, the K-class role was to pick off surviving enemy warships. They had twice the torpedo armament of an ordinary patrol submarine (a total of ten tubes).

They were not fast divers, having to close up their steam plant, which took at least five minutes. They never saw combat action, although two were lost and four damaged in collisions in the "Battle of May Island" on 31 January/1 February 1918, a major fleet exercise marred by fatal accidents.[106] In some RN circles the K designation was understood to stand for "Kalamity". A total of six were lost in accidents, including two after the war ended.

Tactical communications between the Fleet and the Submarine Flotilla Leader were by wireless, but the Submarine Flotilla Leader also had the Fessenden Submarine Signal apparatus that was installed in all K-class submarines. The Submarine Flotilla Leader and the K-class submarines communicated with this early underwater telephone.[107]

---

106 Hezlet, The Submarine and Sea Power, p. 75
107 Hezlet, Electronics and Sea Power, p. 135

The last three K-class hulls were modified during construction and they were commissioned as M-class submarines. Each was equipped with a 12-inch naval gun mounted forward of the conning tower. The guns were taken from pre-Dreadnought battle ships. The guns could be elevated but the submarine had to turn to train them on a target. Only M-1 was completed before the war ended and she did not see action. M 1 and her two sisters carried the largest caliber guns ever installed in submarines.[108] This particular submarine development avenue turned out to be a dead end.

Specialized British ASW submarines (R class)

In January 1917 the U-boat arm had 111 U-boats, and maintained about 46 at sea on any given day. The increasing German U-boat threat led directly to the development of the British R class submarine, optimized for submerged passive listening operations and firing a killing torpedo salvo against a surfaced submarine target. The R class carried five listening hydrophones in the bow and the largest number of bow torpedo tubes of any British submarine – six torpedo tubes. They were ordered in December 1917 and one, operating out of Killybegs, Donegal in Ireland, fired a salvo at a surfaced U-boat in October 1918. Only one torpedo hit but it failed to detonate.

---

108   Later, French submarine Surcouf carried several 8" guns, and some U.S. WW II submarines carried 6" guns.

Their submerged speed of 14 knots was phenomenal, although they made only nine knots on the surface.[109] Their small diesel engine took forever to recharge the battery.[110] They were highly streamlined with a single propeller shaft. However they did not handle well, either submerged or on the surface. Twelve were ordered and ten were completed. Eight were scrapped in 1923. The remaining two were used as high speed submerged targets for ASW training during the 1920s. R-4, the last one, survived until 1934.

COMINT role in Submarine Warfare

The role of "comint" in naval warfare and particularly in submarine warfare was a deep, dark compartmented secret for many years. Comint is an acronym for communications intelligence, referring to intelligence gained through interception and deciphering of enemy communications. It played a major role in World War I. At the time knowledge of the role of comint was

---

109   The submerged speed designation of a battery powered submarine is somewhat deceptive. It refers to the highest speed the submarine can make while submerged and operating on the battery as a power source. What it doesn't say is that it can make that high a speed for only one-half hour before the battery is exhausted. Thus the "R" class submarine could go only seven nautical miles submerged before it was out of power.

110   After WWII the U.S. Navy inflicted a somewhat similar type submarine on itself, the K-class, a very small submarine equipped with an extremely good passive sonar but with a very slow transit speed that gave them very poor strategic mobility. They took forever to get anywhere.

strictly limited to those with an absolute need to know. Comint was used by both sides, with varying degrees of effectiveness.

Room 40 was key to many British comint-related successes, some strategic and some tactical. In November 1916 U-30 suffered a casualty and had to return home. U-20 was sent to escort her. In fog both grounded along the Dutch coast and radioed for assistance. The High Seas Fleet commander, Admiral Scheer, dispatched several large warships to assist. Room 40 intercepted and broke the traffic and alerted British submarine J 1. J 1 torpedoed German battleships *Grosser Kurfurts* and *Kronprinz*, seriously damaging them. The Kaiser subsequently called Admiral Scheer on the carpet for risking such large and valuable ships on a rescue mission for two small U-boats.[111]

The following incident in April 1918 illustrates another use of comint by the British. Admiral Scheer planned some High Seas Fleet operations to attack British convoys to Norway, and to destroy their supporting battleships, thus reducing Grand Fleet strength. The High Seas Fleet sailed 22 April, and was sighted by British submarine J 6 which was on patrol. HMS J 6 had been informed that a Royal Navy surface force might be conducting mine laying operations in the area, consequently the submarine assumed the wrong identity and did not report. Later, German battleship *Moltke* lost a propeller

---

111   Hezlet, Electronics and Sea Power, p. 137

off Norway which reduced her speed to six knots. The on-scene commander sent her home. Soon she lost all propulsion power and had to radio for assistance. Room 40 intercepted her message and thus the Admiralty had its first belated intimation that a portion of the High Seas Fleet was at sea.

Comint was critical to maintaining an overall picture of the deployment of U-boats. Their positions were posted on a master plot in the Admiralty, updated each time a U-boat reported its position to headquarters. Once convoy procedures were placed in effect, this information was used to advise convoy commodores of the location of threatening U-boats and directions were provided to avoid them. This was a key factor in the success of the convoy scheme.

Effectiveness of British submarines

An evaluation of British submarines' effectiveness during wartime operations must rank them very high. During the Dardanelles Campaign they seriously interfered with Turkish logistics in the Sea of Marmara, operating under extreme conditions to penetrate the straits. That the Dardanelles Campaign ultimately failed was not to RN submarine discredit.

In the Baltic they provided the "punch" that the Russian submarines seemingly could not, and thus inflated the "threat" that the larger number of Russian submarines presented to German naval operators. Almost single handedly they stopped iron ore traffic between Sweden and Germany in 1915, and were only prevented from continuing their depredations by the German introduction of convoy in 1916 and its continued use in 1917. Since Germany depended upon Swedish ore for its industrial processes the effect was strategic and significant.

Although ASW patrols at that time by surface ships and submarines tended to fall into the naval category of "when in danger or in doubt, run in circles, scream and shout", British submarines proved deadly to 18 U-boats and were the fifth leading cause of U-boat losses.

In the North Sea, they along with their U-boat opponents, changed naval warfare forever. No longer could large surface warships steam majestically along, buoyed by pride and tradition, respecting only enemy warships of heavier tonnage and larger caliber gunnery installations. Now, all had to keep a wary eye out for the least sign of submarine activity. Higher speeds were required, as were zigzag steering patterns and escorts of destroyers positioned to keep submarines outside of effective torpedo firing range. The German High Seas Fleet found its operations limited by numbers of destroyers available to screen them from British submarine attack.

Chapter Seven –
Italian Submarine
Operations

Italy allied herself with France and Great Britain in opposing Germany and Austria-Hungary. The French blockade of the Adriatic Sea had already put paid to any Austria-Hungarian merchant shipping to and from the Mediterranean Sea. Merchant traffic in the Mediterranean was either allied or neutral shipping. The Italian submarine service therefore focused on sinking A-H warships or A-H coastal shipping along the northeastern edge of the Adriatic. German U-boats also operated from A-H ports in the northern Adriatic, and consequently were targets for Italian submarines after Italy declared war on Germany.

In June 1915 Italian submarine *Medusa* (class leader) was torpedoed near Venice by German UB 15. UB 15 recovered 5 survivors.[112] In August 1915 Italian submarine *Nereide* was torpedoed off Pelagosa Island with the lost of the entire crew. She was a victim of A-H U V commanded by von Trapp. That same month Italian *Medusa* class submarine *Jalea* struck an A-H mine in the Gulf of Trieste and was lost with 19 dead and only one survivor.

In July 1916 *Balilla* was lost with all hands to an explosive sweep off Lissa Island (Vis on current maps).[113] She had been driven under by gunfire from two A-H destroyers which then deployed their sweeps. One connected and *Balilla* was lost. *Balilla* featured four 17.7 inch torpedo tubes and two 76 mm guns. Later that month, *Giacinto Pullino* ran aground off Istria. Her crew survived but she was captured by A-H forces. She sank while being towed to port. Most of the losses occurred in forward operating areas and indicated offensive patrols by Italian submarines.

---

112   UB 15 was actually a German U-boat on 10 June 1915 when she sank Medusa. She was under command of *Oberleutant* Heino von Heimburg, and carried an Austro-Hungarian naval officer for liaison duties. Germany and Italy were not yet at war although Germany's ally, the Austro-Hungarian Empire was at war with Italy. On 14 June 1915 UB-15 was transferred to the A-H Navy as U-XI, but retained its German crew until 18 June when they were replaced by A-H sailors.

113   *Balilla* was originally built for Germany by Fiat-Laurenti so the German Navy could compare competitive submarine technologies. With the entrance of Italy into WWI on the Allied side in May 1915, U 42 was delivered to the Italian Navy and commissioned 4 August 1915 as *Balilla*. Also see Messimer, Find and Destroy, p. 255.

During the period 1916 – 1917 some 21 Fiat-Laurenti "F" class coastal submarines were built. They featured two 17.7-inch bow torpedo tubes and a 14 pounder (3 inch) deck gun.[114] All 'F' class submarines survived the war. During 1917 Italy also acquired 8 Holland class patrol submarines built by Canadian Vickers shipyard at Montreal in Canada. They had four 18-inch bow torpedo tubes. During 1916 two submarines of the *Pacinotti class* were commissioned (*Pacinotti* on 13 March, and *Guglielmotti* on 4 June). In addition Great Britain transferred four "V" class submarines, designated W 1 through W 4, to Italy. They were partially constructed by Vickers and completed by Armstrong Whitworth and transferred in July 1916. They displaced 508 tons, had two bow TT, two diesel engines and could make 14 kts. surfaced and 9 kts. submerged.

On 10 March 1917 *Alberto Guglielmotti* was lost east of Corsica in the Mediterranean Sea near Capraia Island, with her crew of 14. She was the victim of "friendly fire", having been accidentally attacked by a British ASW sloop.

---

114   A 14 pound shell equates to a 3 inch quick-firing Maxim-Nordenfelt deck gun shell. The shell weighed 14 pounds, hence the designation In the days of muzzle-loading canon, the canon ball weight was the common designation for a gun. In British service it continued even when breech-loading shell guns took over, and continues to confuse people (including the author) to this day. The Wikipedia entry for the "QF 14 pounder Maxim-Nordenfelt naval gun" goes on to say that the same ammunition was fired in the QF 12-pounder gun.

In August 1917 submarine W 4 went missing, the presumed victim of an A-H mine in the area between Cattaro and Durazzo in the Adriatic Sea.

On 26 November 1917 *Zoea*, a *Medusa* class submarine, ran aground off Rimini, and was later towed to Venice for repairs. Two days later, *Galileo Ferraris*, one of two *Pullino* class boats, also went aground off Porto Garibaldi. She was finally salvaged in January 1918.

The last war loss for the Italian submarine service was H. 5, which was torpedoed in error by British submarine H 1 off Cattaro in April 1918, with only five survivors. The fact that there were some survivors indicates that H. 5 was probably torpedoed at night while on the surface charging batteries. This was the second Italian submarine lost to British ASW forces in error. The incident does not speak well about Allied coordinated submarine operations command and control. Adequate separation of assigned submarine patrol areas by a central submarine operating authority should have precluded an encounter between two friendly units.

On 12 June 1918 Italian submarine F 12 sank A-H U XX off the mouth of the Tagliamento River with two torpedoes.[115]

---

115   Messimer, Op cit., p. 202

Chapter Eight – Russian Submarine Operations

During WW I Russian submarines were involved in combat operations in two theaters of operations: the Baltic Sea, and the Black Sea. Although it was possible to ship small submarines internally using Russia's river system or railroads, movement of large submarines between the two theaters was not practical. British submarines were sent into the Baltic Sea to assist the Russians but also with a British eye to disruption of the flow of Swedish iron ore that fueled the German war machine.

Baltic Sea Operations

1914

Russian naval plans for the Baltic Theater of Operations called for a defensive posture at the entrance to the Gulf of Finland (see Baltic Sea Area map on page 61).[116] The intent was to protect the capital at St. Petersburg and its industrial facilities. Large scale mining (over 2,200 mines laid on the eve of war) and use of submarines were featured in the plans, as well as the surface ships of the Russian Baltic Fleet and coastal artillery (up to 14-inch guns). The Russian Submarine Brigade operated from the port of Revel (now Talinn in Estonia). The Russian Baltic Fleet also established a forward operating base for destroyers and submarines in Moon Sound, just north of the Gulf of Riga. Russian plans had last been revised in 1912. Because of inadequate surface and air reconnaissance capability, the Russian Navy employed shore radio direction finder stations to provide enemy force locating data.

German U-boats U-23, U-25 and U-26 deployed to attack Russian surface warships patrolling at the entrance to the Gulf of Finland. On 11 October 1914, U-26 sank armored cruiser *Pallada* with one torpedo amidships. Over 570 officers and men were lost.

That same month the Royal Navy looked closely at the Baltic and realized that there might be an opportunity to interdict Swedish iron ore moving by ship from Swedish ports to northern Germany, providing the basic input for weapons manufacture. Great Britain offered to send some of its submarines into the Baltic to assist the Russian government. The Russians were more concerned with

---

116   At this time, 1914, Russia included current day Finland, and
        the Baltic states of Estonia, Latvia and Lithuania in its empire
        as well as Poland.

immediate operational matters and would put the British submarines to work on naval support for Russian armies in the Baltic Theater. Later, in 1915 they would have an opportunity to attack the iron ore trade.

Great Britain sent E 1, E 9 and E 11 to attempt the dangerous journey through the Skagerrak and Kattegat passages between Denmark and Norway and Sweden to enter the Baltic Sea. All three countries were neutral but the passages were narrow and at least in theory the British submarines were constrained to stay out of neutral territorial waters. German patrols could be expected to add to the difficulties.

E 11 had to turn back, but E 1 and E 9 successfully ran the straits and arrived at Libau on 17 October and 19 October respectively. Later, Libau being threatened by German land force advances, they moved to Hango. The Russians furnished liaison officers and a depot ship to provide crew berthing in port, and repair facilities. After several unsuccessful attacks, E 1 and E 9 moved to Revel for engine repairs during the winter.

From the time war began in August 1914 until ice closed the Gulf of Finland that year, eleven Russian submarines attempted 14 patrols without any successful attacks on German ships. Mine laying by Russian surface ships was the only successful naval action taken. The Gulf of Finland froze over every fall for about six months so surface ship and submarine operations were curtailed until the following spring.

1915

In April 1915 the Germans sent a diversionary naval raid into the Gulf of Riga shortly after the ice had disappeared. Libau fell to German ground forces on 8 May. The inoperable Russian submarine *SIG* was abandoned there. On 7 May E 1 fired at light cruiser *Amazone* and missed. That same day E 9 fired two torpedoes at destroyer S.20 at a range of 500 yards and missed. On 14 May *Drakon* fired three torpedoes in two attacks against light cruiser *Thetis*, which was towing U-4, intended for operations inside the Gulf of Finland. *Drakon's* torpedoes missed *Thetis*. U-4 cast off her tow and *Drakon* fired a fourth torpedo at her, but it also missed. What German naval authorities could not miss was the high level of submarine activity directed at them. As a result of the Russian and British submarine operations and botched attacks, the German naval command canceled planned mine laying operations and sent their forces back to Danzig.[117]

On 21 May the old German coast defense ship *Beowulf* was sent to Libau to bolster forces there. Enroute she was attacked by *Akula* but missed. The following day a German aircraft responded to a submarine sighting report by U-26 and dropped four bombs on *Akula*. These also missed and *Akula* got away. The incident illuminates the fast German ASW response to the Russian submarine threat, and the rapid integration of aircraft into German ASW forces.

---

117   Polmar, Op cit., p. 39

On 3 June a German surface warfare group assembled at the Irben Straits in preparation for conducting mine laying operations. *Okun'* was on scene and attempted an attack that failed. Her periscope was struck by a German motor torpedo boat, but *Okun'* escaped with relatively minor damage. The German forces, having experienced a number of submarine sightings, canceled their planned operations and withdrew. Along with *Okun'*; *Makrel*, *Minoga*, *Krokodil*, and British E 9 were in the area. On 28 June *Okun'* fired two torpedoes at light cruiser *Augsburg* but missed.

In June 1915 German naval forces laid a large number of antisubmarine mines. 580 mines were laid in the Irben Straits exit. Another 60 were laid inside Irben Straits. Minelayer *Albatross* laid 200 mines southeast of Bogskar Island, screened by three cruisers as she went about her work. Russian submarine *Drakon* fired three torpedoes at her at a range of 1,640 yards and missed.

On 3 June 1915 Russian sub *Okun* was detected and attacked with an explosive sweep by German destroyer SMS G-135. G-135 rammed her but *Okun* escaped and got home safely.[118]

On 26-27 June 1915 Russian submarines *Makrel*, *Minoga*, *Krokodil* and *Okun'* deployed off the Kurland coast (north of Libau). On the evening of 28 June, *Okun'* fired two torpedoes at light cruiser *Augsburg* without any hits.

On 1 July 1915 five Russian cruisers bombarded Memel. On 28 June several Russian submarines had been

---

118   Messimer, Op cit., p. 232

deployed in advance to cover their foray, including *Makrel* and *Okun'*.[119]

On 2 July E 9 struck armored cruiser *Prinz Adalbert* with a torpedo below the bridge and caused severe damage. *Prinz Adalbert* took on 2,000 tons of sea water and her draft was increased so much she could not enter port at Danzig but had to steam all the way to Kiel for repairs, arriving 4 July.

On 9 August E1 attacked light cruiser *Stralsund* but missed. *Gephard*, a *Bars* class submarine, fired five torpedoes at light cruiser *Lubeck* which *Lubeck* managed to avoid.

During the period 10 – 15 August the Germans again attempted to force the Irben Straits. *Akula*, *Bars* and *Gephard* were all on patrol in the vicinity. Three more Russian subs were inside the Gulf of Riga, waiting: *Makrel*, *Minoga* and *Okun'*. They made several unsuccessful torpedo attacks. On 19 August E 1 hit battle cruiser *Moltke* and flooded her bow compartments. On 20 August the German Fleet Commander ordered his forces to withdraw. All battleships and battle cruisers were withdrawn to the North Sea, reportedly at the Kaiser's direction, because of the enemy submarine threat in the Baltic, They did not return until 1917.

In response to the submarine threat, the German naval command established regular antisubmarine

---

119   Polmar, Op cit., p. 41

warfare patrols in the Baltic Sea. These included the use of zeppelins and seaplanes for aerial reconnaissance. Some 800 regular and 410 ASW mines were laid to protect the port of Riga from Russian submarine inroads. At the time the Russian operational command had 8 large submarines (including 3 British) and 13 small submarines available.

On 14 August E 9 had an interesting encounter with UC-4. E 9 was submerged and spotted UC-4 on the surface. She fired two torpedoes at about 150 yards range. The torpedoes passed underneath UC-4, which then conducted a "crash dive". E 9's third torpedo, a stern tube shot, passed over UC-4 as it went down. If UC-4 were a cat it had just used up three of its nine lives.

On 15 August E 8 and 13 departed the port of Harwich in England bound for the Baltic. E 8 arrived Revel about 21 August. E 13 stranded off Denmark and was destroyed by German forces that ignored territorial waters. E 18 and E 19 departed Newcastle 4 September and arrived safely. There were now five British submarines attached to the Russian Baltic Fleet (E 1, E 8, E 9, E 18 and E 19).

On 28 September *Akula,* E 8 and E 19 sailed to attack the Swedish iron ore trade with Germany. *Akula* found no targets, but E 8 and E 19 were more successful. The reader is referred to the section on British submarines in the Baltic for their exploits.

E 19 went on patrol on 30 October. It sank freighter *Suomi* on 2 November, and light cruiser *Undine* on 7

November, before returning to port 9 November. E 8 was also out looking for targets but had worse luck. On 6 November she missed cruiser *Lubeck* with a torpedo, and on 7 November struck collier *John Sauber* with a dud torpedo that failed to explode.

Alligator, Kaiman, Drakon, Makrel, Krokodil and *Som* were all operating in the Gulf of Bothnia from 23 October through 30 October. On 24 October *Alligator* tried to stop two German steamers and captured *Gerde Vith* (1,801 GRT). *Kaiman* captured *Sta Hleckc* (1,127 GRT) five days later. Perhaps in response, two light cruisers and two torpedo boat flotillas were dispatched from the North Sea to the Baltic.

Russian submarines *Akula, Vepr'* and *Bars* were back fitted with mechanical arrangements on their after decks so that they could lay mines. *Akula* could dispense four mines, while *Vepr'* and *Bars* carried eight apiece. *Akula* departed Revel on 27 November on her first mine laying mission and was last sighted on the 28th. She failed to return and presumably fell victim to a mine.

On 30 November light cruiser *Berlin* was missed by four torpedoes, probably fired by an unidentified Russian submarine. On 4 December E 19 sank steamer *Friesenberg* to wind up the 1915 Baltic Sea submarine campaign for the allies.

Russian submarines fired 50 torpedoes during 1915 without scoring any hits.[120] Messimer offers the theory

120   Ibid., p. 45

that their commanding officers fired at long ranges, thus giving the targets an opportunity to see and evade the torpedoes. [121] Their only successes (sinking's or captures) were accomplished with their gun armament. However, the fact that they were active in the theater, bolstered by British successful torpedoing, served to keep the submarine threat very prominent in German naval commanders' minds, and affected their operational thinking.

1916

When the ice receded enough to begin submarine operations in spring 1916 Russia had a total of 12 large submarines available in the Baltic (7 Russian and 5 British), plus a few short range coastal submarines. The stated Russian Fleet objective for the submarine group was to attack major enemy warships. This focused on surface combatants that had large caliber guns that could be used to support German army advances on land. Attacks on merchant shipping were left up to the discretion of the submarine division commanders.

On the German side all main sea routes involved convoys, the lessons of 1915 having been learned. Shipping would stay in Swedish territorial waters as much as possible. One of three Q-ships equipped with 105 mm (4.1 inch) guns accompanied each convoy.

As it worked out, attacks on enemy merchant ships took top priority with the allied submarine commanding

---

121   Messimer, Op cit., p. 230

officers. On 17 May *Volk* sank three cargo ships. On 27 May, *Gepard* was rammed by a Q-ship but escaped with some damage.

E 1 and E 9 went on patrol in May with Russian torpedoes, having run out of British torpedoes.[122] E 9 fired at two minesweeper support ships but the torpedoes proved to be "surface runners" and did no damage. *Bars* also had a Q-ship encounter from which it escaped. On 1 or 2 June E 18 was lost, most probably to a mine. On 8 July *Volk* sank a freighter. On 17 July *Vepr'* torpedoed a freighter. On 18 August *Krokodil* captured a freighter and sent it into port. However it was later released under the Laws of Maritime Warfare. *Krokodil's* capture was the last success of the 1916 season.

Between July and November seven new and three old Russian submarines and four British submarines carried out 31 short patrols (180 days at sea) but no further losses were inflicted on the enemy. Submarine operations shut down for the winter by the end of November.

During 1916 the United Kingdom transferred four "C" class submarines to Archangel in northern Russia. They were then barged down the inland waterway system to St. Petersburg. C-26, C-27, C-32 and C-35 left England under tow on 3 August, arrived in Archangel on 21 August and at St. Petersburg on 9 September. However

---

122   Most navies of the day used Whitehead torpedoes which were fired on a fixed gyroscopic course and the depth was set by hand before loading into a tube or drop collar, so interoperability was probably not a problem.

there were battery problems and new batteries had to be sent from England. Two C-class submarines made short patrols but scored no successes. In the latter half of 1916 Russian morale was noticeably dropping.

1917

The winter of 1916-1917 was very severe. There was still pack ice in the middle of the Gulf of Finland in the first half of May. During the summer Russian minelayers renewed mine fields in the approaches to the Gulf of Finland and the Gulf of Riga and the Irben Straits. Some 13,418 mines were placed. While that was going on German minelayers were also at work. UC-78, UC -58 and UC-57 planted mines in the Gulf of Bothnia.

In the second half of May, Russian submarines *Bars, Gephard, Vepr'* and *Volk* patrolled toward the Swedish coast, without results, except for the loss of *Bars*. On 21 May 1917 *Bars* was sunk in the Norrkoping Bight while attempting to attack a small German convoy consisting of two merchant ships and four escorts. *Bars'* periscope was sighted as she made her approach, and an escort dropped a dud depth charge and then trailed an explosive sweep. The sweep, towed at 65 foot depth, exploded in a 150 foot deep area. Oil and debris on the surface soon followed. Two more depth charges were dropped in the immediate vicinity and both exploded. *Bars* failed to return to base.[123] *Bars* class submarines had no internal bulkheads, so any

---

123   Ibid, pp. 223 – 224, also 239 - 240

sizeable hull breach would doom therm. The attacking units used a *Berghoff* curve scheme, which had them mark the initial submarine sighting position with a buoy, then spiral outward with their explosive sweeps. In theory the submarine could not escape.

Pantera was attacked by a German airship on 14 June and damaged seriously enough that she had to return to base. Another Russian submarine, *Lvitsa,* failed to return from patrol, probably mined south of Gotland on 11 June. E 19 was on patrol in that area and recovered some torpedo parts that belonged to *Lvitsa.*

On 6 July AG-14 was lost while on patrol near Libau, possibly mined.[124] On 17 July AG-15 accidentally submerged with an open hatch. Eighteen men were lost, but there were eight survivors. She was later salvaged and returned to service.

The Russian fleet commander directed that British E class subs take position off Libau or seaward of the Irben Strait. Small C-class subs were sent into the Gulf of Riga.

In August Revel had to be abandoned as a base because of German ground force advances. The submarine depot ship moved to Hango in late August. The C-class boats in the Gulf of Riga were based at Rogekul. Patrols by E-class subs proved fruitless.

On 8 August *Vepr'* sank transport *Friedrich Carow* about 50 nm. south of Lulea. On 20 September *Gephard*

---

124 AG stood for Ameranski Golland (American Holland), indicating a class designed by Electric Boat Company

attacked German escorts east of Oland but missed with three torpedoes. She suffered four hours of counterattack. When that ordeal was over her crew forced the commanding officer to take her back to Hango. While perhaps technically not quite a mutiny, it was a disturbing sign of disaffection and plummeting morale.

Volk was sent out to replace *Gephard*, but about 20 nm out of port she suffered a damaged main bearing, probably as a result of sabotage by her crew, and had to return to port. Both incidents were clear indications that Russian Navy morale was falling sharply.

On 1 September a major German ground offensive seized Riga. C 27 and C 32 were the only allied subs available. *Edinrog* had grounded and was being repaired. *Tur* damaged herself and *Tigr* while mooring alongside. *Ugor* had been damaged and partially flooded by a destroyer propeller. E 9 and C 26 were at sea off Hango. C 26 was sent down to Moon Sound to join C 27 and C 32 in opposing German naval forces. C 26 attempted an attack on a force that included two battleships but ran aground, was hunted and finally extracted itself and got back to Hango.

C 27 missed battleship *Konig* with a torpedo but severely damaged minesweeping support ship *Indianola*. In turn C 27 was damaged by depth charges. She escaped and followed the damaged *Indianola* through the Irben Straits mine fields and got back safely in Hango on 19 October.[125]

---

125   Polmar, Op cit., pp. 50-51

C 32 sailed for the Irben straits but ran across UC-57 which spotted her first and fired at her with its deck gun. C 32 escaped by diving. Later while making an approach on cruiser *Strasburg*, C 32 was attacked by a seaplane. On 20 October she attacked net tender *Eskimo* which had three escorts. C 32 fired two torpedoes but missed. She was depth charged in return and suffered major damage. She had to be beached near Pernau, and was destroyed with explosives by her crew.

By 18 October 1917 German forces controlled the Gulf of Riga. Russian battleship *Slava* was heavily damaged in a gun action with *Konig* and *Kronprinz Wilhelm* and had to be scuttled in Moon Sound Channel. On 19 October the Russians evacuated.

Submarines *Vepr', Rys, Gephard*, C 35, E 9 and E 19 were deployed to protect the approaches to the Gulf of Finland until winter ice closed down operations. *Gephard* was lost in a mine field about 29 October.

1918

In March 1918 German naval forces began an offensive in the Baltic because armistice negotiations had broken down. On 21 March they landed 9,000 troops at Hango. The Russians responded by scuttling submarines AG-11, AG-12, AG-15 and AG-16. In early April, at Helsingfors (Helsinki) British forces also scuttled their submarines lest they fall into German hands. E 1, E 8, E 9, E 19, C 26, C 27 and C 35 were all scuttled between 3 and 5 May off Helsingfors.

Black Sea Operations

The Ottoman Empire's (Turkey) control of the Bosporus blocked the only sea route to the Mediterranean Sea from the Black Sea. No Russian warships or merchant ships could pass without Turkish permission. There were two possible employments for Russian submarines, the first against Turkish warships in the Black Sea; and the second to interdict movement of coal by sea from the coal mines near Zonguldak to Constantinople. The Zonguldak region was famous for its coal mines and supplied the capital with most of its fuel.

1915

Although the war actually began in late October 1914 when German and Turkish ships bombarded Russian ports in the Black Sea, no Russian submarines saw action that year. Older Russian submarines in the Black Sea Fleet were too short ranged for offensive operations, having been designed for port and coast defense. The first new construction submarines became available beginning in late 1914.

Six boats moved from the building yard at Nikolayev (on the Black Sea) to Sevastopol to begin their trials on the following schedule: *Nerpa* (12/14/14), *Tyulen* (2/15/15), *Morzh* (3/15/15), *Narval* (7/15/15), *Kit* (9/15/15) and *Kashalot* (11/15/15).[126] All were products of the 1911 Russian submarine building program.[127]

Russian battleships began operating off the Bosporus, the narrow passage between the Black Sea and the Sea of Marmara that separates the two parts of the city of Constantinople. On 15 March they were supported by seaplane transport Nikolai I, whose seaplanes spotted the ships' fall of shot.

Nerpa made the first Russian submarine war patrol off the Bosporus from 5 to 8 March 1915. This set an early pattern of Russian submarine operations. From Sevastopol to the Bosporus is about 260 nm. With no air opposition at least initially, and at a surface speed of 8 kts. *Nerpa* and her sisters would have required about 33 hours for each of their outbound and return legs. There were no enemy submarines in the Black Sea at that time. Turkey never acquired any that operated, and German U-boats did not enter the Black Sea until later. *Nerpa* was heavily armed with 2 bow torpedo tubes, 2 stern torpedo tubes, and an additional 8 torpedoes carried topside in Dzhevetskiy drop collars, for a total of 12 torpedoes. Later in March, *Tyulen* and then *Nerpa* again made patrols off the Bosporus.

On 3 April Russian surface forces encountered battle cruiser *Yavuz* (former *Goeben)* which withdrew in the face

---

126   The author uses the common American English scheme for dates (month/day/year)

127   *Schukat* and *Som* arrived at Nikolayev in August 1915 from the Far East but were sent on to the Baltic Fleet.

of superior forces. *Nerpa* was present but was unable to attack. Later, on 10 May, *Tyulen* observed *Yavuz* but could not close to attack either.

In June 1915 German submarines U-21, UB-7 and UB-8 arrived at Constantinople after their journey from northern Germany and through the Med. From August through October additional U-boats arrived: UB-14, UC-13 and UC-15. The UC class were minelayers. From 5 through 22 July UB-7 conducted a patrol without seeing any Russian targets. In September U-boats were off the Odessa and Crimean coasts.

Krab, a purpose built Russian mine laying submarine, carried out her first mine plant in July. She was screened by *Morzh, Nerpa* and *Tyulen*, and laid 58 mines off the eastern end of the Bosporus on 10 July 1915. The mine planting operation was designed to prevent battle cruiser *Yavuz* from entering the Black Sea while newly built Russian battleship *Imperatritsa Maria* was vulnerable, moving from the building yard at Nikolayev to the fleet base at Sevastopol to complete fitting out. The operation was a success although the mines were discovered on 11 July and cleared by the 16th. A Turkish gunboat was heavily damaged by one of the mines.

In August and September Russian submarines scored their first successes against Turkish merchant ships. In response the Turks set up shore observation towers with gun batteries in support to prevent Russian submarines from operating on the surface close to the Turkish coast.

On 5 September off Kefken Island (Kirpen) Turkish cruiser *Hamideh* was escorting merchant ships when two Russian destroyers attacked. *Hamideh* got separated from the convoy and *Nerpa* took the opportunity to attack the merchant ships on the surface with her deck gun. The merchant ships were driven ashore and destroyed by gunfire, the water being too shallow to use torpedoes. Turkish battle cruiser *Yavuz* was called upon to help. She encountered *Nerpa* on the surface on the morning of 6 September at close range. *Nerpa* made a crash dive to escape a salvo of five 11-inch shells delivered at only 1,750 yards, narrowly escaping the fame, or ignominy, of being the first submarine to be destroyed by battle cruiser gunfire.

In late September Russian surface forces, now including battleship *Imperatritsa Maria*, resumed shelling Turkish ports. Bulgaria entered the war on 6 October 1915 – on the side of the Central Powers. Germany sent two U-boats to operate from the Bulgarian port of Varna in mid-October. On 27 October they attacked a Russian squadron without success. On 14 November *Morzh* launched two torpedoes at battle cruiser *Yavuz*, but they passed close astern of her.

1916

In July 1916 Admiral Eberhard was replaced as the Black Sea Fleet commander by Vadm. A, V. Kolchak. Kolchak was a mine warfare expert and looked at mining as a way to close the Bosporus to Turkish shipping On 29 July *Nerpa* conducted a periscope reconnaissance of the Bosporus and reported that a submerged expedition could probably plant mines without detection. On 30 July *Krab* sailed and successfully laid two lines of 30 mines each off the eastern entrance. On 2 August *Nerpa* and *Kit* sailed to act as navigation beacons for destroyers to use while they laid 820 mines off the Bosporus.[128] On 21 August *Nerpa* was ambushed off Sevastopol by UB-7, which fired two torpedoes at her. One hit but it was a dud. She survived.

Krab was underway from Sevastopol in early September on another mine laying mission. Bad weather and engine problems forced her into Constanta in Romania for repairs. On the night of 15/16 September she laid 28 mines off Varna, then had to abort operations when her portside mine track jammed leaving the 29th mine stuck.

During 1916 Russian submarines did not enjoy much success in the Black Sea. Communications were inadequate and torpedo boats had to be used for relay. A similar situation was observed by British and French submarines in the Sea of Marmara during 1915, and a RN destroyer had to be positioned on the east side of the Gallipoli Peninsula to act as a communications relay ship. However submarine *Kit* received new equipment that increased transmitter range from 80-100 miles to 300 miles.

---

128   The use of submarines as navigation beacons, particularly for
        amphibious operations became widespread in WW II.

Black Sea Map

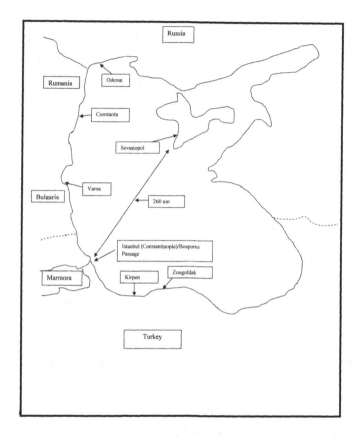

Russian subs patrolled all the way from off Zonguldak on the Black Sea in north central Turkey to the Bulgarian coast. On one of these patrols on 2 March *Morzh* spotted former cruiser *Breslau*, but misidentified her and so missed an attack opportunity. She also sighted *Yavuz* on 7 July but the battle cruiser's high speed prevented *Morzh* from reaching a firing position.

There was a great deal of German seaplane ASW activity which interfered with Russian submarine movements. As a result the commanding officer of *Morzh* recommended removal of the topside drop collar torpedo carriers in favor of installing a dual purpose gun that could be used for antiaircraft fire.

During the period 19-21 August *Tyulen* made a reconnaissance of Varna and Euxinogrod searching for targets for naval gunfire.

During October the Russian fleet commander tried to establish a blockade of the Bosporus using submarines alone. They had limited success. *Tyulen* fought a hour-long gun battle with armed freighter *Rodosto*, which mounted an 88 mm gun manned by a *Breslau* gun crew. Surprisingly *Tyulen* captured her and sent her into Sevastopol as a prize.

After Rumania entered the war on 27 August on the allied side, Russia stationed *Karas* and *Karp* at Constanta. However on 22 October Constanta fell to Central Power attack and the submarines had to depart.

UB-46 was mined and sunk on 7 December 1916 in a Russian surface laid mine field.

1917

Four new *Bars* class submarines were delivered from Nikolayev Shipyard during 1917. *Burevestnik*, *Gagara*, *Orla* and *Utka* moved from the building yard to Sevastopol for final fitting out and training. *Lebed* and *Pelikan* were still uncompleted at Nikolayev.

Normally there was at least one Russian submarine on patrol in the Black Sea, with two or even three on occasion. Usually their targets were sailing vessels, barges and tugs, which although not prominent targets had an impact on Turkish logistics.

On 11 May *Morzh* with 24 patrols under her belt, failed to return. She was believed to be a victim of either a mine or a seaplane off Cape Ercgli. On 17 June *Kashalot* attempted to land operatives near Cape Kerempa, but was detected, fired on, and forced to abort. This mode of submarine operations foretold many such missions during WW II, particularly in the South Pacific by U.S. submarines.

On 25 June *Nerpa* had an opportunity to torpedo *Breslau* near the Bosporus but a seaplane escort forestalled the attack. That month there was a great deal of unrest in the Black Sea Fleet, reflecting political events in St. Petersburg. Admiral Kolchak was deposed by a delegate assembly of soldiers and sailors.

On 25 October *Gagara* forced a Turkish freighter aground using her deck gun. She returned to port on 27 October, ending the last Russian submarine patrol in the Black Sea. On 26 October 1917 the Russian Kerensky regime fell to the Bolsheviks. Russian hostilities against the Germans and Turks ended shortly thereafter.

During 1917 some ten Russian submarines conducted 111 patrols, most several days to two weeks in length. Only one submarine was lost – *Morzh*.

CHAPTER NINE – U.S. SUBMARINE OPERATIONS

President Wilson was determined to keep the United States out of World War I. Although there were strong language and cultural ties between England and the United States, there was also a history of bloodshed in two wars, the Revolutionary War and the War of 1812, In addition there were two large immigrant groups in the United States who had reason to either actively dislike England or to instinctively choose to sympathize with Germany. They were the large body of Irish immigrants and their descendants who populated the northeastern area, and the equally large group of German immigrants and descendants who lived in the mid-West.

However, both Wilson and most of the American public were shocked by German savagery displayed in Belgium during their invasion in 1914. The use of poison gas and flamethrowers in ground warfare by the Germans increased the repulsion felt by the general American public. The introduction of unrestricted submarine warfare did nothing to offset that impression. Sinking of the British passenger liner Lusitania on 7 May 1915, with the loss of life of a large number of American citizens including women and children cost the Germans heavily in U.S. public opinion.

President Wilson tried to intervene in the conflict to bring the opposing parties to negotiations, dispatching his personal envoy, Colonel House, to Europe twice during 1915, without success. However, American diplomatic protests succeeded in causing the German government to change its unrestricted submarine warfare policy during 1915.

Wilson was so concerned about trying to stay out of the conflict that he forced the U.S. Army to officially eliminate the War Plans Division of the Army Staff, lest its mere existence be seen as a sign that the U.S. planned to enter the war. In November 1916 President Wilson ran for reelection, using the slogan "He kept us out of war", and won narrowly.[129]

In December 1916 the German government opted for resumption of the unrestricted submarine warfare campaign beginning in early 1917, its leaders convinced that such a move would lead to knocking Great Britain out of the war by the fall of 1917, well before American troops could be trained, transported and put into the trenches

---

129   Wilson had a winning edge of 579,511 votes out of 18,535,022 votes cast, a 3% margin in the popular vote.

in France. The resumption of an unrestricted submarine warfare campaign in February 1917 brought American protests, the severing of U.S. diplomatic relations with Germany, and in April 1917 a declaration of war against Germany and her allies.

In late March 1917 the President of the Naval War College, Rear Admiral William Sims, received a message from the Navy Department directing him to proceed to Washington, D.C. and to check in with officials there by telephone, avoiding any public scrutiny. He did so and learned that the American Ambassador in London had called for a senior naval officer to come to London to represent the United States in what looked more and more like U.S. participation in the Great War.

Sims went to England, traveling in civilian clothes with an aide, aboard SS New York, both under assumed names. His journey was politically sensitive since the nation was not yet at war.

He arrived at Liverpool on April 9th and was met by a Rear Admiral dispatched from the British Admiralty, and taken to London aboard a special train. Shortly afterwards he met with the First Sea Lord, Sir John Jellicoe, RN, with whom he had a previous acquaintance dating back to the Boxer Rebellion in China in 1901.

After a little initial reluctance the Admiralty finally revealed the true state of affairs facing Great Britain – they were only a few months away from having to enter negotiations to end the war. In April 1917 they had only enough foodstuffs in the United Kingdom to feed the populace for several months. What the unrestricted submarine warfare advocates in Germany had predicted was coming true. The rate of loss of shipping was so high that Great Britain could not support its population food requirements and obtain raw materials for war production.

Shipping losses in February were 536,000 tons; in March 603,000 tons; and in April were approaching 900,000 tons. Sims was dismayed and shocked. The shipping losses were three to four times those reported in the press of the day and known in Washington. British authorities did report numbers of British ships lost fairly accurately, but not the tonnages. In addition they did not report losses of neutral shipping. Against the background of heavy Allied troop losses in fierce ground fighting in France, the true facts were shattering. The general public in Great Britain and the United States were blissfully unaware of the real state of affairs, so thoroughly had British censorship accomplished its mission.

On 17 April 1917, not long after Radm. Sims had arrived in London, the United States Congress declared war on Germany. Now the job began. He set to work in an office in the U.S. Embassy with only the help of his aide. Before long volunteers had been recruited to help with administrative work. Additional office space was obtained and ultimately his headquarters involved 1,200 personnel, with 200 naval officers, only 60 of whom were regular navy. By the time of the Armistice on November 11, 1918 U.S. naval forces in Europe would expand to include 370 ships, 5,000 naval officers, 75,000 enlisted men, and 45 bases. The U.S. Navy successfully transported two million American troops to France without a single loss despite German predictions that U-boats would prevent such a movement.

Sims' immediate and strong advice to the Secretary of the Navy, Josephus Daniels and the Chief of Naval Operations, Admiral William Benson, was to concentrate on helping the Royal Navy defeat the German U-boat threat before it forced Great Britain into negotiations. He also suggested that capital ship building programs be slowed in favor of destroyers and other escort vessels capable of helping solve the current problem. This later advice was somewhat unwelcome and to some extent relations between Sims, the Secretary and the CNO, became a bit testy.

He called for dispatch of destroyers to assist in ASW operations as soon as possible. On May 4, 1917 Destroyer Division Eight, arrived at Queenstown, Ireland to begin American naval participation in the Great War.

The Royal Navy had been debating the concept of convoy as a defense against U-boats for some time. Troops of the British Expeditionary Force transported from England to France had traveled in escorted convoys, safely. Other controlled traffic back and forth between England and France also traveled in escorted convoys.

The Admiralty had a clear example of the value of convoy in preventing submarine attack - from the other end of the periscope. British submarines had stopped iron ore transport by sea from Sweden to northern Germany in 1915. In 1916 German naval authorities instituted strict convoy procedures in the Baltic which then kept British submarines from interfering with the same sea transport in 1916 and 1917.

The arguments against convoy were largely from the merchant captain viewpoint. They deeply believed that it would not be possible for them to maneuver their ships safely in unison to conform to zigzag procedures. Rear Admiral Sims was one of those who encouraged the Admiralty to adopt convoy procedures on a wide scale.

In May 1917 a test convoy sailed from Gibraltar to England. All ships arrived safely. Another test convoy left from Norfolk, Virginia to England with similar results. The case was proven, and the Admiralty instituted widespread convoy procedures in the Atlantic and Mediterranean Sea. The key to defeating the U-boat threat had been adopted although many more independently-sailing ships would be lost before the German surrender.

Meanwhile additional U.S. destroyers were arriving. A second Destroyer Division arrived May 17th. The U.S. 6th Battle Squadron consisting of five dreadnought battleships, later joined the British Grand Fleet at Scapa Flow to help ensure the defeat of the German High Seas Fleet if it should sortie again in a test of main strength. In addition, three U.S. battleships were based at Bantry Bay in southern Ireland to take on the task of surface escort for troop convoys from the United States. Although German submarines with rare exceptions only operated fairly close to the British Isles during WW I, the possibility of a German surface raider interfering with trans-Atlantic convoys was alive and well.

The terrible damage that was being done to merchant shipping was accomplished by a relatively few German U-boats. Sims noted that usually there were only 8 – 10 U-boats on patrol station off the United Kingdom, with perhaps fifteen at a maximum.[130] Of course for each U-boat on patrol, another one was either enroute home or to the patrol station and a third was in a repair period.

Room 40 of British Naval Intelligence was able to use its DF network to keep track of each U-boat as it left port in Germany and used its wireless freely to communicate its progress to home authorities. Room 40 operators probably came to know many individual U-boat radio operators by their "fist", that is the manner in which they keyed the Morse code signal when they transmitted. The Admiralty maintained a large plot of all known or estimated U-boat positions. That didn't do much good as long as most ships were individual sailers. It would help greatly when convoys were formed and a convoy commodore could be kept advised of submarine threats in the path of his convoy.

---

130   Sims, The Victory at Sea, p. 9

In addition to battleships and destroyers the United States also deployed some submarines to assist in ASW operations overseas. Two divisions of submarines were deployed. The first was Submarine Division Four consisting of four K-class boats which went to Punta Delgado in the Azores. Division Four submarines were towed from Halifax to Punta Delgado. They conducted ASW patrols to a radius of several hundred miles. K-2 left on the first U.S. submarine ASW patrol on 1 November 1917. The K-class was 153'7" in length, and displaced 392/521 tons. They carried four bow 18" torpedo tubes and had a crew of 28.

They were followed by Submarine Division Five, seven L-class submarines, which followed them to Europe via Punta Delgado and then on to Bantry Bay, Ireland. They were also towed across, by USS Bushnell and a couple of ocean tugs. L-10 lost a man overboard during the transit. Another submariner, a Lieutenant from L-2, was lost aboard British submarine HMS H-5 when it was rammed by a British merchant ship in March 1918, mistaking it for a U-boat.

The L-class was slightly larger than the K-class. They were 165' in length and displaced 463/532 tons. They had four bow 18" torpedo tubes and a crew of 28. Both K and L classes could make 14/10.5 kts.

The American L-class submarines were re-designated as AL to distinguish them from British L-class submarines operating in theater. The AL submarines normally made

7-8 day patrols from Bantry Bay, returning for several days of rest and repairs before heading out again. They operated submerged all day attempting to get a periscope sighting of a U-boat that would normally be operating on the surface while searching for ship targets.[131] At night both U-boats and Allied ASW submarines would be on the surface recharging their batteries. While the surfaced U-boat could usually detect any surface or air enemy unit in daytime well before they could see the small surfaced U-boat, the U-boat watch would be highly unlikely to spot a submarine periscope.[132] The first AL submarine patrol from Bantry Bay began 6 March 1918.

Allied ASW submarine patrols were tedious and dangerous. Any Allied destroyer or air unit that spotted a surfaced submarine immediately assumed that it was a U-boat and attacked. Although there was recognition signals, many Allied submarines came under friendly gunfire or had bombs dropped on them. Several were sunk by "friendly fire".

One American submarine, AL-2, was credited with sinking a U-boat, although the circumstances were very

---

131   With two feet of periscope exposed above the waves the submerged watch officer has a horizon of only 1.6 nm, whereas from the bridge of a surfaced submarine with a height of eye of 20 feet the lookouts have a horizon of 5.1 nm.

132   Although submarine ASW patrols were tedious and dangerous and usually fruitless, eighteen German U-boats were lost to torpedo attacks by Allied submarines during the war. Not all of these sinking's were to ASW submarines. Some were chance encounters while Allied submarines were engaged in offensive patrols themselves.

murky. AL-2 was returning to base at Bantry Bay when a lookout sighted a periscope. The officer of the deck immediately changed course and ordered a torpedo made fully ready and prepared to dive. Before AL-2 could dive there was an explosion in the water near its port quarter. AL-2 then dove and the CO attempted to ram the U-boat. He got close enough that the AL-2 sonar man could hear high speed propellers. That was followed by underwater sound signals. Eventually, with no further contact AL-2 surfaced and proceeded to port where the CO reported the encounter. British authorities later noted through radio intelligence that U-65 had failed to return to port in Germany after a patrol in that area and officially credited AL-2 with the sinking. The CO was awarded the DSO.

No surface ship was sunk by American submarines during WW I. Other U.S. submarines conducted ASW patrols in home waters and the Panama Canal area during the conflict without any significant incidents. U.S. submarine operations during the period November 1917 to November 1918 must be rated as relatively ineffectual despite the questionable "sinking" of a U-boat off Bantry Bay.

PART FOUR

SUBMARINE OPERATIONS OF THE CENTRAL POWERS

WORLD WAR ONE

(1914 – 1918)

CHAPTER TEN –
AUSTRO-HUNGARIAN
SUBMARINE OPERATIONS

The Austro-Hungarian (A-H) Navy was relatively small and focused on Italy as its probable opponent in any war. In 1914 it consisted of 3 dreadnoughts, 9 pre-dreadnoughts, 3 armored cruisers, 5 protected cruisers, about 26 destroyers and 6 submarines (2 designated for training only). In addition the A-H navy possessed about 42 torpedo boats, 12 of them designated as coastal torpedo boats.[133] Most were based at Pola at the northern end of the Adriatic Sea. Some operated from the naval port of Cattaro, located further to the south.

Italy possessed a distinct geographic advantage. Italian naval forces could block the Strait of Otranto,

---

133 The automotive (self-propelled torpedo) had been developed in Trieste and the first models were very short range, their propeller being run by compressed air alone. Later models were powered by an oil-fuel/compressed air combustion system and had longer ranges.

an 80 mile stretch between the southeastern end of the boot of Italy and Albania, and preclude A-H access to the Mediterranean Sea. As a potential ally of Great Britain and France, an Italian blockade of the Adriatic Sea would complement the British blockade of the North Sea and severely limit the amount of foodstuffs and raw materials able to be imported by the Central Powers. Although A-H entered the war at its onset against Serbia, Russia, France and Great Britain, Italy held back from hostilities.

Italy was formally allied with the Central Powers (Germany and A-H) but was only required to support them in the event that they were attacked. It was clear that that was not the case, and Italy remained at peace while weighing the advantages of joining either the Central Powers or the Allies, depending upon which side offered her greater territorial gains in the event of victory. By allying herself with Germany, A-H found herself at war with France, a Mediterranean power with a strong surface navy, and France soon established a blockade of the Adriatic Sea at the Straits of Otranto that prevented the A-H fleet from entering the Mediterranean Sea.

In May 1915 Italy entered the war on the side of the Allied Powers, and A-H and Italy were now at war. Austria was concerned over its lack of border defenses on its frontier with Italy and therefore dispatched its fleet on 23 May into the southern Adriatic to attack Italian military installations and ports from Ravenna to Barletta as a diversion. It hoped that this action would delay an

Italian ground advance to the Isonzo River. In response to the Austrian naval attacks, an Italian squadron set out to raid the Austrian naval base at Cattaro.[134] A-H submarine U-IV, in refit at the time, was rushed into action and on 19 June sank the Italian cruiser *Giuseppe Garibaldi* with two torpedoes.

Emperor Franz Joseph died 21 November 1916. He was succeeded by his great-nephew Karl. In April 1917 Karl and his chief of staff visited Berlin to complain, ostensibly about the lack of coordination between Berlin and Vienna when Germany announced the reinstatement of the unrestricted submarine campaign. In reality they were there to press for a peace settlement. At that time the position of Austria-Hungary was relatively satisfactory: Serbia had been crushed; Romania had been overrun; and Russia was essentially out of action because of the fall of the Czar. A-H had no real quarrel with Great Britain or France. In fact Karl was already engaged in secret, back door discussions with the United Kingdom and France. However the German government (essentially Generals Hindenburg and Ludendorff) would not back down on its war aims: to retain parts of Belgium and France. Karl's initiative went nowhere.[135]

By early1918 Austria was worried about food shortages. On 17 January 1918 over 200,000 workers went on strike in Vienna over food. By 19 January a general strike was in

---

134   Currently Kotor in Montenegro.
135   Strachan, The First World War, p. 281

progress. The other half of the Dual Monarchy, Hungary, had enough food and was even shipping some overland to Germany which had its own food problems, while ignoring food shortages in Austria. In early February 1918 there were mutinies at the A-H naal base at Cattaro

A-H Submarine Operations in the Adriatic and Mediterranean

Austria-Hungary began the war with six submarines in commission. During the war twenty-one additional submarines entered service. Eight submarines were lost during the war, all in the Adriatic Sea: U-III and XII in 1915; U-VI and XVI in 1916[136]; U-XXX in 1917, and three: U-X, XX, and XXIII in 1918. That equated to a 29.6 % attrition rate.

France established a distant blockade of Austria-Hungary ports in the Adriatic Sea at the Strait of Otranto. In October 1914 A-H submarine U-XII missed French cruiser *Waldeck Rousseau*, but hit and seriously damaged battleship *Jean Bart* in December.[137] As a result French battleships were withdrawn to Malta and Bizerte, and

---

136 U-VI was lost in the Otranto Barrage in May 1916. She became fouled in a drifter's nets, surfaced, was taken under fire, and was scuttled. Her crew of 15 survived.

137 U-XII was the third U-V class submarine, completed in 1914. U-VII though U-XI were being built in German shipyards but were sold to the German Navy in December 1914, when it was thought that they would be unable to transit from Germany to the Adriatic (they were too large to ship overland).

subsequent patrols were conducted by cruisers and smaller craft. In April 1915 the cruiser *Leon Gambetta* was sunk by A-H submarine U-V. Thereafter Otranto Strait patrols were limited to destroyers.[138] In August of that year U-IV sank Italian cruiser *Giuseppe Garibaldi* in the central Adriatic.[139]

The commanding officer of A-H submarine U-V which sank *Leon Gambetta* was Georg Ritter von Trapp, later to be better known as the father of the von Trapp Family Singers of *Sound of Music* fame.[140] He reported that he made a night submerged attack on his target, something not previously done in the A-H submarine service. He fired two forward tubes at the target at 500 meters range around midnight. Torpedo speed was 40 knots according to von Trapp's book.[141] He watched the air bubble trail and saw the hits. *Leon Gambetta* listed to port and sank in nine minutes. Von Trapp reported that five life boats cleared her sides.[142]

U-V was a Holland boat design based upon USS Octopus (SS-9) (later re-designated as SS C-1 in the U.S.

138 Hezlet, The Submarine and Sea Power, p. 31
139 Italy entered the war against Austria-Hungary in May 1915.
140 Von Trapp was married to one of Whitehead's granddaughters.
141 Germany's best performing torpedoes of that day were listed with a speed of 40 km/hour, which would equate to a speed of about 24 knots, which is much more likely than 40 knots.
142 Von Trapp, To the Last Salute, pp. 20 – 23. The torpedoes he used were compressed air powered. Some of U-Vs stores were canned meats taken from the French submarine Marie Curie captured when she became entangled in an antisubmarine net while attempting to penetrate the harbor at Pola, Austria in December 1914.

Navy). U-V and U-VI were built by the Electric Boat Company in New York, then disassembled and shipped to the Whitehead & Company firm in Fiume, where they were reassembled. She had gasoline engines for surface propulsion. She handled very well submerged because of her tear drop hull shape.

In 1915 German U-boat U-21 arrived at the A-H naval base at Cattaro where U-V was moored alongside S.M.S. Gaa, the A-H submarine tender. Lt. Hersing, CO of U-21 showed von Trapp around U-21. Von Trapp was filled with envy. U-21 had powerful diesel engines and torpedo tubes both forward and aft, and had completed a successful 18-day trip around the British Isles using only on-board fuel, a matter of wonder for the CO of a very short range A-H submarine. In return Hersing was shown around U-V by von Trapp and disparagingly remarked "I would refuse to travel in this crate".

When Italy entered the war against Austria in May 1915, Austrian U-boats were postured for defense: 2 at Trieste, 1 at Pola, 1 at Lissa, and the remainder in the Gulf of Cattaro.[143] On 12 August 1915 U-XII hit a mine while trying to enter Venice Lagoon, and was lost with 17 men. U-III attacked an Italian auxiliary cruiser *Citta di Catania* in the Otranto Straits, was rammed and damaged but got away. The following morning U-III was sighted by French destroyer *Bisson* and sunk with gunfire with the loss of seven crew members. U-VI got entangled in a net at

143   Ibid, p. 36

the Otranto Barrage, could not get free and was scuttled when armed Italian trawlers approached. Her entire crew was taken prisoner.

Adriatic Sea Map

During 1915 on another patrol after Italy entered the war, U-V was near the Pelagosa islands, hunting for an Italian submarine that had been reported operating in that vicinity. Conditions on board were marginal as usual. There were no berths for officers or crew, merely several air mattresses laid beside the machinery. Sighting the Italian submarine *Nereide* on the surface U-V began a submerged approach but was sighted in turn. *Nereide* fired a torpedo that missed. U-V fired two torpedoes. One hit and *Nereide* went down with all hands,[144]

Still on patrol in 1915 U-V was operating on the surface. Suddenly an Italian cruiser emerged from the fog. U-V dove but there was no time to ventilate to remove gasoline fumes. Once the boat was sealed the crew began to succumb to 'gasoline intoxication'. The CO was among those affected. Depth control and rudder control were erratic. U-V broached several times and was sighted by the cruiser. The cruiser thereupon rapidly cleared the area,[145]

Later, in command of U-XIV and operating off the Greek island of Corfu, von Trapp detected an older warship and six escorting torpedo boats. He attempted an approach on the main target but found her zigzagging and was unable to get within torpedo range. The zigzag (steering evasive courses) was a new antisubmarine warfare tactic. Later von Trapp learned that General Kitchener

---

144   Ibid, pp. 44-49

145   Ibid, pp. 57-59. U-V was extremely lucky not to have been rammed and sunk by the enemy cruiser. The Germans lost several U-boats to ramming by warships.

was on board the target, traveling from Patras in Greece to Brindisi in Italy.[146]

U-XIV had an interesting history. She was originally the French submarine *Marie Curie*. In December 1914 her commanding officer daringly attempted to penetrate the Austrian harbor of Pola. The sub got entangled in antisubmarine nets, was detected and fired upon and sunk. She was later raised, repaired and refitted and commissioned as the A-H U-XIV. Her commanding officer fell ill and von Trapp was ordered to take command in late 1916. She had only one internal torpedo tube forward but also carried six tubes topside, some firing ahead and some broadside.[147] Later U-IV and U-XIV attempted to attack a steamer off the port of Durazzo (now Durres in Albania), and U-XIV was depth charged. She escaped but all her unprotected topside torpedoes were wrecked.[148]

On 17 October 1916 U-XVI sank Italian destroyer *Nembo*, but was rammed and damaged by steamer *Borminda,* and was damaged beyond repair. Two of

---

146   Ibid, pp. 81-82. Although General Kitchener escaped this submarine encounter he later drowned when HMS Hampshire was sunk by a German submarine mine in May 1916.

147   In the days before torpedoes with settable gyros were developed, the torpedo gyro was only used to maintain the torpedo on a straight course. That required the approach officer to rapidly calculate a firing bearing that would allow the torpedo to intercept the target ship track. If the target changed course just before the submarine reached its intended firing position, the solution was frequently worthless. Having some tubes that could fire at a 90 degree angle off set from the bow offered more possibilities for a hit.

148   Ibid, pp. 66-67

U-XVI crew died and the rest became prisoners. On 3 March 1917 U-XXX sailed from Cattaro and was not heard from again, presumably falling victim to a mine.

In early 1917 A-H received word that the German government had declared a return to unrestricted submarine warfare. U-XIV was in refit at Pola at the time. In April U-XIV was able to sneak through the Otranto Barrage (drifters with nets dangling to catch and indicate submarine positions) and entered the Mediterranean Sea. U-XIV sank a 6,000 ton steamer headed from the Strait of Messina towards Cape Matapan in Greece. She made a submerged approach at night, then surfaced with a full moon and sank the ship with gunfire.

Several days later a convoy hove into sight. The ships were in two columns, protected by trawlers. U-XIV stayed ahead on the surface checking the formation zigzag pattern. The convoy zigged every 15 minutes, about 20 degrees right or left alternately. When the CO believed he had the routine figured out he submerged ahead and let the convoy overtake him. Von Trapp selected torpedo tube #3 (outboard) and headed between the columns. He fired and missed. A steamer tried to ram him but he evaded, going to 20 meters depth. He then fired tube #7 (also outboard) and got a hit which sank the second target. U-XIV then departed the immediate area submerged. He surfaced when the range opened to 6,000 yards and exchanged gunfire with the trawlers.

The visibility decreased and the convoy then disappeared in the mist heading west.[149]

The Austro-Hungarian Empire was a polyglot empire, with different nationalities speaking different languages. The U-XIV crew mirrored the various ethnic/language groups within the Empire. This could be a problem. An attack on a yacht was aborted when a Czech crewman didn't understand the torpedo firing order (in German). After that fiasco, and some intensive and focused German language lessons for the offender, U-XIV headed back for Cape Matapan. There she sank steamer *Marianga Gulandris* from Baltimore with 4,500 tons of wheat. She then moved over towards North Africa and torpedoed another steamer. It was hit aft and damaged but continued towards the port of Derna in Cyrenaica (current day Libya). Von Trapp pursued on the surface, unwilling to let a valuable target escape, but had to withdraw when taken under fire by Italian shore batteries. Having been at sea for 30 days, running sort of fuel and fresh water, U-XIV headed for Cattaro, her home port. She had no difficulty in getting through the Otranto Barrage on her return transit. A-H Admiral Horthy had taken most of his fleet to sea in May 1917 and cleared out the Otranto Barrage drifters and their nets. His ships sank 14 drifters.[150]

The Otranto Barrage was actually fairly formidable although U-boats could very carefully pick their route

---

149   Ibid, pp. 95-96. The tactics were classic and were used again on many occasions.

150   Ibid, p. 102

through it. The Barrage stretched from Italy in the west some 80 miles eastward across to the island of Fanio near Corfu close to Greece. Trawlers stretched steel wire nets with explosive charges attached. Tethered balloons with embarked observers were flown from steamers to look for approaching surfaced submarines. Aircraft were also used during daylight. U-XIV ran the Barrage at night on the surface, going between two motor torpedo boats (MTB), each about 600 meters to port and starboard. Finally she submerged and worked her way through the drifters and their nets. Once through she sank a French steamer. After that she hunted along the convoy route between Post Said at the north end of the Suez Canal and Malta. She detected a small convoy of 5 steamers and 4 escorts. Submerged, she let the escorts pass by and fired – a miss. U-XIV was attacked by a destroyer, and then fired a second torpedo at a steamer – a hit. She then dove to 25 meters, and went under the port column to get clear.

The next evening another convoy came into view, this time steering eastward toward Port Said. The convoy changed course and no immediate attack was possible. U-XIV overtook the convoy on the surface (called an "end around run" by U.S. submariners during WW II) and sank an 8,000 ton steamer. She kept after the convoy, sinking another steamer the following day.

She then shot a large steamer that didn't sink. U-XIV surfaced and started using her deck gun to finish her off but found that she had apparently walked into a U-boat trap.[151] Hurriedly diving she fired a torpedo – missed, then another – a hit and the steamer broke up. With all torpedoes gone after nine hectic days at sea, U-XIV returned to Cattaro.[152]

U-XXIII was sunk by an Italian torpedo boat towing an explosive sweep on 21 February, 1918. On 7 June 1918 U-XX was torpedoed by Italian submarine F 12 off the mouth of the Tagliamento River. On 9 July 1918 U-X hit a mine off Caorle, was beached and subsequently towed to Trieste for repairs but was out of service until the war's end.

The Austro-Hungarian submarine service was small but very professional. It sank a number of capital ships, both French and Italian, and limited the operations of opposing large warships in the Adriatic Sea through its demonstrated capability. However, there were too few A-H submarines to seriously affect events. The large majority of Allied and neutral ships that were sunk in the Mediterranean Sea were sunk by German U-boats, which operated from A-H bases in the northern Adriatic Sea, mainly Cattaro. The A-H U-boat Service was a poor cousin to the German U-boat Service. This relationship reflected the relative economic strengths of the Dual Monarchy and Germany.

---

151   From Von Trapp's memoirs it isn't clear whether the intended target was a Q-ship or merely a merchant ship with an eager gun crew.
152   Ibid, p. 123.

CHAPTER ELEVEN – GERMAN SUBMARINE OPERATIONS

The modern German Navy had been built by Admiral Tirpitz to challenge Great Britain's Royal Navy for command of the seas. However when the war started in 1914 the Royal Navy was still greatly superior in numbers of capital ships, "dreadnought" type battleships, 24 British to 16 German, enough so that it was clear that the Royal Navy would be the victor in an all out battle at sea. Therefore German Navy capital ships stayed in port as a "fleet in being" that forced the Royal Navy to maintain its superior numbers of ships in position to respond if the German High Seas Fleet sortied into the North Sea. This stalemate offered independent German Navy cruisers and disguised surface raiders some opportunity to sink or capture British merchant ships in distant locations. Meanwhile the High Seas Fleet sat waiting for an opportunity to conduct operations that could isolate and destroy small segments of the Royal Navy's Grand Fleet. If these operations were successful, the High Seas Fleet might be capable of engaging the reduced Grand Fleet on nearly equal terms. On an individual ship basis German dreadnoughts were superior in both gunnery and damage control arrangements.

Lesser units of the Royal Navy operating in the North Sea immediately established a distant blockade of Germany, captured German merchant ships, and blocked neutral nations from supplying war materials to Germany. They also tried to hunt down and sink German raiders.

1914

Major political/diplomatic events: The Dual Monarchy (Austria-Hungary) declared war on Serbia; Russia declared war on Austria-Hungary and Germany; France declared war on Germany and Austria-Hungary; Germany declared war on France and England; and England declared war on Germany when Germany violated Belgium's borders. In August Japan declared war on Germany, looking for an opportunity to acquire German colonial possessions in the Far East. In October 1914 Turkey attacked the Russian Black Sea Fleet, bringing the two countries into conflict. Italy maintained tenuous neutrality waiting to see which alliance might offer her the best deal in terms of territory.

Major ground operations: The German Army invaded Belgium and swept toward Paris. It was stopped at the Marne in September and a race to the sea ensued as armies tried to outflank each other, leaving the opponents entrenched. The Germans attacked at Ypres in Flanders in late October and early November. The British Expeditionary Force held, with the loss of over 50,000 casualties.

Trench lines stabilized. By late 1914 General von Falkenhayn, the German chief of staff, realized that German hopes for a short war had been dashed. The German Army adopted a defensive stance on the Western Front. But von Falkenhayn then looked to the East, where maneuver warfare was still possible, hoping to quickly knock Russia out of the war. Generals von Hindenburg and Ludendorff had succeeded in crushing the initial Russian offensive in August.

Major naval operations: The Royal Navy established a distant blockade of Germany in the North Sea. The German Pacific Squadron was engaged and defeated at the Falklands after having earlier destroyed a British squadron off Chile. The Royal Navy successfully transported the British Expeditionary Forces to France. The German General Staff had not included the German Navy in its war planning and thus the German Navy did not attempt to interfere with the transport of British troops across the channel to France.

Admiral von Tirpitz thought that Great Britain would institute a close blockade of German ports in the event of war, and planned to use submarines and torpedo boats to reduce their capital ships' advantage. In the event, the Royal Navy understood that the submarine had made close blockades no longer viable and settled on a distant blockade in the Channel and North Sea.[153]

U-boat operations during 1914:

At the war's beginning there were about 20 U-boats in the German High Seas Fleet. They were commanded by *Korvettenkapitan* Hermann Bauer, Commander U-Boats. They operated from an advanced base at the island of Heligoland in the North Sea. When hostilities started with Russia on 1 August, they were deployed immediately as a defensive screen in the North Sea.

On 3 August Great Britain declared war on Germany in response to the invasion of Belgium. Bauer as *Fuhrer der Unterseeboote, FdU,* immediately sent U-5, U-7, U-8, U-9, and U-13 through U-18 to attack the British Grand Fleet in its anchorage at Scapa Flow. U-5 and U-9 turned back with engine problems. U-13 disappeared without a trace. U-15 was rammed and sunk by light cruiser HMS Birmingham on 9 August while attempting to torpedo Birmingham. The daring attack on a major British naval anchorage achieved nothing.

On September 14, 1914 U-21 (diesel-electric) torpedoed and sank light cruiser HMS Pathfinder in the Firth of Forth, the first submarine success in wartime since the American Civil War.[154] Pathfinder's forward magazine exploded and she sank with the loss of over 250 men.

---

153   Lyons, World War I, pp. 62-63
154   Vause, Wolf, p. 9

Several weeks later U-9 (paraffin-electric) was on patrol in the Channel. She had 2 bow and 2 stern torpedo tubes plus 2 reload torpedoes for her bow tubes. She had been swept south from her patrol area by a strong gale. On 22 September she came upon three armored cruisers, HMS Aboukir, Cressy and Hogue, off the Dutch coast. Bad weather had forced their accompanying destroyers back to port and as a result the cruisers had no protection. U-9 torpedoed Aboukir first. Aboukir's commanding officer thought his cruiser had hit a mine. U-9 went below periscope depth to reload. When U-9 returned to periscope depth she observed Aboukir sinking and the other two cruisers standing by to rescue survivors. U-9 fired 2 bow torpedoes at Hogue and got two hits. Hogue sank in ten minutes. U-9 then fired 2 torpedoes at Cressy, hit with one, and finished her off with her last torpedo. There were over 1,400 casualties. The Royal Navy at first thought that an entire German submarine flotilla had been involved.[155]

Orders were soon issued to RN warship captains to maintain speed in submarine waters and not to stop their ships to rescue survivors. The submarine, thought to only be useful in close defense of a harbor, had suddenly emerged as a major threat to large warships at sea. The complexion of naval warfare would never be the same again.

---

155 Hezlet, Submarines and Sea Power, pp. 27-29. Lieutenant Otto Weddigen, former CO U-9, was lost in March 1915 when his boat, U-29, was rammed and sunk by HMS Dreadnought.

In addition to attacking British warships, German U-boats were tasked to conduct mercantile warfare against enemy merchant ships. International law regarding commerce warfare required that suspected enemy ships be warned to stop, then an inspection party could then board and inspect ship's papers, bills of lading and cargo, seizing contraband, and capturing the ship as a prize of war if warranted and sailing it to a neutral port where a Prize Court would adjudicate disposition of cargo and ship. This was a relatively simple matter for a surface warship but submarines with low freeboard had a much more difficult time and were much more vulnerable.

Great Britain established a distant naval blockade of Germany upon the beginning of hostilities, and was in a geographic position to interdict German and neutral merchant traffic in the North Sea. German ships had only a 20 nautical mile (nm) exit from the North Sea to the south through the English Channel, and a 200 nm exit to the north between Scotland and Norway.

During 1914 U-boats sank only 13 ships totaling 64,163 tons.[156] However the losses included warships HMS Pathfinder, HMS Aboukir, HMS Cressy, HMS Hogue, HMS Hawke, HM submarine E-3, and HMS Hermes. In addition the French battleship Jean Bart was damaged. Five U-boats were lost. In late November the German Navy commander in chief recommended that an unrestricted submarine campaign be conducted in a

---

156   Sinking totals include ships taken as prizes of war.

war zone around the British Isles as a countermeasure to the British naval blockade of Germany. The submarine had clearly shown that it could be considered a factor in distant blockade operations as well as close blockades. It had not yet clearly demonstrated its capabilities in "cruiser warfare", that is in attacks on maritime commerce.

Ship sinking's, tonnage sunk, and U-boats sunk
through the end of 1914[157]

	1914	1915	1916	1917	1918	Totals
Number of ships sunk	13					13
Tonnage sunk	64,163					64,163
Number of U-boats sunk	5					5

1915

Major political/diplomatic events: Italy declared war on Austria-Hungary in May, but not Germany at this time. Her ground forces attacked Austria-Hungary on her northern border. Bulgaria joined the Central Powers. In late 1915 the U.S. government provided an opinion about armed merchant ships that assisted German government factions favoring unrestricted submarine warfare. In January and again in December 1915 President Wilson sent his personal representative, Colonel House, to Europe to attempt mediation between the warring powers and to arrange a peace conference. Neither side would agree to abandon their war aims.[157]

---

157   Lyons, Op cit., pp. 226-227

Major ground operations: 1915 saw the introduction of the flame thrower and poison gas into modern warfare, both deadly novelties wielded by the German Army. A combined British-French amphibious operation was launched at Gallipoli in Turkey to seize the Dardanelles in April and May, after earlier naval attacks to force the Dardanelles had failed due to mines.

Major naval operations: In January British and German naval forces clashed at the Dogger Bank in the North Sea. In February and March a combined British-French naval force tried to force the Dardanelles and seize Constantinople thereby forcing Turkey out of the war. Turkish mines sank several battleships and damaged others, ending the purely naval thrust. The ensuing Allied amphibious landing was initially successful but a spirited Turkish defense of the Gallipoli Peninsula heights sparked by Kemal Ataturk, later ruler of Turkey, halted the invading forces not far from their beach landing sites. Finally in January 1916 the landing forces were withdrawn, the operation a failure. The debacle led to Winston Churchill stepping down from civilian leadership of the Royal Navy.

U-boat operations during 1915:

On 1 January 1915 U-24 sank the old battleship HMS Formidable in the Channel with over 500 lives lost. This and previous warship sinking's had a major effect on British naval operations. High speed now had to be used at sea as well as zigzag steering patterns to make submarine approaches more difficult. This required greater fuel expenditure. The Grand Fleet was forced to leave its covering position in the North Sea and relocated to its bases, which moved to the west coast of Scotland and to Ireland. So far the submarine campaign had been carried out with only 25 U-boats.

Two new classes of small U-boats had their launch dates in 1915. They were UB-1 class: 127/142 tons, 92 feet in length, 6.5 kts/5.5 kts, two 18-inch TT, with a crew of 14; and UC-1: 168/183 tons, 111 feet long, 6.5 kts/5.25 kts, no TT but 12 mines, with a crew of 14.[158] UC class boats would specialize in laying mines off the East coast of England.

At the Battle of the Dogger Bank in January, U-boats that were not present strongly influenced the battle. Room 40 had warned of planned operations by Admiral Hipper's Scouting Squadron, and the Royal Navy assumed a raid against the English east coast. Actually Hipper intended to reconnoiter the Dogger Bank area and destroy any British fishing trawlers encountered, and lay mines in the Firth of Forth. Forewarned, Beatty and his Battle Cruiser Fleet surprised Hipper and began a hot pursuit. Suddenly Admiral Beatty thought he saw a U-boat periscope and ordered his force to turn away, fearing a U-boat trap. Room 40 knew that no U-boats were involved but had neglected to pass that information along. Beatty's force

---

158   Grey, Edwyn A., *The Killing Time*, p. 228

finished off one German capital ship and badly damaged another but their bag might have been much larger. The incident clearly points out the effects of losses of capital ships to submarines in 1914 had on the minds of the Royal Navy's leaders.[159]

In February 1915 the main U-boat effort shifted to an unrestricted war on merchant ships in the area around the British Isles. The German Navy had not originally planned to attack British commerce with submarines. The General Staff had focused on a short war and the Western Front deadlock came as a complete surprise. The British naval blockade of Germany was being felt on the home front by 1915. It was apparent to the naval staff that the attrition policy currently being pursued would not lead to defeat of the Royal Navy's Grand Fleet. Cruiser warfare had already failed. Nine German cruisers/raiders had been sunk for a bag of only 52 merchant ships. There was no hope for a decisive victory in that direction. On the other hand U-boats had been able to operate all around the British Isles.

A few words on antisubmarine warfare (ASW) are appropriate at this time. Sonar as we know it today did not

---

159 Strachan, Op cit., pp. 205-207. Room 40 was the heart of British naval intelligence focused on code and cipher breaking. Within four months of the beginning of the war Room 40 had access to three German codes: merchant ship, Imperial German Navy code, and a German destroyer code book. In addition, Room 40 received and plotted bearings on German Navy radio transmissions intercepted by stations along England's east coast.

exist.[160] Neither did radar. In daylight a U-boat could be spotted by alert lookouts when it was on the surface, and then it could be attacked with gunfire or rammed. Depth charges had not yet been developed. While it was possible to spot a submarine periscope during the submarine's submerged approach on a target, it was not likely if the submarine approach officer was careful to limit the height of periscope above the water and the length of time it was up. Submarines carried torpedoes and a deck gun. Either could be used to sink an enemy ship. Often the first indication of a submarine attack was the detonation of a torpedo against the target ship's hull.

In November 1914 the Commander in Chief, German High Seas Fleet suggested that U-boats be used against British commerce in retaliation for the British blockade. Admiral von Pohl, the Navy Chief of Staff, thought that a ruthless submarine campaign would frighten neutral nations and sharply reduce their trade with Great Britain. He knew that about one-third of all imports into the British Isles were carried in neutral shipping.

After a lively debate, political approval to carry out an unrestricted U-boat campaign was finally granted. A War Zone was declared on 4 February 1915 to take effect 18 February around the British Isles. On 18 February 1915 there were 27 operational U-boats, 21 in the North Sea,

---

160   Hydrophones lowered into the water could sometimes detect submarine propellers or machinery noise but their use was just beginning. In any case they could only provide a rough bearing to the noise.

and 6 in the Baltic Sea. An additional 75 were building. Six U-boats were usually at sea at any given time, 4 in operational waters including 2 west of the British Isles. Losses to U-boats that had averaged about 8 – 10 ships per month in January and February, tripled in March. U-boats began to take a heavy toll of British and neutral merchant ships. However, strong neutral nation reaction forced some changes almost immediately. U-boat commanding officers were directed not to attack merchant ships flying the flags of neutrals.

During the first three months of the campaign there were 57 torpedo attacks without warning of which 38 were successful. Four ships that were hit made port in spite of damage. Fifteen ships were missed. There were 97 attacks made with gunfire. 43 ships escaped. In addition to 54 ships sunk by gunfire attacks, an additional 28 small ships and fishing vessels were sunk by gunfire. The sinking's that took place were mainly in the southwestern approaches to the UK.

In April U-boats largely abandoned use of the Dover Strait for passage around the British Isles due to mine barriers and ASW patrols. Nets had been laid with indicator buoys. A U-boat attempting submerged passage could get caught in the net and the dragging buoys indicated its position to watching ASW forces. They could then drop explosive charges. Mine barriers consisted of anchored mines, floating below the surface at different depths.

Twenty-five new U-boats were delivered during this period, all UB or UC class submarines.[161] Operational strength in May 1915 was 35 U-boats.[162] 19 U-boats were lost during 1915, but another 17 were delivered from the builders, mostly UB and UC types. 72 more UB and UC class U-boats were ordered. A total of over 100 U-boats were now under construction.

On 7 May 1915, without warning U-20 torpedoed and sank a large British passenger liner, SS Lusitania, off the southeast coast of Ireland with the loss of over 1,198 lives including 139 American citizens. American and international opinion were outraged. British propaganda made the most out of the horrible event.

On 15 September 1915 the passenger liner SS Arabic was sunk with the loss of two more American lives, leading to further strained relations between Germany and the United States. Under American diplomatic pressure, the German government then issued orders that no further ships were to be sunk without warning, and no passenger ships were to be sunk at all. As a result, on 18 September 1915, Commander in Chief, High Seas Fleet called off all submarine attacks on commerce west of the British Isles.[163] A total of 546 ships had been sunk since the beginning of the unrestricted campaign, an average of 78 ships per month.

---

161   UB were coastal submarines, smaller and shorter range than the U-class. UC submarines were primarily minelayers that carried a number of mines in vertical tubes in their ballast tanks.

162   Hezlet, Submarines and Sea Power, pp. 43-47

163   Hezlet, Submarines and Sea Power, p. 49

In the Mediterranean Sea a combined British – French naval force attempted to steam through the Dardanelles into the Sea of Marmara to attack the Turkish capital of Constantinople and knock Turkey out of the war. That would assist the Russians and provide access to badly needed Russian grain. This strategic plan was the brainchild of Winston Churchill, then serving as First Lord, civilian head of the Royal Navy. The Dardanelles were defended by mines and shore batteries. Turkish forces were assisted by German advisers. Newly laid mines sank several British and French battleships and damaged others. On 25 May 1915 German submarine U-21 arrived on scene and sank battleship HMS Triumph. On 27 May it sank another capital ship, HMS Majestic. Subsequently all capital ships were withdrawn to a protected anchorage, and hence unavailable to provide supporting gunfire to the landing party.

In the Mediterranean Sea during the period September – December 1915 a total of 100 ships were sunk with no U-boat losses:[164]

Mediterranean ship sinking's September – December 1915

Month	Ships Sunk
September	18
October	17
November	41
December	24

---

164   Ibid, p. 55

During 1915 U-boats sank a total of 660 ships totaling 1,302,822 gross register tons, compared to only 15 ships sunk in 1914. Nineteen U-boats were lost.

During the next 16 months sea commerce proceeded as before under international law with submarines having to stop suspect vessels and identify any contraband before action could be taken. By the end of 1915 Germany ordered construction of another 52 U-boats and took possession of 6 that were building in German yards for other countries. 32 of these were small boats intended for operations in the southern North Sea or Adriatic Sea.[165]

Another significant diplomatic event took place in late 1915. The U.S. government offered the opinion that an armed merchant ship fell into the category of a naval auxiliary. That was agreeable to German naval ears since under international law naval auxiliary ships could be attacked without warning. British merchant ships had been armed in order to make it more difficult for U-boats to attack and sink them with gunfire while surfaced. Gun ammunition was relatively cheap compared to torpedoes. A number of armed merchant ships were able to fight off their attackers. This U.S. interpretation offered assistance to the faction inside the German government that strongly advocated unrestricted submarine warfare against Great Britain.

---

165 The term "boat" is used in the U.S. Submarine Service to refer to a submarine (which is officially a ship). It goes back to the term "submarine torpedo boat" used to distinguish submersible torpedo boats from torpedo boats.

Ship sinking's, tonnage sunk, and U-boats sunk
through the end of 1915

	1914	1915	1916	1917	1918	Totals
Number of ships sunk	13	660				673
Tonnage sunk	64,163	1,302,822				1,366,985
Number of U-boats sunk	5	19				24

1916

Major political/diplomatic events: In Germany the Navy chief of staff, Admiral von Tirpitz, became the chief advocate for resumption of an unrestricted submarine campaign against Great Britain. He used widespread publicity to make his point. The public, already suffering from the economic effects of the British blockade, and the Reichstag, agreed with him. The Army chief of staff, General von Falkenhayn also agreed.

On August 16 Italy declared war on Germany. Also in August General von Ludendorff replaced General von Falkenhayn as German chief of staff. That same month Romania declared war on the Central Powers. Toward the end of the year Generals von Hindenburg and Ludendorff allied themselves with the Navy chief of staff and the High Seas Fleet commander in urging resumption of an unrestricted submarine campaign. The Navy Chief of Staff predicted Great Britain would be driven to make peace within five months.

In late 1916 British concern over increasing shipping losses led to the move of Admiral Sir John Jellicoe from

Grand Fleet commander to the post of First Sea Lord in the Admiralty. He was a natural but not a good choice. He initially opposed the concept of convoy, dismissing it as a "defensive" strategy in favor of an "offensive" strategy – using destroyers, submarines, trawlers, aircraft and airships to search for and destroy submarines.[166] The arguments against convoys included: it would be too hard to coordinate the actions of individual merchant ship captains; the convoy would be limited to the speed of the slowest ship present; and that convoys would be easier to spot from a U-boat bridge. These arguments ignored the fact that convoys had been used successfully to transport the BEF to France and to transport coal from the UK to France. They also ignored the successful use of convoy in the Baltic Sea by the German Navy during 1916 to protect ships carrying iron ore from Sweden to Germany.

Major ground operations: The German Army attacked the French fortress at Verdun in February, planning to draw large French infantry units into an artillery killing zone and inflict enough casualties to bring France to the negotiating table. However the intense fighting consumed both German and French troops in almost equal numbers.

---

166   Similarly during the 1942 Battle of the Atlantic, USAAF and RAF leaders opposed using long range aircraft to support convoys, dismissing the tactic as "defensive". They failed to realize that convoys could protect most ships, and would lead submarines to focus on convoys and thus open themselves to attack. Hunting submarines in the open ocean was and is a fool's game.

Perhaps more soldiers died in the Verdun sector than at any other battlefield in history. In July the British attacked at the Somme, attempting to provide some relief to their French allies, incurring 60,000 casualties on the first day. The British introduced a new weapon of war, the tank, a tracked armored vehicle, during that offensive. However, too few were used to provide a breakthrough. The British suffered about 400,000 casualties during the period of the Somme offensive. On the Eastern Front Russia launched the Brusilov offensive, named for the Russian Army commander.

Major naval operations: 1916 was marked by a number of German naval raids or attempted raids, trying to bring smaller segments of the British Grand Fleet into action. The Germans had a strategic advantage in the operation of zeppelins which provided long range visual reconnaissance. The Royal Navy enjoyed the advantage of the code-breaking services of Room 40 whose decryptions of German naval messages often led to early knowledge of German intentions. On 31 May 1916 the two major fleets clashed at the Battle of Jutland in the North Sea. Tactically the Germans won but they suffered a strategic defeat and never again emerged in strength to challenge the Royal Navy. In July Admiral Scheer, commander High Seas Fleet, decided that a fleet action between the German High Seas Fleet and British Grand Fleet was no longer a viable option. Failing to succeed on the surface during 1916, the German Navy returned to unrestricted submarine warfare to attack Britain's mercantile fleet during 1917.

In June 1916, U-75 laid some 22 mines close inshore off the west coast of the Orkney Islands, which contain the naval anchorage of Scapa Flow. Several days later HMS Hampshire set out for Russia carrying the Secretary of State for War, Lord Kitchener, for consultations. That evening Hampshire struck one of U-75's freshly laid mines and sank. There were only 12 survivors. Kitchener and his staff were among those lost.[167]

U-boat operations during 1916

The U-boat Arm had 154 U-boats operational. At any one time some 70 were on or enroute station.[168] In general terms during 1916 the U-boat war continued the way it had since the end of the unrestricted campaign in September 1915. U-boats operated under international law. They could stop and inspect and sink ships carrying contraband. Their toll increased as their commanding officers and crews gained experience. Their victims were individual ships in all cases. The Royal Navy did not

---

167   Hoehling, Op cit., p. 158
168   An operational-boat had completed construction or repairs, and its initial or refresher training, and was considered available for war patrol operations. Usually a ratio of one submarine on station for each three submarines in an operational status is considered normal. The second is on passage to or from a war patrol station, and the third is undergoing repairs and crew rest period.

institute widespread convoy procedures although convoys of sailing ships had been used in the early 1800s during the Napoleonic Wars to thwart privateers carrying out mercantile warfare. Faulty operations analysis led the Royal Navy to the conclusion that concentration of ships in convoy increased the probability of visual detection at sea by U-boats, and the same concentration increased the number of targets that might be sunk.[169]

The main area of U-boat concentration was around the British Isles southwest of Ireland, although some U-boats operated in the Mediterranean against traffic to and from India. Meanwhile Flanders-based U-boats mostly laid mines in the southern North Sea. About 12 to 14 ships per month were sunk or seriously damaged by U-boat mining operations.

The battle of Jutland in May 1916 essentially confined the German High Seas Fleet to harbor. However it still was a 'fleet in being' and the British Grand Fleet had to remain on guard. The winter of 1916 – 1917 was very difficult for the German people. Food was in short supply

---

169   Actually the probability of visual detection of a 40 ship convoy is only marginally greater than that of a single ship sailing by itself. A single submarine might get off up to 4 torpedoes in a submerged attack on a convoy, hitting perhaps two ships, while the remaining 38 ships cleared the area as fast as possible. The same submarine could sink as many ships going by individually as it had torpedoes.

because of the blockade.[170] It appeared that a victory on the ground was no longer likely and that the only possibility for Germany to "win" the war was to reopen an unrestricted submarine campaign against Britain. Major shipping losses might force Great Britain to the negotiating table and end the paralyzing blockade. However there was a very strong possibility that another result would be to bring the United States into the war on the side of the Allies. Proponents of an unrestricted submarine campaign argued that Great Britain could be forced to negotiate before an adequate number of U.S. troops could be raised, trained adequately, transported to France, and put into the battle in significant numbers.[171]

The new Chief of Naval Staff, Admiral von Holtzendorff, calculated that Great Britain could be forced to negotiate within a six month period if an unrestricted submarine campaign were carried out. Some German politicians disagreed, greatly fearing the effects of United States entry into the war. The Army chief of staff, General von Falkenhayn, agreed with his naval counterpart's opinion.

---

170 Strachan, Op cit., p.219. Between 1913 and 1918 areas under cultivation in Germany fell by 15%. Cereal production (grains) fell by greater than 30%. The first German food controls were instituted in 1914. Pre-war average daily calorie intake was 2240 calories. It fell to 1000 calories in February 1917. The winter of 1916-1917 was called the "turnip winter" because of having to substitute turnips for potatoes.

171 Vause, Op cit., pp. 11-12

In November 1915 the United States had expressed the view that merchant ships could be sunk if their crews were allowed to debark first, and that merchant ships should not be armed lest they be classed as "naval auxiliaries". Based on those views Germany revived its U-boat campaign against commerce in late February 1916. The rules of engagement (ROE) promulgated to U-boat commanding officers allowed armed vessels to be sunk without warning if the armament could be seen by the U-boat. Later, orders were modified to spare passenger liners even if armed.[172]

On 4 March the Kaiser agreed to an unrestricted campaign to begin 1 April. However, two days later he withdrew his permission with the consequence that the German Navy chief of staff, Admiral von Tirpiz, who was not consulted about the sudden reversal in policy – resigned his position in disgust.

On 13 March new orders were issued – all British ships in the "war zone", except passenger ships, were to sunk – whether armed or not. On 24 March the French cross-channel packet Sussex was sunk with large loss of life. The United States protested strongly and threatened to break diplomatic relations with Germany.[173] New orders followed – U-boats were again to operate under international rules. Admiral Scheer recalled all U-boats under his command, about 50% of the U-boat fleet.

---

172 Hezlet, Submarine and Sea Power, pp. 55-56
173 Terraine, Business in Great Waters, p. 11

During May 1916 the German High Seas Fleet commander, Admiral Reinhard Scheer, attempted to set a U-boat trap for the RN battle cruiser fleet. On 16 May he ordered 19 U-boats positioned off the Firth of Forth. The RN battle cruisers were based at Rosyth in the Firth. He planned to raid Sunderland and assumed that the battle cruisers would sortie from Rosyth in response. He also planned on zeppelin strategic aerial reconnaissance to detect any sortie of the Grand Fleet from its base at Scapa Flow, further north. However bad weather ruled out zeppelin operations Scheer then revised his plan, to sortie to the Skagerrak between Denmark and Norway. On 28 May Room 40 was able to give Grand Fleet commander Admiral Jellicoe early warning of German intentions. Late on 29 May, actually two hours before the German fleet got underway, both the Grand Fleet under Jellicoe and the Battle Cruiser Fleet under Beattie, left port headed for the Skagerrak. The subsequent famous Battle of Jutland took place without any U-boat participation.[174]

In the Mediterranean some submarine attacks without warning still took place, and in the absence of U.S. protests, such attacks continued and increased.

In 1916 the German government dispatched a commercial submarine to the United States. It was *Deutschland*, a 315 foot long submarine of 2,000 tons submerged displacement. It departed Bremen June 14, 1916 with a cargo of dye stuffs and chemicals, arriving in

---

174   Strachan, Op cit., pp. 209-214

Baltimore in early July. It departed Baltimore 1 August and arrived in Bremen on 15 August with a return cargo of rubber and metals, having successfully dodged Royal Navy patrols in the North Sea. The United States was neutral at the time and although strongly leaning toward the Allied cause was free to trade with both Allied and Central Power nations. *Deutschland* later departed on a similarly successful second voyage in October headed for New London, Connecticut.[175] After the United States entered the war Germany had no more need for commercial submarines and converted *Deutschland* into a long range U-boat.

Another German submarine visit to the United States took place that year. On October 7, 1916 U-53 surfaced off Newport, Rhode Island and proceeded into port accompanied by U.S. submarine D-2 that had been on offshore patrol. U-53's commanding officer made several courtesy calls on U.S. naval officials at Newport and handed over some papers for delivery to the German ambassador in Washington. After a 24 hour port call permitted to belligerent warships in neutral ports, U-53 got underway. She moved into international waters and there stopped and sank five merchant ships, towing ships boats, crew and passengers to the safety of the Nantucket Light Ship. They were then taken aboard U.S. destroyers and taken into port.[176]

175   Abbot, Aircraft and Submarines, pp. 364-378
176   Hoehling, Op cit., pp. 170-178

During 1916 the Kaiser agreed to a new set of rules governing submarine warfare: restricted (limited) around the British Isles; but unrestricted in the Mediterranean. In 1916 U-boats increased their toll to 1,390 merchant ships totaling 2,239,162 tons. 22 U-boats were lost. So far U-boats had seriously damaged British sea commerce but had not yet placed it in severe jeopardy.

From January through July 1916 U-boats sank fewer than 100 ships per month, on average 63.4 ships per month. But in August the toll rose to 146 ships; in September to 191 ships, in October to 202 ships, in November to 199 ships, and in December to 208 ships.

If U-boats could sink that many ships while abiding by international law, what would the score be in an unrestricted submarine campaign? Those in the German government who favored reinstituting an unrestricted submarine campaign had two powerful arguments: first, that the increased rate of loss of merchant shipping would bring Great Britain to the negotiating table in an estimated 6 – 8 months; and that although the campaign would probably bring the United States into the war on the side of the Allies, it would take the U.S. about 18 months to raise and train a large army, transport it overseas and get it into combat. Long before then, Great Britain would have been forced out of the war.

During 1916 a rather unusual court-martial took place. In July a German court-martial in occupied Belgium tried and convicted a British civilian ship captain of violating the international laws of war for attempting to ram a German submarine that had stopped and challenged him. He was tried, convicted and executed at Bruges, Belgium. The British took great exception to the affair and threatened to execute German prisoners of war in retaliation. The German government then pointed out that they held a large number of British prisoners of war, and could reciprocate if necessary. The matter was allowed to die. [177]

Ship sinking's, tonnage sunk, and U-boats sunk through the end of 1916

	1914	1915	1916	1917	1918	Totals
Number of ships sunk	13	660	1390			2,065
Tonnage sunk	64,163	1,302,822	2,239,162			3,606,147
Number of U-boats sunk	5	19	22			46

1917

Major political/diplomatic events: In January 1917 representatives of Great Britain and France met with the Russians and came away with the clear understanding that no Russian offensive activity was possible during the year because of political unrest in Russia. In March, Czar Nicholas of Russia came under heavy political pressure and abdicated. Later in the year Russia suffered revolution and essentially withdrew from the war, thereby freeing large numbers of German troops for employment on

---

177   Hoehling, Op cit., p. 178

the Western Front. The United States entered the war in April in response to the German unrestricted submarine campaign. At the start of hostilities between Germany and the United States in April 1917, Admiral Sims, the senior U.S. naval officer in Europe, asked Admiral Jellicoe about possible solutions to the U-boat problem. Jellicoe replied "Absolutely none that we can see now."[178] On 13 July Bethmann-Hollweg resigned as German Chancellor because he had found that he was unable to manage the Reichstag. In August some mutinies broke out in ships of the German High Seas Fleet based at Wilhelmshaven.

Major ground operations: The German Army was content to remain on the defensive during 1917 while the unrestricted U-boat campaign was carried out. General Ludendorff, effectively running Western Front operations, directed German forces to withdraw slightly to the east to the Siegfried Line (called the Hindenburg line by the Allies). The Allies mounted several Western Front offensives. The first was by the French in April. The French had long planned this offensive, which was keyed to a similar planned offensive on the Eastern Front by the Russian Army. As planned, the two relatively simultaneous offensives would prevent the Germans from shifting troops from one front to the other. Despite the Russian cancellation, the French decided to carry through

---

178   Lyons, Op cit., pp. 238-239

with their offensive.[179] It failed with very heavy casualties, and led to widespread mutinies in April, May and June within the French Army. French soldiers would defend their trenches but could no longer be forced to "go over the top" in futile attacks. General Petain was called in to deal with the delicate situation. A few mutineers were shot and others sent to military prisons, but for the remainder of the year offensives by the French Army were out of the question due to the need to rebuild morale.[180] In the summer and fall the British again tried to pick up the slack with offensives at Ypres. They both failed with resulting large casualty lists.

Major naval operations; The German High Seas Fleet remained in port, ever threatening and thus tying up Great Britain's Grand Fleet. The real work at sea was carried out by U-boats. After prolonged discussion and argument the faction demanding a return to unrestricted submarine warfare won out. In late December 1916 Navy chief of staff Admiral von Holtzendorff had recommended that Germany resume an unrestricted submarine campaign, stating that severe shipping losses could knock Great

---

179   Strachan, Op cit, pp. 242-244. Logic called for cancellation of the French offensive once it was realized that there would be no Russian offensive. However, General Neville who had taken over as French Army chief of staff, threatened to resign if the offensive was cancelled. The French government was weak and felt that it had to attack or fall politically.

180   The French government took strong steps to limit public knowledge of the mutinies, depriving the Germans of that information.

Britain out of the war by August 1917. On 8 January 1917 the Army and Navy chiefs of staff met with the Kaiser and recommended the renewed submarine campaign. Chancellor Bethmann-Hollweg was not present at the meeting. The Kaiser assented, and Bethmann-Hollweg later went along with the decision, announcing it to the Reichstag at the end of January. February 1st, 1917 was announced as the date for opening the new campaign. It would continue without letup through October 1918.

U-boat operations during 1917:

On 31 January the German government announced that as of 1 February 1917 it would resume an unrestricted submarine campaign, fully realizing the possible implications for U.S. entry into the war on the Allied side. Shipping losses mounted astronomically in the New Year:

February:	520,412 tons
March	564,497 tons
April	860,334 tons[181]

On 3 February the United States sundered formal diplomatic relations with Germany. On 2 April President Wilson responded further to the German government action by requesting that the Congress issue a declaration

---

181   At the end of April 1917 Great Britain had only six weeks of wheat supply remaining in the United Kingdom.

of war against Germany. After substantial debate, on 17 April 1917 the U.S. Congress declared war.[182]

In April Admiral Roger Keyes, RN led a "death or glory" raid on the U-boat base at Zeebruge in Belgium. A number of casualties were experienced but the raid was ineffective despite heroic efforts. The following day U-boats were still using the Bruges Canal for transit.

On May 24, 1917 the Royal Navy finally began a test of the convoy system. Sixteen merchant ships were escorted from Gibraltar to the UK without loss. That same day a 12 ship convoy left Norfolk, Virginia enroute the UK, escorted by a UK cruiser and 6 U.S. destroyers. Two ships fell out and one was torpedoed while enroute Halifax, Canada. The convoy speed was 9 knots.

Based on these and other test results, the Royal Navy formally adopted convoys in August 1917. The widespread institution of the convoy system was a key to defeating the U-boat campaign of unrestricted attacks.[183] By December monthly losses fell to <u>only 399,000 tons</u>. For

---

182 On 3 February the United States severed diplomatic relations with Germany. On 12 February Admiral 'Blinker' Hall, R.N., Great Britain's Director of Naval Intelligence, briefed the American Ambassador on the contents of the Zimmerman telegram to the German Ambassador to Mexico. In it Zimmerman, the German Foreign Minister, offered financial support to Mexico if it went to war with the United States, and indicated that Germany would help Mexico reclaim New Mexico, Arizona and Texas. That revelation did not go over well with the U.S. government or American citizens.

183 Doenitz, Memoirs, pp. 18-19. Doenitz writes "The German submarine campaign was wrecked by the introduction of the convoy system".

the year the average monthly shipping loss was 516,666 tons (about 250 ships per month). Although still in a serious position, it was apparent that Great Britain would survive.[184] On the map of Europe on the preceding page a U-boat danger zone is overlaid. Most ship sinking's by U-boats took place in that area. Unlike WWII, during WWI very few sinking's took place in the open Atlantic Ocean. When convoys were finally instituted destroyers escorted the convoys through the "danger zone" to or from their arrival/departure ports. However, unlike the North Atlantic the entire Mediterranean Sea was a U-boat danger zone.

Writing many years later in his Memoirs, Admiral Doenitz noted that WW I submarine flotillas were under separate commands rather than under one overall operational commander. He stated that there was "no unity of effort" and never any coordinated attacks. He was presumably correct about the absence of coordinated attacks, but substantial unity of effort was in evidence despite the lack of a central U-boat command. No German U-boat flotilla commander was able to "solve" the convoy problem, which removed the many vulnerable individual merchant ships from the sea and substituted large packets of 40 or more ships protected by escorts.

---

184 Keegan, An Illustrated History of the First World War, pp. 333-334.

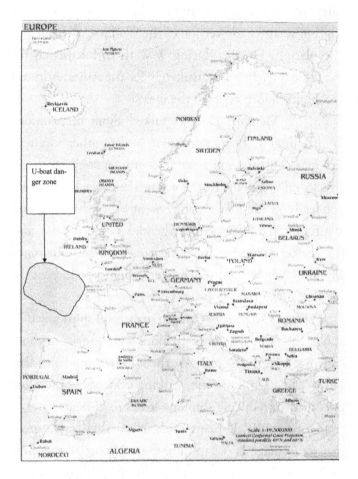

CIA World Factbook

In April 1917 *Kommodore* Hermann Bauer proposed using U-155, former *Deutschland*, as an offshore command post. Aboard U-155 a commander would coordinate radio intelligence about incoming convoys and direct U-boats to concentrate on attacking them. In addition, U-155 would carry torpedoes, fuel and supplies for other U-boats. This concept was an early version of the Wolf pack scheme put into place by Doenitz during WW II. Unfortunately for the U-boat effort and fortunately for the Allies, Admiral von Holtzendorff rejected the idea.[185]

In his Memoirs Doenitz talked about preparations for his final U-boat patrol. He and another German commanding officer planned to coordinate night surfaced attacks on a convoy. In the event, the other U-boat was not ready to sail and Doenitz went off on his own and wound up in a POW camp. The idea would not die, and the correct tactic for attacking convoyed ships at night would be worked out much later using torpedo boats in the Baltic and then U-boats.

Prior to October 1917 more than 1500 ships sailed in about 100 convoys. Only 10 ships were lost from those convoys, a 1:150 loss ratio. At the same time independent sailers had a 1:10 loss ratio, striking evidence of the value of convoy in reducing shipping losses to U-boats.

During 1917 U-boats sank 3,000 ships for a gross register tonnage of 6.2 million tons. Almost all the ships sunk were independent sailers. While U-boats would continue to sink ships, the very severe threat to Great Britain was over. She could continue to import adequate foodstuffs to feed her population, albeit on a rationing system. In addition her supply of raw materials for war production continued to arrive.

---

185   Messimer, Op cit., pp. 155 - 156

Sixty-three U-boats were lost during the year. By late 1917 it was clear to many that the unrestricted U-boat campaign had failed in its goal of bringing Great Britain to the negotiating table. Although Admiral von Holtzendorf had thought that if U-boats could sink 600,000 tons of shipping per month for five months, the Great Britain would enter peace negotiations, his assumptions proved faulty. A large number of ships, submarines, aircraft and blimps were involved in convoy escort and independent ASW patrols, and an increasing number of U-boats were sunk.

ASW activities were not the key to the defeat of the U-boat campaign. Rather the defeat was due to: the refusal of neutral nations to be terrorized into withdrawing their vessels from trade with Great Britain; to the increased efficiency of handling cargo offloading in the United Kingdom; to the greatly increased merchant ship production in United States shipyards; and last but not least by any means – the introduction of convoy on a large basis.

However, the war was not over and the remaining Allies were still in a very serious position at the end of 1917. Russia had essentially folded thus freeing a large number of German divisions for use on the Western Front. Victory for the Allies was not a "given" as 1918 began.

Ship sinking's, tonnage sunk, and U-boats sunk
through the end of 1917

	1914	1915	1916	1917	1918	Totals
Number of ships sunk	13	660	1390	3,000		**5,063**
Tonnage sunk	64,163	1,302,822	2,239,162	6,200,000		**9,806,147**
Number of U-boats sunk	5	19	22	63		**109**

1918

Major political/diplomatic events: At Brest-Livosk in Russia on 3 March the new Russian government signed a peace treaty with Germany, officially freeing German armies on the Eastern front to redeploy to France. On 7 May Romania signed a peace treaty with the Central Powers. Between 1 November 1917 and 21 March 1918 Germany shifted 44 divisions from the Eastern Front to the Western Front. Meanwhile increasingly large numbers of American troops landed in France. By June over 274,000 American troops had arrived, and ten U.S. divisions were manning front line positions. The overall line up was 207 under-strength German divisions opposing 203 Allied divisions. U.S. divisions were 20,000 men apiece, twice the size of European divisions.[186]

Major Ground Operations: The German High Command believed that an intense spring offensive on the Western Front, using divisions diverted from the now quiet Eastern Front, coupled with the ongoing U-boat

---

186   Lyons, Op cit., pp. 270-271

campaign could still knock Great Britain out of the war before significant numbers of fresh American troops could enter combat. Storm troops, using new tactics developed on the Eastern Front, would lead the 1918 Spring Offensive, or *Kaiserschlacht* (Kaiser's Battle). On March 21, 1918 General von Ludendorff launched an all-out German offensive with three armies. Initially it succeeded very well. There were four separate German attacks, named *Michael, Georgette, Gneisenau*, and *Blucher-Yorck*. However by July 18th all the attacks had been repulsed and the front stabilized. The German Army suffered very heavy personnel casualties and had no hope of providing adequate replacements.

Major Naval Operations: The German High Seas Fleet remained in port, with morale crumbling. Eventually in October mutinies began to form. News of a planned last minute suicide clash with the British Grand Fleet leaked out and led to direct mutiny of many sailors in the High Seas Fleet, who refused to raise steam and get underway. U-boat crews, who fought to the last, wound up training their torpedo tubes on German capital ships to bring the mutineers under control.

The U.S. Navy and Royal Navy laid a very large number of mines from Scotland to Norway to attempt to close off that passage that U-boats were using to attack British maritime trade. The mine field was called the North Sea Mine Barrage and contained about 100,000 mines. The mines featured a special antenna that effectively increased the depth of coverage of each mine. The U.S. Navy claimed at least four and perhaps up to eight U-boats sunk. The Royal Navy credited the mine lines with six U-boats sunk. Given Room 40's clear look into German naval communications the RN estimate was probably correct.[187]

U-boat operations during 1918:

U-boats continued to attack British and Allied shipping without letup. However the convoy system, now fully in place for most inbound and outbound shipping to and from the British Isles, reduced shipping losses dramatically. Ship loss rates fell by two-thirds from those experienced in 1917. A total of 1,133 ships were sunk during 1918, but 999 (88%) of those lost were independent sailers. During 1918 only 134 ships were lost from convoys. [188] The introduction of convoys, which had been implemented during the Napoleonic Wars against French and American privateers in the early 1800s, proved equally useful against the far deadlier U-boat threat in the new century. While convoys could not win a war by themselves they enabled Great Britain to continue in the war and contributed greatly to the ground victory won on the Western Front by Allied troops.

187   Hoehling, Op cit., p. 256
188   i Blair, Hitler's U-boat War, pp. 16-17

Although U-boat operations off the east coast of the United States during WW I were not nearly as extensive as later in 1942, a few ships were sunk and some mines were laid. The latter resulted in the sinking of armored cruiser USS San Diego southeast of Fire Island, New York on July 19, 1918 with the loss of six lives.

On the night of 3-4 October the German government, reeling from setbacks on the Western Front and threatened with revolution in major cities of Germany, sent a note to President Wilson requesting an armistice and the start of peace negotiations.[189] While President Wilson was discussing the basis for acceptance of an armistice with British and French representatives, U-boats sank a Japanese liner on 4 October and a British mail packet on 10 October. A total of over 800 lives were lost. In response, on 14 October President Wilson demanded that the U-boat campaign be ended as a prelude to further peace negotiations. The German cabinet met on 17 October to consider the demand, and finally accepted it on 20 October despite General Ludendorff's opposition.[190]

Seventy-three U-boats were lost in combat during 1918. The last U-boat activity of the period was not directed at the Allies, but rather against ships of the German High Seas Fleet whose crews had mutinied. U-boat crews, who

---

189   Lyons, Op cit., pp. 290-291 Also see Strachan, The First World War. Over 772,736 deaths in Germany during the war were attributed to starvation by an official British history. The 1918 civilian death rate in Germany was 17% greater than that of 1913.
190   Lyons, Op cit., pp. 295-297

fought to the bitter end and were untainted by Socialist and Communist propaganda emanating from Bolshevik Russia, trained their torpedo tubes on German Navy warships flying the red flag of revolution in German ports.

Ship sinking's, tonnage sunk, and U-boats sunk
through the end of fighting in 1918

	1914	1915	1916	1917	1918	Totals
Number of ships sunk	13	660	1,390	3,000	1,133	6,196
Tonnage sunk	64,163	1,302,822	2,239,162	6,200,000	2,632,115	12,438,262
Number of U-boats sunk	5	19	22	63	73	182

Mediterranean submarine operations

On 25 April 1915 Germany dispatched U-21 from Kiel, Germany to Pola, Austria at the northern end of the Adriatic Sea. Germany was not at war with Italy but apparently was well aware of behind the scenes Italian diplomatic maneuvering with the Allies. On 26 April Italy secretly signed the Treaty of London with Britain, France and Russia, committing herself to go to war within a month. On 23 May 1915 she declared war on Austria (but not with Germany). After a week layover at Pola, U-21 proceeded to the Dardanelles where Allied forces had conducted an amphibious assault landing at Gallipoli. The Royal Navy was aware of her journey but was unable to intercept her.

On arrival 25 May at the Dardanelles U-21 missed both HMS Swiftsure and HMS Vengeance. But later that day she sank pre-dreadnought battleship HMS Triumph.

Two days later she sank another older battleship HMS Majestic. As a result of these losses all Allied battleships were withdrawn to the port of Mudros in Greece where they rested safely behind an antisubmarine boom. They could no longer provide much needed gunfire support for ANZAC troops fighting the Turks.[191] This was another significant punctuation point in naval warfare, attributable to the power of the new submarine.

U-21 was joined in the Mediterranean Sea by several more medium size submarines that transited around the British Isles and into the Mediterranean through the Straits of Gibraltar. U-34 and U-35 were sent from the Baltic Sea on 21 July 1915. They went to Cattaro in the Adriatic, which was used by the Austro-Hungarian Navy as a submarine operating base. In August 1915 they were joined by U-33 and U-39, after pleas from the German Naval Attaché in Constantinople, who was concerned over Turkish ground force casualties at Gallipoli caused by Allied naval gunfire support.

In addition nine small UB and UC class U-boats were shipped overland and assembled at Pola at the north end of the Adriatic Sea. From September 1915 through January 1916 the Adriatic U-boat Flotilla sank 106 ships without losing any U-boats. Antisubmarine forces in the Mediterranean were under French command and included 65 destroyers, 79 sloops, and 200 trawlers operating in 18 different areas.

---

191   Hezlet, Submarines and Sea Power, p. 38

The German Adriatic Flotilla began serious operations against British, French and neutral trade in the Mediterranean Sea in October 1915. They sank 18 ships (63, 848 tons), concentrating on the approaches to Salonika and Kavalla. Another large U-boat, U-38, sailed that month to augment the U-boat flotilla in the Adriatic. In November 44 ships (155,882 tons) were sunk. In December the sinking rate fell off, down to 17 ships (73,741 tons). This last figure was slightly over half the U-boat tonnage sunk worldwide.

A sinking in November caused serious diplomatic problems. U-38, commanded by Max Valentiner, and sailing under the Austrian flag, sank Italian passenger liner *Ancona* off the coast of Tunisia. Over two hundred lives were lost including nine American citizens. The U.S. Secretary of State filled a strong diplomatic protest in Vienna.[192]

In the summer of 1916 a large number of German U-boats were shifted from the Atlantic theater to the Mediterranean where there were very few American-flag ships and hence few restrictions on unrestricted submarine attack.[193] During 1916 the Allies lost 415 ships in the Med

---

192   This incident points to a certain casualness on the German side. Italy and Germany were officially at peace. German U-boats at times operated under the Austrian flag, and of course Austria and Italy were at war. The German government could be a bit officious about international law when it chose, as it did in July 1916 when it tried, condemned and executed a British merchant captain for attempting to ram a U-boat in violation of the Laws of War (see German U-boat operations: 1916).

193   Von Trapp, To The Last Salute, p. 60

(1,045,058 tons) almost half of all their tonnage losses that year.

The U-boat Service fought two different wars simultaneously during 1915 and 1916. In the Atlantic it dithered, going from observance of international law to unrestricted submarine warfare, and back again as diplomatic pressures built. The main concern was of alienating the United States to the point that she would join the Allies. The German government was well aware of American industrial potential and did not wish to add the United States to her enemies' list. In the Mediterranean Sea, where few American flag vessels sailed, U-boat operations were much less restricted since there were fewer chances of major problems. During 1916 U-boat operations in the Med approached an unrestricted nature. Finally on 1 February 1917 the German government committed itself to unrestricted submarine warfare worldwide in the belief that U.S. entry into the war would not seriously affect the balance of power.

In May 1916 UC-12 was lost in the approaches to the port of Taranto, Italy, an important Italian naval base. She was sunk by a mine, apparently her own. Italian divers went down to the wreckage and positively identified her as a German mine-laying submarine.[194] This incident helped tip the balance. Germany had been too clever by half, operating U-boats under the Austrian flag and expecting to continue to get away with that subterfuge. Sinking

---

194   Showell, *The U-Boat Century*, p. 135

an Italian-flagged passenger liner at sea was one thing, directly attacking a major Italian naval base was not to be tolerated. On 28 August 1916 Italy declared war on Germany. The incident may have been an excuse rather than the primary reason, but Italy was now fully engaged against the Central Powers.

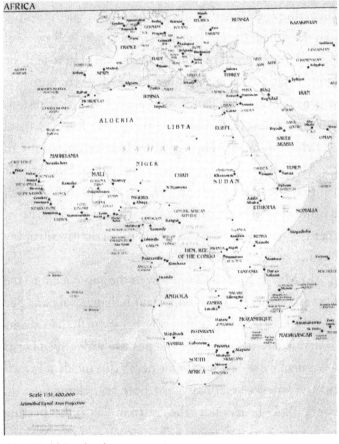

CIA World Factbook

The U-boat campaign in the Mediterranean Sea was quite effective up to a point. Of some 14 million tons of shipping sunk by U-boats during WW I, 3.2 million tons (23%) were sunk in the Mediterranean. Eight of the top twelve "U-boat aces" served in the Pola Flotilla. However, the imposition of convoy in the Med during 1917 did much to bring their depredations under control.[195] Convoy thwarted them as it did U-boats commanders in the Atlantic. Doenitz had to surface his submarine and scuttle it during an attack on a convoy in the Med in 1918. His experience there rankled and led him to theorize on a way to deal with the convoy system. While a POW he began to devise a method, too late for WW I but carrying a threat for the future.

The Imperial Japanese Navy joined the Allies in the Med in April 1917. It contributed fourteen destroyers with cruiser flagships based at Malta. They helped with ASW and convoy escort duties although not sinking any German or Austrian submarines. One destroyer, IJN ship Sakaki, was sunk by U-27.

1918 ship losses to U-boats fell to 325 ships (761,060 tons). Nine German U-boats left for home waters in October as Germany reeled under the threat of revolution, and ten U-boats were scuttled. UB-50 exacted a final revenge on the Royal Navy on 9 November 1918 near Cape Trafalgar when it torpedoed and sank battleship HMS Britannia.

---

195   The Italian Navy instituted convoy procedures in April, and the Royal Navy followed suit on the Alexandria-Malta route in May.

Chapter Twelve –
Effectiveness of German
U-boat campaigns

G ermany operated a total of 351 U-boats during WW I. They sank slightly more than 6,000 Allied ships including 10 battleships and 18 cruisers. In all they sank about 12 million tons of shipping.

At the time of the Armistice signing on November 11, 1918 there were 179 operational U-boats. 224 more were on the building ways, and another 200 were projected. By 1919 the German Navy planned to have 300 operational U-boats.

Both the restricted and unrestricted U-boat campaigns were devastating to Great Britain's and neutral nations' merchant shipping. Belated introduction of a convoy system finally reduced shipping losses by over 60%. Without that factor, Great Britain would have been forced into negotiations with Germany, thus ending her own slow but very effective economic blockade. If that had taken place, it is likely that Germany would have secured a peace with France that left significant portions of French territory in German hands.

Germany came very close to winning World War I with her unrestricted submarine campaign. There is no doubt that the unrestricted U-boat campaign was a potential war winning strategy for Germany. The U-boat Service involved fewer men than a standard German Army division. There is also no doubt that *convoy* was the key to defeating that strategy. It was not necessary to destroy U-boats in order to defeat them; it was only necessary to prevent them from sinking enough British, Allied and neutral merchant ships to ensure that the United Kingdom could feed its population and import an adequate supply of raw materials to continue its vital support for land operations on the Western Front. Chapter 17 of Messimer's excellent book *"Find and Destroy"* about ASW during WW I deals in detail with the mechanics of the convoy system, and is highly recommended reading.

One could argue that the German leaders should have foreseen the implementation of convoy on a wide scale by the British to combat the unrestricted attack. After all the German Navy had defended their vital iron ore trade in the Baltic Sea using convoy. But perhaps it did not occur to them to admit that by late 1916 Germany had been stalemated and should agree to negotiate a settlement.

On 21 October 1918 Germany recalled all U-boats as a condition of commencing preliminary peace negotiations. On 22 October 1918 the U-boat campaign officially ended. During WW I, 178 U-boats were lost for all reasons with the loss of 5,000 crew members killed, captured or missing in action. The following table shows those losses categorized by cause:[196]

World War I German U-boat losses by cause[198]

Surface warships	55
Probable mines	48
Unknown causes	19
Known accidents	19
Submarines	18
Q-ships	11
Merchant ships	6
Aircraft	1
Unexplained explosion	1

From a tactical and operational point of view it is hard to imagine that U-boats could have been better utilized than they were by the German Navy during WW I. They were finally and only narrowly defeated by a strategy that selected a correct measure of effectiveness (MOE). That MOE was the percentage of merchant ships that arrived in UK ports. If that percentage was high enough, Great Britain would survive and maintain its killing economic blockade of Germany. To cope with the convoy strategy, Germany would have had to concentrate U-boats in large enough numbers, outside of air cover, to overwhelm the convoy escorts with night surface attacks. That operational technique was not developed until many years later.

---

196   Blair, Op cit., p. 18

CHAPTER THIRTEEN – GERMAN SPECIAL SUBMARINE OPERATIONS[197]

German U-boat operations were focused initially on sinking enemy warships. Later they became involved in mercantile warfare, attacking shipping carrying war material to Great Britain. Established rules and regulations came into play and hampered submarines with their low freeboard, small crews, and inherent vulnerability. The German Navy and government, facing in their view a merciless British blockade designed to starve Germany into submission, cast off adherence to the Rules of Civilized Warfare, and commenced an unprecedented unrestricted submarine warfare campaign against Great Britain, its allies and any neutral nations engaging in maritime trade with Great Britain. Previous pages have

---

197   This chapter is published here with permission from the April 2010 issue of THE SUBMARINE REVIEW, a quarterly publication of the Naval Submarine League of Annandale, Virginia – of which the author is a life member.

dealt with that theme in great detail. Now it is time to turn to some "special submarine operations".[198]

During the First World War strategic communications used two modes of transmission: underwater telegraph cable and long range radio. Great Britain, France, Germany and a few other countries had invested in underwater cables but Great Britain led the world in the number of cables it controlled. The British government well understood the importance of strategic communications and the advantages that such control could bring them. Plans had been formulated to attack German cables in the event of war. The desired result would be to force German cable traffic to flow through British controlled cables, where the messages could be intercepted and read, or to force the traffic into radio transmission mode where it could be intercepted. British plans were to impose an information blockade on Germany in parallel with the economic shipping blockade it envisioned if a war occurred.

This story begins with British attacks on German undersea cables using surface ships, and the inevitable German countermoves, but segues into little known German "special operations" using submerged U-boats to attack British and Allied cables.[199]

---

198   U-boats were used during WW I to insert agents behind enemy lines in the Mediterranean and other theaters. Perhaps the most famous was the use of a U-boat to land Sir Roger Casement in Ireland in 1916 in the hope of fostering an Irish rebellion against Great Britain. Casement was rapidly "policed up", tried, convicted and hung for treason.

199   Edwyn A. Gray, The Killing Time, p. 189

In 1911 in Great Britain a Special Subcommittee of the Committee of Imperial Defense considered the role of undersea cables in strategic communications in the event of war. Plans were made to sever enemy cables at the start of war. The General Post Office, which controlled cable laying and repair operations, and the Royal Navy, agreed to cut five major German cables in the English Channel. The British army was tasked with plans to defend cable landing sites against enemy raiding parties that might come ashore to destroy British cable facilities.[200] The Eastern Telegraph group agreed to stockpile cable supplies and cable repair ships at appropriate locations within the Empire.

For Great Britain the First World War began on 4 August 1914 when Germany invaded neutral Belgium in violation of treaty, and refused a British demand to withdraw its forces. The British Empire immediately set its operations into gear to sever German cable connections. On the second day of the war, British civilian cable ship *Alert* left the port of Dover and sailed into the English Channel. When it reached the appropriate location it dragged for and pulled up five German undersea telegraph cables to her deck and cut them.[201] This severed many of Germany's cable links to its colonies in Africa and other locations, and forced German authorities to send a great deal of message traffic from their high powered radio

200   Jonathan Winkler, Nexus, pp. 16 - 17
201   Ibid, pp. 5 - 6

station at Nauen, near Berlin. That traffic was subject to interception and could possibly be deciphered.

That day, 5 August 1914, the Joint Naval and Military Committee, a Special Wartime Subcommittee of the Committee of Imperial Defense, met to consider further action against German communications with her overseas colonies. Prior to the war mainland Germany and her colonies in Africa and the Pacific were connected by cable and radio, and it was feared that those communications would be used to direct German naval units against British seaborne trade. Personnel from the Foreign Office, the Colonial Office and military representatives attended. In addition to the Channel cables that had already been cut, the Joint Committee directed attacks on German radio stations in her African colonies and the destruction of the German-controlled cable facilities at Yap Island in the Pacific.[202] On 12 August HMS Triumph destroyed the Yap Island cable facility with naval gunfire. Operations to capture or destroy radio stations in West and East African colonies began. Later that year, in November, the Royal Navy cut another German cable near the Azores which carried traffic from Tenerife to Monrovia in Liberia. The following year, in September, 1915 the British cable ship Transmitter cut the German cable to Brazil, off Monrovia.

The German government also understood the importance of strategic communications, and had similarly planned to sever its enemies' cables in the event of war.

---

202   Ibid, pp. 23-24, 27.

In the Baltic the Germans attacked the Great Northern Company cables that linked Russia with its allies, France and Great Britain. Later, between September 29 and November 30, German warships attacked the cable connecting Denmark with Russia at the ports of Libau and St. Petersburg. In the Black Sea German battleship *Goeben* cut the cable between Sevastopol and Varna, Bulgaria. Russia was now without direct cable links to Great Britain and her principal ally – France. Since Russian and French military operations were supposed to be coordinated against the common foe Germany, that situation presented a serious problem.[203]

In the Pacific area, German cruisers attacked British cable stations on small islands to destroy terminal equipment and cut the cables on shore. But before long the German cruiser squadron departed the Pacific and this threat ended. In the Atlantic, British naval superiority limited German surface force activities to the Baltic Sea and close-in operations in the North Sea.

Since British naval superiority prevented ordinary hostile surface ship operations against British and allied cables, the German Navy turned to its submarine arm which had demonstrated a capability to operate all around the British Isles.

In 1915 German U-boats began submerged attacks on cables in the North Sea and Adriatic at depths of 40 fathoms or less (240 feet). The submerged U-boat trailed a grapnel,

---

203   Ibid, pp. 28 - 30

attached to a wire rope, and trolled in the approximate position of the cable until the grapnel caught (on something). Cable locations were no secret but navigation out of sight of land had a fairly large area of uncertainty in the days before electronic navigation using GPS. The wire rope was attached to one of two motor-driven winches driven by the capstan and controlled from inside the U-boat. An engineer monitored a strain gage attached to the wire rope. Increased tension indicated that something had been snagged. The grapnel apparatus contained a shearing mechanism and if everything went well, the U-boat was able to snag and cut the cable. The U-boat operated at slow speed on the battery about 10 to 20 feet above the sea bed while carrying out this operation.[204]

Training operations were carried out in German waters, near the port of Emden on the North Sea. The mechanism used may have been a "Lucas" cutting and holding grapple. Germany operated cable ships of her own and her engineers would have been very familiar with the technology involved.

U-47 "distinguished" itself in the northern Adriatic Sea by accidentally cutting an Austro-Hungarian cable while conducting training operations near Pola in Austria, a major naval base.[205] Since the Germans and the Austro-Hungarians were allies, there had to have been some embarrassment. How do you say "Oops" in German?

---

204   Ibid, p. 31
205   Ibid, p. 295

To reach cables beyond the North Sea required the use of specially outfitted and trained long range submarines. The German Admiralty proposed the use of U-cruisers (U-151 through 157). They were large (65 meters in length, and 1,875 tons submerged displacement) with a range of 25,000 miles at 6 knots. They were designed and built in 1916-1917 to be commercial submarines to import critical goods through the British naval blockade. *Deutschland* made two successful round trips to the United States in 1916. *Bremen* was lost early in 1917 on her first voyage, possibly due to a mine. They were unarmed.

Six more cargo submarines were still under construction. They, along with *Deutschland,* were converted into U-cruisers, long range submarines, equipped with torpedo tubes and two 105 mm. guns. *Deutschland* became U-155.

The German High Seas Fleet staff objected to the Admiralty scheme on the grounds that cable attack operations were too difficult technologically and that the diversion of the U-cruisers would interfere with the ongoing unrestricted submarine campaign that commenced on 1 February 1917. The Admiralty won the argument, not unexpectedly, and the U-cruisers were equipped, trained, and detailed to cable cutting duties in addition to attacks on Allied merchant ships.

From 10 to 12 February 1917, U-155 cut British cables between the British Isles, Portugal, Gibraltar, and the

Azores.[206] After the United States entered the war in April 1917, the German Admiralty identified cables off the U.S. coast as possible targets.

During the period March – April 1918 four cables were attacked off the Iberian and African coasts. Three U-cruisers damaged cables to the Mediterranean, Africa and America at points off Lisbon, and Sierra Leone in West Africa.

On March 7 – 8, U-155 attacked cables off the Spanish coast. In April U-153 and U-154 attacked cables off West Africa. Room 40 of British naval intelligence intercepted and deciphered a radio message setting up a rendezvous on 11 May between U-153 and U-154. Two British submarines, J 1 and E 35, were sent to the rendezvous area to ambush the German boats. E 35 was submerged and sighted U-154 on the surface, and made a submerged approach. She missed her with one torpedo which was not seen by the target's lookouts and sank her with two more torpedoes. U-153, in the vicinity and operating on the surface, saw the explosion and sighted E 35 on the surface briefly. E 35 then re-submerged and moved away before U-153 could avenge her comrade.

On 28 May 1918, U-151 succeeded in severing two cables off New York City. In June 1918 the British Admiralty complained that six different cruiser U-boats had attacked cables off the Azores, Lisbon, Gibraltar, Dakar, Freetown, and off the United States. In mid-September 1918 British cables off Portugal were attacked.

---

206   Ibid, p. 106

However, it was difficult for the U-boat to know if it had severed a cable, merely damaged it, or at worst had just moved it a short distance along the sea bottom. In one instance U-157 had to abort her cable operations off the Azores when she lost both grapnels. U-156 was probably lost to a mine in September 1918 while returning to base through the North Sea Mine Barrage.

The British undersea cable infrastructure was too strong to fold under what were essentially pin prick attacks. The author of *Nexus* opines that an attack on the vital and scarce British cable ships might have been more productive. However the British Admiralty was well aware of their value and vulnerability while lying to, conducting cable repair operations, and regularly assigned escorts to them.

In early 1918 the U.S. Army was faced with an increasing volume of cable traffic to France to support the American Expeditionary Force in France. Laying additional cables would take far too long, so other means to increase capacity were examined. One idea looked feasible. If messages were not enciphered, more information could be pushed through the cable per time unit. The Army Chief Signal Officer was not completely comfortable with that proposal, although it was commonly believed that underwater cable traffic was not capable of being intercepted. He contracted with AT&T to test that assumption. AT&T, in connection with Western Union and Western Electric, pulled up an operating cable to Europe from the sea bed, placed an induction sleeve around the cable, and discovered that they could read the cable traffic without the cable operators on shore having any indication of their eavesdropping. The neat assumption died, and the Army continued to encipher its traffic.[207]

Some may have read the book, *Blind Man's Bluff*, about the use of U.S. submarines in clandestine surveillance operations against the Soviet Union during the Cold War. The authors reported that USS Halibut (SSN 587) entered the Sea of Okhotsk and used an induction pod to record important Soviet cable message traffic between their commands on the Kamchatka Peninsula and headquarters further west.[208] I believe that the official U.S. Navy comment about Blind Man's Bluff, published in 1998, was "no comment". It is fascinating to realize that the same basic technology reportedly used by Halibut was developed in 1918 to test the vulnerability of cable traffic from the United States to France.

---

207   Ibid, pp. 131 - 133
208   Sherry Sontag and Christopher Drew,, Blind Man's Bluff, chapter 8

PART FIVE

SUBMARINE OPERATIONAL EFFECTIVENESS DURING WORLD WAR ONE

(1914 – 1918)

Chapter Fourteen – Effectiveness of WWI Submarine Operations

The submarine was the second stealth weapon employed at sea. It was preceded by the much older sea mine. The submarine was unlike the mine that usually was anchored in place at a fixed depth and was limited to fairly shallow water. The submarine had some submerged mobility, although limited by its battery capacity and the need to surface to replenish its air supply at intervals. During World War I the submarine graduated from a mere theoretical threat to close blockade forces operating in the immediate vicinity of an enemy port or coastline, to a very serious threat to naval forces at sea and particularly to merchant shipping. German U-boats conducted a limited number of trans-Atlantic operations and as well closely investing the ocean areas around the British Isles. They developed the range capability to transit from Germany, around the British Isles, and into the Mediterranean Sea without port stops or at sea refueling. Unsatisfactory gasoline engines were replaced with sturdy, reliable diesel engines that would power submarines during two world wars.

Against large naval ships they proved deadly, sinking a number of battleships and cruisers. Their constant threat required the development of a host of antisubmarine warfare equipments and tactics as well as strategies. These included sustained high speeds and steering zigzag courses when in submarine waters, leaving rescue efforts to smaller ships, the stationing of destroyer screens at a range outside normal torpedo ranges, passive hydrophone installation on small ships to detect submarines, depth charges, and improved mines designed to sink submerged submarines. Despite all these measures the threat remained to the very end. HMS Britannia, a battleship, was sunk off Gibraltar on 9 November 1918, only two days before the armistice took effect.

Against merchant ships, submarines proved devastating even when constrained by the Rules of Maritime Warfare, which required them to challenge and stop merchant ships, and check their cargos for contraband before taking action to sink or capture them. During the period August 1914 through January 1917, U-boats sank or captured 4,316,515 tons of Allied and neutral merchant ships, despite massive ASW force deployments. These sinking's or captures were conducted against independently sailing ships.

In 1916 the German High Command calculated that based on U-boat successes against merchant ships under

Maritime Warfare Rules, an abandonment of those rules in an unrestricted submarine campaign would result in the destruction of so much British and supporting neutral shipping that Great Britain would be forced to enter negotiations. They were nearly correct. However the widespread adoption of the convoy system defeated the U-boats.

The unrestricted campaign began in February 1917 and sank or captured 5,867,357 gross register tons by the end of the year.[209] The strategic solution, convoy, lay at hand but the Royal Navy somewhat inexplicably declined to implement it across the board until August 1917. Thereafter, losses of escorted, convoyed merchant ships fell off rapidly. The strategic problem was solved. The German U-boat Arm had no tactical or technical answer to convoy procedures. The failure to knock Great Britain out of the war, coupled with the unexpectedly fast pace of training and sending American divisions to the Western Front, doomed Germany to defeat.

A submarine tactic for dealing successfully with convoy operations was not worked out during WW I. Both British submarines in the Baltic Sea in 1916-1917 and German U-boats in the Atlantic in late 1917-1918 were rendered relatively ineffectual by convoys. In the Atlantic the kill ratio of 1 out of 10 for submarines against independent sailers as opposed to the kill ratio of only 1

---

209   The data concerning tonnage sunk was taken from John Terraine's *Business in Great Waters*, p. 766, Appendix C.

out of 150 for ships in convoy was a remarkable measure of the success of the convoy system.

Karl Doenitz, a former U-boat commanding officer in the Mediterranean, began to attempt to solve the convoy problem in theory, while sitting in a British POW camp after his capture in 1918. His theorizing, and later involvement in torpedo boat and U-boat exercises in the Baltic Sea and the Atlantic during the mid-1930s, would lead him to develop a practical theory of anti-convoy submarine warfare that would nearly defeat Great Britain during WW II. As commander of all U-boats in that war he was in a unique position to test his theories.

The German strategic submarine campaign of WW I came close to forcing Great Britain out of the war and ending the conflict in an entirely different fashion than the one recorded in history books. It came much closer to success in accomplishing its goals than the early German and Allied strategic air bombing campaigns of WW I.[210] H. G. Well's *The War in the Air*, which foretold war-ending destruction from the sky missed its mark entirely. Jules Verne's *Twenty Thousand Leagues Under The Seas*, which portrayed the submarine as an unstoppable ship killer, came much closer to an accurate prediction.

Looking far ahead, both German and American submariners would learn how to deal with enemy convoys during WW II. The Germans were ultimately unsuccessful

---

210 See O'Connell, John F., *The Effectiveness of Airpower in the 20th Century Part One (1914-1939)*

as the Allies introduced long range aircraft equipped with air-to-surface radar that drove U-boats underwater by day and night, depriving them of their previous ability to use relatively high surface speed to reposition for attacks and to concentrate against slower convoys.

American submarines, with even higher surface speed and equipped with surface search radar, would wreak havoc on Japanese convoys, principally at night. Starting on 8 December 1941, U.S. submarines waged an unrestricted campaign against the Japanese merchant marine. A major factor in their success was the relatively low level of Japanese ASW capability and effort.[211]

---

211   U.S. submarines suffered a loss rate of about 25% during WW II.

PART SIX

SUBMARINE DEVELOPMENT
BETWEEN THE WORLD WARS

(1918 – 1939)

Chapter Fifteen – International Law Limitations on Submarine Warfare

After WW I ended, the Treaty of Versailles, imposed by the victorious allies, forbade the German nation from having submarines, building them, or buying them. They were required to turn over all submarines to Allied and Associated nations, along with submarine salvage vessels and submarine-related material. The Allies and Associated Powers had had quite enough of unrestricted submarine warfare. Although no German officials were tried for war crimes because of the unrestricted submarine campaign, there was no doubt in the victors' ranks that there would never be another unrestricted submarine warfare campaign, or so they thought at the time.[212] Submarine warfare would properly return to its roots, to attacking naval vessels as an integral part of the fleet structure.

Great Britain tried to abolish the submarine as part of the Treaty of Versailles in 1919. The United States agreed with her at the time. In fact the U.S. Navy Department provided a memorandum to President Wilson urging the abolition of the submarine as a naval weapon. However France and Italy did not agree. They feared the overwhelming power of the Royal Navy and wanted to retain submarines to partially offset that advantage.[213] Because of the opposition of France and Italy, President Wilson did not push the issue.

From 1919 through 1921 Great Britain's official views of the submarine firmed up – the primary goal was to get rid of submarines. Among other arguments put forward by the Royal Navy were that the submarine was the most expensive warship to construct (in British pounds per ton) and had the shortest operating life.

Later there were a series of international conferences which dealt with submarine warfare among other naval

---

212   Articles 227 – 230 of the Treaty Of Versailles dealt with war crimes and penalties. Although the allies were empowered to convene courts to try war crimes charges, none were established. In early 1921 a reduced list of war crimes was submitted to the *Reichsgericht* at Leipzig for trial. Britain submitted seven cases, several involving war crimes in connection with submarine sinking's of ships. However no one was tried for the unrestricted submarine campaign. The failure of German war crimes trials after WW I led to the Nuremberg Trials following WW II.
213   Andrade, New Interpretations, pp. 67-68

matters discussed. The leading concern was to avoid a major naval armaments race that could beggar some of the participants and that might lead to war.

In 1921 the United States invited other major nations to a conference in Washington, D.C. to discuss measures to reduce the dangers of a naval armaments race. The United States surprisingly proposed a radical move to scrap a number of battleships if other participants would do likewise. Eventually the participants (Great Britain, the United States, France, Italy and Japan) agreed to a set of limitations on large warship quantity and quality. Limiting numbers of battleships and cruisers were established along with limitations on individual ship displacement and size and number of guns.

The British goal regarding submarines was still to abolish them if possible, but failing that - to limit their numbers and tonnage. However the U.S. had changed its views and France and Italy were still emphatic on the need for submarines to offset the large surface warship advantage held by the Royal Navy.[214] The United States, which had the second largest submarine fleet at the time, now opposed abolition. It argued that submarines did not have to violate international law and pointed out submarine effectiveness against naval warships. However it would accept some limitations. The Conference failed to limit submarines but did include a statement that submarines would not be used for wholesale commerce destruction. However, France

---

214   Ibid, pp. 68 - 70

would not ratify the statement with that clause in it. One can conclude that British shipping presented a potentially lucrative target for a French *guerre de course*.[215]

In 1927 at Geneva another Naval Conference was held. On the submarine issue Great Britain attempted to establish limiting tonnages for coastal submarines at 600 tons surface displacement and seagoing submarines at 1600 tons. She also tried to limit submarine gun armament to not larger than a 5-inch gun. The Technical Committee agreed on no greater than 1800 tons for submarines and no gun larger than 5-inches, and set a submarine replacement age of not earlier than thirteen years after commissioning. Because of unsettled arguments over classes of cruisers, no treaty was promulgated by the Conference. In 1929 British Prime Minister Ramsay MacDonald was very concerned over the increasing cost of weapons and issued an invitation to meet in London the following year.[216]

On 21 January 1930 the London Naval Conference convened. The British Admiralty proposed submarine limitations of not greater than 1800 tons surface displacement, no gun with a diameter greater than 5-inches, and a replacement life of 13 years. France wanted larger displacements. Italy and Japan argued for 2000 tons instead of 1800 tons. That was tentatively accepted with the proviso that each Navy could have three submarines with not greater than 2800 tons displacement.

---

215   Hezlet, The Submarine and Sea Power, pp. 110 -111
216   Andrade, Op cit., pp. 70 - 72

Japan would not agree to accept a total tonnage level (in submarines) of less than that of Great Britain and the United States. The French would not accept any submarine tonnage limitation. Italy would not accept a limit unless the French agreed to it.

Japan, Great Britain and the U.S. all eventually agreed to accept a total tonnage limitation on submarines of 52,700 tons per nation by the end of 1936. The treaty was to run for five years. Part IV of the Treaty precluded the use of submarines against merchant shipping Finally Great Britain got France to accept a limit of 81,989 tons. All these provisions were put together to form a "Bases of Agreement" to be ratified at a League of Nations Conference, scheduled to be held in Geneva in 1932. The Conference began as scheduled but 18 months later Adolph Hitler, Chancellor of Germany since early 1933, took Germany out of the Conference and out of the League of Nations.[217] All bets were now off.

217   Andrade, Op cit., pp. 73-77

CHAPTER SIXTEEN – TECHNICAL AND TACTICAL DEVELOPMENTS AFFECTING SUBMARINE WARFARE

Active sonar, or **ASDIC** as the British termed it, employed projectors to send acoustic energy into the sea. When it reached a target, some of the energy was reflected back to the point of origin, allowing measurement of range to a submerged target.[218] The Royal Navy equipped most of its destroyers with ASDIC between the wars and became expert at tracking submerged, but somewhat constrained, submarines. It was convinced that ASDIC provided an antidote to submerged submarine attacks.

Night surfaced torpedo attacks by U-boats as a standard tactic were developed in the middle and late 1930s by Germany's Karl Doenitz as one step in a plan to defeat the convoy system that had outwitted Germany's

---

218 Since the speed of sound in sea water is a known quantity, the time required to obtain an echo provides the range to a target, very similar to radar.

unrestricted submarine warfare campaign in 1917 and 1918. Doenitz worked out the tactics on paper and then used torpedo boats in the Baltic to test the theory. Finally he extended the tests to U-boats in the Baltic and the Atlantic.

Wolf pack tactics (*Rudeltaktic*) were the second step in Doenitz's plan to defeat convoy tactics. They involved concentrating a large number of U-boats to overwhelm escorts and ravage convoys while conducting torpedo attacks from the surface at night.

The **snorkel** was developed in Holland during the early 1930s as a means to allow a submerged submarine on patrol in enemy waters to ventilate its atmosphere. In 1938 a Dutch "O" class submarine stopped at the U.S. submarine base at Pearl Harbor on its way to the Netherlands East Indies (now Indonesia). A visiting American submarine officer took note of the device.[219] There were two basic limitations on submarine submergence at the time.[220] One was battery capacity. Once the battery charge is depleted the submarine must surface to recharge the batteries by running its diesel engines. The second limitation is the

---

219 Galantin, Take Her Deep, pp. 58-59. He described her as an "O" class Dutch submarine but doesn't give her hull number. See also Showell, Op cit., p. 98.

220 Neither limitation applies to current nuclear submarines. The nuclear power plant provides almost unlimited endurance. On board oxygen generators and carbon dioxide burners maintain a normal atmosphere for the length of the submerged patrol.

internal atmosphere in the submarine. Once the submarine shuts its hatches and dives, respiration by the crew consumes oxygen and generates carbon dioxide. A U.S. WW II fleet class submarine contained enough breathable air to support life for a crew of about 80 men for eighteen hours. Slowly but steadily oxygen is consumed and carbon dioxide is produced and the atmosphere deteriorates. Assuming a dive in the early morning hours and continued submergence thereafter, it got difficult to light a cigarette by mid-afternoon. Carbon dioxide produces headaches in the crew as its percentage increases. Thus a means to raise a pipe just out of water to run a blower for a few minutes and replenish the atmosphere offered a large advantage for submerged patrol operations.[221]

After the defeat of Holland in 1940 the German U-boat service adopted the Dutch snorkel device but further modified it to allow the running of diesel engines while submerged.[222] This innovation allowed snorkel-equipped U-boats to reduce detection by radar-equipped ASW aircraft while maintaining some mobility (5 - 6 knots). However it did not restore the relatively high

---

221   At that time radar did not exist so the snorkel head valve could only be detected visually during daytime.

222   In his *Submarines of World War Two*, Erminio Bagnasco states that the Dutch 0.19 and 0.21 classes of submarines were provided with an experimental device that allowed the running of diesel engines while submerged. He notes that the rudimentary snorkel device was on several Dutch submarines that joined with the Royal Navy, but was not very reliable and was removed. The British saw little utility in the device and did not try to develop it further.

surface speed (17 knots) of the U-boat that allowed it to overtake convoys.

Magnetic (torpedo) Exploders were developed by both the new German Navy and the U.S. Navy. The theory promised to economize on expensive torpedoes by guaranteeing hits. The magnetic exploder sensed the magnetic field of an iron or steel ship as the torpedo approached it underwater, and could be set to detonate at the closest point of approach. Whereas a contact exploder would function to punch a hole in the target ship's side and flood one or several compartments, the magnetic exploder torpedo would detonate underneath the keel and literally break a ship in half. Prior to WW II in the U.S. Navy the magnetic exploders were classified Top Secret and only a submarine commanding officer and his torpedo officer had access to information about them. Depth settings for magnetic exploder torpedoes were chosen to cause the torpedo to run underneath the target. Great Britain's Royal Navy also experimented with magnetic exploders but abandoned them in favor of contact exploders after a series of problems.

Chapter Seventeen – Submarine development 1920s and 1930s

Submarine development during the 1920s and 1930s took place within the framework of well intentioned international efforts to limit the horrors of unrestricted submarine warfare. Another major factor was economic. WW I had eaten deeply into each nation's coffers.

Great Britain was the most powerful nation in terms of sea warfare, and the Royal Navy set a standard for other navies to try to approach. It is not surprising then that Great Britain and the Royal Navy should play a prominent role in future discussions about submarines. In 1918 Great Britain had 137 submarines in commission. This was the largest number of all the world's navies, after Germany had handed over her U-boats in accordance with the dictates of the Versailles Treaty. Great Britain then scrapped 90 older submarines including all of the small defensive type, and in addition canceled orders for 31 new construction submarines.[223] The Royal Navy accepted delivery of 24 new construction boats, and also experimented with surrendered German U-boats to gain whatever technical advantages might be possible.

The British "E" class had proven reliable and served as the RN's principal patrol submarine during WW I. It had two bow TT, one stern TT and 2 beam TT. However, these arrangements limited a torpedo salvo to two or fewer torpedoes, entirely inadequate to sink a modern large warship. When hits were obtained they seldom accomplished more than serious damage, and the target frequently was able to limp back into port for repairs. This situation led to replacement of beam TT with a larger number of bow TT. The L 50 class was designed with six bow TT. Torpedo diameter was increased from 18 " to 21", providing greater volume and doubling the explosive warhead weight as well as providing a longer torpedo run.

Submarine development during the 1920s and 1930s was strongly limited and influenced by the events and outcome of WW I. The Treaty of Versailles, forced on Germany by the Allied and Associated Powers, severely limited German ground force strength and naval strength. It denied submarines and military aircraft to the new, small German armed forces. Although no German officials suffered war crimes trials for instituting unrestricted submarine warfare, it was clear that unrestricted submarine warfare was considered a breach of International Law and

---

223   Hezlet, The Submarine and Sea Power, pp. 108 - 109

thus unacceptable among civilized nations. This point of view was punctuated by the London Convention of 1930. We shall examine German efforts to work around these limitations in the section on German submarine development.

Thus, following the conclusion of WW I, submarine development focused on traditional submarine roles, attacking enemy warships and naval auxiliary vessels, and conducting cruiser warfare, that is attacks on mercantile traffic within the approved rules. The standard European submarine was a hybrid diesel electric submarine that had to surface to recharge its batteries. It was relatively small and short ranged. It usually had two to four torpedo tubes forward and perhaps one aft and torpedoes were carried internally. The external *Dzhevetskiy* drop collars used during WW I by the Russians and the French proved ineffective, their exposed torpedoes subject to being put out of commission by close depth charges.

Command and control was exercised by radio signals from the operational commander to submarines on patrol, and return radio reports from submarines. Both sets of signals were subject to interception and decryption efforts by a hostile nation. Normally a submarine on patrol would surface after darkness fell, start a battery charge, dispose of garbage over the side in weighted bags, and cruise at slow speeds keeping an alert watch for enemy units. The order of preference for dealing with merchant ship targets was: (1) sink with explosive charges placed in the holds,

(2) sink with gunfire, and (3) sink with torpedoes. This last method was the most expensive.

The development of submarines in the other nations basically followed similar paths with a few exceptions. Diving depths increased as did hull strength. Welded or partially welded hulls replaced riveted hulls that were prone to leakage from fuel tanks, leaving a tell-tale oil slick behind the submerged submarine. Most submarines sported a small deck gun, perhaps 3 or 4 inch in caliber.

Some experiments with large guns took place. The British modified three steam powered K-class submarines into a new "M" class late in WW I. Each of the three carried a 12 inch naval gun although the entire submarine had to be maneuvered to train the gun. The French built submarine *Surcouf* mounted a pair of eight inch guns. Three U.S. large V-class submarines each carried a pair of six inch guns. However these large gun equipped submarines were exceptions and did not prove particularly useful in combat.

Experiments with small seaplanes carried in submarine hangars also took place. Great Britain modified one M class boat (M-2) to carry a seaplane, removing the 12 inch gun in the process. She was lost in 1932 when the hangar flooded during an exercise, taking her to the bottom with all hands.

The U.S. modified an S class submarine, S-1, to carry a seaplane in a small hangar and carried out experiments in the early 1920s.[224] The U.S. Navy did not follow up at the time.

Japan fully embraced the concept of seaplanes aboard submarines and took it further than any other nation. It fit the Imperial Japanese Navy plan of using long range submarines for reconnaissance and scouting of an approaching enemy battle fleet. The IJN built a number of I-class submarines, each with a hangar that carried one seaplane. A significant step up were three larger I-400 class submarines, later laid down in 1943 which carried three seaplanes each in a long hanger forward of the conning tower.

During the 1930s the Dutch uniquely experimented with a ventilation pipe that could be used to refresh the air in a submarine while it was at periscope depth. After their defeat early in 1940, the Germans seized the idea and turned it into the *snorchel*, allowing submerged U-boats to run their diesel engines at periscope depth.

To a large extent torpedoes were still straight runners, controlled on a fixed course by a gyroscope. However, settable gyros were introduced in some navies so that the torpedo turned to a new course to intercept its target after leaving the torpedo tube. The exploders were usually contact type, having to strike a solid object to initiate the detonation chain. There was experimentation with magnetic exploders, to take advantage of a steel target ship's inherent magnetic

---

224 A movie serial "Don Winslow of the Navy" from the 1930s, features film of S-1 launching her seaplane during exercises, with the sequences neatly shoe horned in to the fictional movie plot involving submarines.

field. A torpedo running at a slightly deeper depth than the target ship could sense the target's magnetic field and detonate underneath, breaking its keel, and ensuring a sinking. Torpedo depth was usually settable and maintained by a depth control mechanism. Torpedo speeds were ether fixed, or variable between high speed (shorter range) and low speed (longer range). Torpedoes all now used fuel burning engines rather than purely compressed air.

Most torpedoes used their air flasks to support fuel combustion. There were experiments with oxygen torpedoes by the U.S. and Japanese navies. The U.S. Navy rejected the concept as too dangerous. The IJN persevered and perfected their Long Lance (Type 93) torpedo used in cruisers and destroyers– a nasty surprise in the South Pacific for the U.S. Navy during WW II.[225] The Long Lance torpedoes had unusually long range and were wake less.

The torpedo fire control problem is a simple exercise in trigonometry as shown in the following diagram. However, to quote from von Clausewitz, "Everything in war is simple, but the simplest thing is difficult". The range to target is an estimate measured by seaman's eye, the course of the target is an estimate again measured

---

225   The American naval attaché in Tokyo correctly reported on the existence of an oxygen-fueled, long range, wakeless torpedo with a 24-inch diameter in 1940. Bureau of Ordnance technical experts rejected the idea as preposterous. Consequently American admirals expected and planned for Japanese surface ship torpedo ranges much shorter than the new torpedo was capable of achieving. The results were disastrous during various night naval engagements in the Solomon Islands during late 1942.

by seaman's eye (through a periscope). The speed of the target is another estimate, although sonar may be able to determine target propeller turn count and hence approximate target speed. The submarine approach officer must close his target while submerged without showing too much periscope for too long or an alert lookout will detect the scope and alert his bridge watch officer.[226] The target would then change course and or speed and evade the torpedo. If the target is a warship, particularly a destroyer or other ASW ship, it would immediately attack the submarine with depth charges or other weapons.

The submarine approach officer must keep in mind sea state, angle of the sun (both compass angle and elevation), wave height, minimum torpedo run necessary to arm the warhead, maximum torpedo run (no point in firing if the target is too far away to hit), and the fact that most torpedoes leave a detectable wake on the surface that may attract a lookout's attention. The approach officer must also choose how many torpedoes to fire, realizing that any misestimate or error in calculations may cause one or more to miss.

Analogue submarine torpedo fire control computers were introduced in some navies towards the end of the 1930s to continuously calculate torpedo gyro angle to better hit the target. Mirroring a latter refrain of "garbage in, garbage out (gigo)" used in today's era of digital computers; the

---

226   In the Pacific Submarine Prospective Commanding Officer School during the 1950s – 1960s, a periscope observation of only six seconds was the goal taught to PCO students.

analogue computer of that day was equally vulnerable.[227] Spreads of torpedoes were used to try to achieve hits while allowing for errors in target speed and range estimates.

A simplified torpedo firing diagram is shown to illustrate the problem. The Torpedo Data Computer (TDC) was introduced into U.S. submarines to accept target data as well as own submarine's course and speed The TDC, an analogue computer, continuously generated the correct gyro angle to hit the target (this assumes that all the input data is correct). A spread of three or more torpedoes would be fired to ensure a hit on a merchant ship or to ensure enough hits on a large enemy warship to cause serious damage or sinking.

Torpedo Firing Diagram

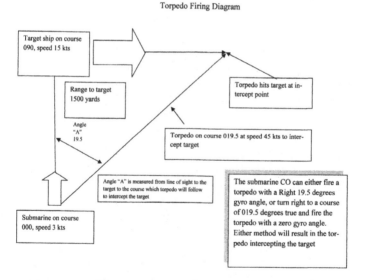

227   Torpedo fire control computers were a follow-on to naval gunfire computers used for many years to direct gun fire against ship and land targets. Both types were analogue computers.

The torpedo fire control solution is a simple trigonometric problem: Sine of angle A = Opposite side/ Hypotenuse; Sine A = 15 kts/45 kts = 0.333; therefore Angle A = 19.47 degrees = 19.5 degrees

Given the circumstances described earlier, each Navy followed at least slightly different paths in the design and building of submarines to meet its own needs. The major nations soon to be involved in WW II are discussed in subsequent chapters, along with their major classes of submarines.[228]

---

228   The author has drawn heavily on Vice Admiral Sir Arthur Hezlet's "The Submarine and Sea Power" for his discussion of national submarine development during the period 1920-1939. It is highly recommended reading.

CHAPTER EIGHTEEN –
FRANCE

F ollowing the end of WW I the French Navy proceeded to build submarines at a fairly fast rate. Although the French had argued that submarines were an offset to an inferior battle fleet and thus presumably would be primarily designed for naval combat, some of their new designs seemed more suited for long range commerce-destroying campaigns.

The French Submarine Service built a number of classes of submarines during the 1920s and 1930s. They included large ocean going submarines, *Requin* (9) and *Redoubtable* (or 1500 *tonne*) classes (31) for a total of 40 long range submarines; medium range submarines 600/630 *tonnes* (26); oceangoing minelayers (*Saphir* class) (5); and one very long range submarine cruiser - *Surcouf.* The various classes are discussed below.

From 1922 to 1927 nine *Requin* class were built. They displaced 1150/1441 tons, were 250 feet long, made 15/7 kts, had a range of 7,700 nm at 9 kts, and carried ten torpedo tubes (6 internal (4 fwd, 2 aft) plus another 4 external amidships in a traversing mount). They had an operating depth of 256 feet and a crew of 54. They carried a 3.9 inch gun and 115 tons of fuel oil.

They were followed by thirty-one Redoubtable (or 1500 *tonnes*) class built from 1924 through 1935. They displaced 1570/2084 tons and were 302 feet long. They made 17-20/10 knots and had a range of 10,000 nm at 10 kts. Operational depth was 256 feet and they carried 95 tons of fuel oil. Crew size was 61. They had a 3.9 inch gun, four internal bow TT plus 3 or 4 stern TT in a traversing mount and 3 amidships TT in another external traversing mount.

Surcouf , a one-off design, was built from 1927 through 1934. She boasted an aircraft hangar and twin eight inch guns. Her displacement was 3250/4304 tons and she had a range of 10,000 nm at 10 kts. Her speeds were 18/8.5 kts and she was 360 feet long. Her operational depth was 256 feet and she carried 280 tons of fuel oil. She had a crew of 118. She embarked a *Besson* MB 411 small reconnaissance aircraft, carried partially disassembled in her hangar. Her 8 inch guns had a range finder to help direct their fire. She had twelve torpedo tubes, 8 x 21.7 inch and 4 x 15.75 inch, and carried 22 torpedoes. Four 21.7 inch torpedo tubes were internal forward. Four more were external aft in a traversing mount. Four 15.75 inch TT were also external aft in another traversing mount.[229]

This is probably as good a time to discuss French torpedo tube arrangements as any. First of all, the French Submarine Service employed two sizes of torpedoes: the larger was 21.7 inch (550 mm) to use against large naval targets. According to one source they could not be set for less than ten feet in depth thus were useless against ASW vessels of shallow draft. The second size carried was 15.75 inch (400 mm), with correspondingly smaller explosive warheads for use against small combatants and merchant ships that lacked the compartmentation found in large warships.

The same source indicates that the reason for the traversing mount, which was operated electrically, was to deal with a difficulty in setting gyro angles in French torpedoes. The traversing mount swiveled to the calculated correct firing bearing and the torpedo went out on its appointed gyro-controlled course without having to make any changes, which had apparently proved a problem. The external traversing mounts could not ordinarily be reloaded except in port. The *Surcouf* was the only French submarine that carried reloads for her external tubes.

Surcouf was quite obviously designed as a merchant raider, and even had provisions to embark a boat to carry out boarding and search of stopped merchant vessels.

---

229   Surcouf was lost in a nighttime collision in the Caribbean Sea in February 1942 with SS Thompson Lykes. See Galantin, Op cit., p. 25

She also had a separate compartment to house up to 40 prisoners. Her aircraft would provide long range search for targets. Her 8 inch battery was powerful enough to deter any single escort save a heavy cruiser or larger. *Requin* and *Redoubtable* classes were also quite capable of conducting mercantile warfare.

Five mine laying submarines of the *Saphir* class were built from 1925 through 1937. They employed the *Normand-Fenaux* mine laying system that consisted of 16 mine tubes, eight on each side within the ballast tanks. Each tube carried two mines, one above the other. Apparently the system was safe and reliable according to French naval records. The Germans had employed a similar system in their mine laying UC class submarines during WW I.

Saphir class boats displaced 761/925 tons and were 216 feet long. They could make 12/9 kts and reach a range of 7,000 nm at 7.5 kts. They carried a crew of 42 men, and had in addition to their mine load, they had five TT, 3 x 21.7 inch and 2 x 15.7 inch. Their operating depth was 256 feet and they carried 90 tons of fuel oil.

The final classes of submarines were medium range types, the 600/630 *tonnes* classes. Twenty six were built between 1925 and 1932. There were two 600 tons classes (*Sirene* and *Ariane*). The 630 tons class was similarly split into four sub-classes: *Argonaute, Diane, Orion* and *Minerve*. The 630 *tonnes* class was an improvement over the 600 *tonnes* class that had some longitudinal stability problems.

The characteristics for the 630 class are as follow: 651/807 tons displacement, 211 feet long, 13.7/9 kts, and a range of 4,000 nm at 10 kts. They had an operational depth of 256 feet and carried 60-65 tons of fuel oil. Their complement was 41. The torpedo arrangements were again somewhat peculiar by U.S. standards. They had seven 21.7 inch TT (2 external forward, 1 aft external in a traversing mount, 2 amidships external in a traversing mount, and 2 internal forward.[230]

The final class of French submarines started prior to WW II was the *L'Aurore* class. Seven were planned but only one, *L'Aurore* was completed at Toulon by 1940. They were 893/1170 tons, 241.3' in length, had nine TT (4 bow internal, 3 external amidships, and 2 stern external). Operational depth was 340 feet. Their range was 5,600 nm at 10 kts, and 17 hours dived at 5 kts. They could make 14.5/ 9 kts.

French submarines did not have a TDC prior to the war. U.S. TDCs were installed on some Free French submarines during the war.

---

230 Some of the information has been taken from a document titled "New Year 1942 Report on the status of *Marine Nationale*", provided by Admiral Lemonnier, Chief of Staff, *Marine Nationale* to the *Council de la Defense Nationale*, dated January 3, 1942, dealing with the status of Free French naval forces and their engagement against German, Italian and Japanese forces in Europe and the Far East.

CHAPTER NINETEEN –
GERMANY

Submarine (U-boat) development in Germany after the end of the First World War falls into two distinct phases. The first phase was under the terms of the Versailles Treaty that forbade Germany from having anything at all to do with submarines. This lasted from 1919 to 1933. The democratic Weimar Republic held office during this period. Senior generals and admirals of the German Army and Navy, and senior civilian officials of the Weimar Republic conspired to develop forbidden weapons systems in violation of the treaty. A secret treaty with the new Bolshevik Union of Soviet Socialist Republics provided for training within the USSR's vast spaces for German development of military aircraft, chemical warfare and tank warfare. German government funds were quietly shuffled and hidden to ensure that these programs did not come into public view.[231] The second phase took place from 1933 to 1939 after Adolph Hitler came to power in a democratic election, and was later voted dictatorial powers by the German *Reichstag*, their legislative body. These developments were no longer hidden.

Germany was forbidden to possess submarines by the Treaty of Versailles. She was directed to turn over all submarine material as well as submarines and submarine rescue ships to the victorious Allies. She did so. However, she did not turn over submarine documentation in the files of the many shipyards that had built U-boats during the war. Under the guidance of the new German Navy a commercial engineering office was set up in Holland and undertook the design of submarines. In this fashion German U-boat designers were able to maintain their expertise.

Several countries contacted German shipyards about either purchasing submarine designs or hiring former submarine personnel. As noted in the section on Japanese submarine development, Japan received a number of U-boats as war reparations and hired a large number of German personnel to help with her submarine programs. The USSR and Argentina also sought German assistance. A number of European and other countries either had or

---

231   See O'Connell, John F. "The Effectiveness of Airpower in the 20th Century, Part One (1914-1939), pp. 47-57 for a discussion of the secret development of German military air power during this time frame. See also Hezlet, "The Submarine and Sea Power", p. 115.

desired to have submarines in their navies. Few except the Dutch had room for many boats in their navies but in total they provided a reasonably large market for submarine designs and submarines.

The name of the cover firm in Holland was *NV Ingenieurskantoor voor Scheepsbouw den Haag (IvS)*. It was set up in 1922 with capital provided by the *AG Vulcan* yard in Hamburg and Stettin, and the two Krupp-owned yards, *Germaniawerft,* Kiel and *AG Weser*, Bremen. The commercial director was ex-Commander Ulrich Blum, of the former U-boat Service. He maintained an office in *Germaniawerft* as he waited for the Dutch bureaucracy to deal with procedural matters in setting up the new firm. Finally in 1925 the company's official office was opened in The Hague. Until then all business was run out of the *Germaniawerft* office in Kiel.

IvS built two submarines for Turkey. Their design was based upon the UB III class of the WW I German Navy, of which type 89 U-boats had been launched in 1917 and 1918.[232] The contracts provided for *IvS* personnel to take part in the service trials as well as crew selection and training.

During its existence *IvS* delivered submarine designs to Italy, Finland, Sweden, Romania, Chile, Argentina, Turkey, Spain, Estonia and the USSR. In addition it built submarines in shipyards in Finland and Spain.

---

232   UB III Class displaced about 500 tons, had four TT and an 88 mm. gun, and was considered a medium-sized U-boat.

In addition to hidden submarine development, German engineers worked in Sweden during the 1920s to develop an advanced torpedo, propelled by batteries thus leaving no surface wake to clearly mark a path back to the firing submarine location. In 1929 the trials were completed, and the plans set aside for production in Germany at an appropriate time. That time came after Hitler's rise to power. On 14 October 1939, U-47 under command of Gunther Prien slipped undetected into the waters of Scapa Flow, a major British naval anchorage. There he sank battleship HMS Royal Oak with the new G7e torpedo. The G7e was a 21" diameter, 20 foot long torpedo, powered by 52 lead-acid batteries, and carrying a 672 pound high explosive warhead. It could do 30 kts for 5,000 yards,

In 1931 *IvS* contracted to design a small submarine for Finland. Newly independent of Russia (now the Soviet Union), Finland had established friendly relations with Germany and entertained a German military mission in Finland. It included naval personnel. Under this arrangement former German submarine officers and men kept their hands in the design and building process of the Finnish boat, a German design, including manning it on sea trials. The Finnish submarine, *Vesikko*, was designed by IvS and was built by the Crichton-Vulcan shipyard in Turku, Finland. It was launched 10 May 1933 and commissioned 30 April 1934. It displaced 254/303 tons, was 134 feet long, made 13/8 knots, and had a range of

1350 nm at a speed of 8 knots. Its test depth was 150 feet and it had a crew of 17 – 20 men. It had three 21 inch torpedo tubes and carried five torpedoes. Handing over *Vesikko* to the Finnish Navy was delayed until 1936. In the interim she was used to train German officers and enlisted men in submarine operations. *Vesikko* became a prototype for the German type II U-boats.

Similar arrangements were concluded with Spain. One submarine of German design was built in Cadiz. E I was not delivered to Spain but was sold to the Turkish government in 1934. The boat was renamed *Gur* and delivered to Turkey in January 1935. The second design, E II, was modified to meet Soviet needs, and led to the construction of three Soviet submarines built at the Ordzhonikidze shipyard in Leningrad in 1934.

Adolph Hitler came to power in January 1933 after a democratic election. Under the Nazi regime, rearmament in violation of the Versailles Treaty was a primary goal. On 16 March 1934 Dr. Goebbels, head of the Propaganda Ministry, announced a new law which reintroduced universal military conscription, and the formation of an army of 36 divisions, in defiance of the Treaty.[233] Great Britain and France did nothing.

A year later Germany and Great Britain signed a Naval Agreement allowing Germany to build up to 35% of the capital ship tonnage allocated to Great Britain, and up to 45% of the submarine tonnage. Hezlet indicates

233   Shirer, Berlin Diary, pp. 28-29

that Great Britain realized that the Germans were going to build submarines in any case so tried to place some limits on their construction.[234]

In July 1935 Captain Doenitz, then commanding German cruiser *Emden*, was told by the Navy commander-in-chief that he would be ordered to take charge of the new U-boat Arm.[235] Prior to that event, in 1932 the Naval High Command had made preparations for resumption of submarine construction. In early 1935 while the Anglo-German negotiations were in progress the German Navy laid down the keels of several new submarines. They were Type II U-boats of about 250 tons displacement. By September 1935 there were six completed, U-1 through U-6, all Type IIA.

The Type II U-boats were based upon the UB III series of WW I, and on *Vesikko*, built for Finland. There were four versions, A through D. Referred to as "canoes" because of their small size, they would be useful only for coastal operations and training. They ranged from 134' in length to 144'. In displacement they started at 303 tons submerged and went up to 364 tons displacement. They had three torpedo tubes forward, a crew of 25, and speeds of 13/7 kts. A total of 47 were built, including two for Yugoslavia.

Another larger type was built. It was Type IA, of 862/938 tons, 238 feet long, with six TT, a crew of 43,

234   Hezlet, Submarines and Sea Power, p. 118
235   Doenitz, Op cit., p. 7

and a 4 inch gun. It could make 18/8 kts. Two of these, U-25 and U-26, were not considered very satisfactory. They didn't handle well, and it was decided to stick with a slightly smaller model, the Type VII. It came in three initial versions, A through C. The Type VII C was to carry much of the burden of the German U-boat effort during WW II. The VII C was 769/871 tons, 220 feet long, had 5 TT (4 bow, 1 stern), 14 torpedoes, could make 16-17/8 kts., had a crew of 44 and a range of 6,500 nm.

The Type VII U-boat was optimized for the night surface attacks that Doenitz designed as the answer to the convoy scheme. They would attack on the surface at night, thus outfoxing the British Asdic capability. Asdic was incapable of detecting a surfaced target. The Type VII superstructure was kept low, so low that the highest point was a lookout's binoculars, thus giving them an advantage over even alert crews of enemy warships whose masts stuck high above their lookouts. Their relatively high speed, 17 kts, allowed them to overtake and "end around" on slow convoys while remaining just outside escort lookout visual range but still within the U-boat lookout visual range.[236]

Doenitz emphasized training of U-boat crews, and especially of his commanding officers. They trained in the Baltic, making approaches on targets again and again until their instructors could find little to criticize. Doenitz used torpedo boats in the Baltic to practice night surface

---

236   Most convoys of WW II were slow, about 10-12 kts on average.

torpedo attacks on surface targets, and when the tactics were formalized he then carried them out with U-boats.

The German submarine school was teaching PCOs to fire at 3,000 yards to avoid Asdic detection. Doenitz changed that doctrine to shoot at 600 yards when either surfaced at night or submerged, thus eliminating errors that arose in longer range shooting. He also required each PCO to conduct 66 night surface attacks and 66 submerged attacks before firing a first practice torpedo.[237] Seldom has a submarine arm been so well trained in advance of war.

---

237   Doenitz, Op cit., pp. 13 - 15

CHAPTER TWENTY –
GREAT BRITAIN

G reat Britain had employed its submarine service to good effect during WW I in the Baltic, North Sea, the Dardanelles and Mediterranean Sea. It had been used primarily against enemy naval units and especially in the North Sea and ocean areas around the United Kingdom to oppose German U-boats, sinking 18 of them.

Its focus subsequent to WW I was on operating under the "Prize Regulations", that is the accepted international rules for submarine warfare. However it had to deal with two distinct geographic theaters, the nearby North Sea and Mediterranean Sea where distances were relatively short, and the Far East and Pacific where the distances were much greater and longer range operations were required. This led to developing two different classes of submarines.

There was no training in night surface attack procedures, unlike the later German U-boat Service under

Doenitz. The Royal Navy had great faith in the utility of Asdic in destroyers to detect submerged submarines. And although to its knowledge no other navy possessed that capability, it encouraged its own Submarine Service to plan on firing large salvos of torpedoes from beyond expected Asdic ranges to be able to sink large enemy warships.

The standard British submarine torpedo was the Mark 8, a steam torpedo with a sizeable warhead, containing 850 pounds (386 kg.) of high explosive, and the detonators were a simple contact type. The Mark 8 torpedo was simple, reliable and did not have the depth nor the magnetic exploder problems experienced later by the German U-boat Arm and by the U.S. Submarine Service.

Shortly after WW I ended, in 1921 the Royal Navy laid down the keel for HMS X1, a huge submarine by any standard and the largest in the world at the time. She was 361 feet 6 inches in length and displaced 3,700 tons submerged. She was commissioned in 1925. She had a range of 14,500 nm, and a design test depth of 500 feet.[238] Armed with six 21 inch bow torpedo tubes, she also carried two gun mounts, each with a pair of 5.2 inch guns for a total of four 5.2 inch guns. She was designed as a long range commerce raider, a seeming contradiction to RN submarine theory. She had a complement of 10 officers and 100 ratings. She was a one-off model, and

---

238   Her depth was limited to 350 feet after commissioning.

had been designed to replicate the German U-173 class of U-cruisers. It was a dead end design, not later repeated. She had many machinery problems, and was placed in reserve in 1930 and scrapped in 1936.

The next class of submarine, optimized for North Sea and Mediterranean operations, was a medium range patrol submarine with a large torpedo salvo capability. The "S" class, ordered in 1929, filled this need. There were three groups ordered, with slightly different specifications, for a total build of 62 units, between 1931 and 1945. Seventeen had been built prior to the start of WW II. Their key characteristics (first group) were: 202 feet in length, and 24 feet in width, with twin diesel engines, surfaced/submerged displacements of 735 tons/935 tons, surface/submerged speeds of 13.75 kts/10 kts, a range of 3,700 nautical miles at 10 kts, and a battery of six torpedo tubes forward. They had an operating depth of 300 feet.[239] The pressure hull was riveted. The "S" class had a crew of 40, and carried 40 tons of fuel. Torpedoes were 21 inch diameter, allowing larger warheads. The placing of six torpedo tubes forward required the use of an oval hull cross section instead of maintaining the optimum circular cross section, which could only contain four tubes. Transition from a circular hull section to an oval hull section weakened the pressure hull; hence the British boats had lesser depth capability than the

239   A few of the last group constructed were welded vice riveted and their operating depth was increased to 350 feet.

equivalent German U-boats that maintained a circular hull section throughout their length.

The following longer range boat was the "T" class. Its dimensions were: 275 feet in length, 26 feet width, twin diesel engines, surfaced/submerged displacements of 1300 tons/1595 tons, surfaced/submerged speeds of 15.25 kts/9 kts, a range of 8,000 nm at 10 kts, and a battery of ten torpedo tubes forward (2 external to the pressure hull).[240] The "T" class had the same operating depth limitation of 300 feet, but had a larger crew of 56 men. They carried an increased fuel load of 132 tons. This class was ordered in 1935. A total of 55 were constructed. Fifteen were available at the start of WW II. Like the "S" class they had riveted pressure hulls.

A third class was originally designed as an unarmed training submarine to perform "electric rabbit" or "clockwork mice" duties for practice tracking and attacking by surface ASW units employing Asdic (active sonar). It was the "U" class, 191 feet in length, 16 feet 1 inch wide, with surfaced/submerged displacements of 630 tons/730 tons, surfaced/submerged speeds of 11.25 kts/9 kts, a range of 3,800 nm at 10 kts, and a battery of six torpedo tubes forward (two external). These were ordered in 1936 when it became apparent that Germany was rearming and might present a U-boat threat again. A total of 30 were built. They would prove very useful in

---

240　The ten torpedo tubes allowed a large salvo of torpedoes to be fired from outside Asdic range, in theory guaranteeing at least one hit

the Med during WW II. Only three had been completed when the war started.

Great Britain still had some submarines left over from WW I, particularly the "H" class. Nine of these were in still in service in 1939. H-28 had the unique distinction of making war patrols during WW I and WW II. Two were lost before the remaining seven were taken off active operations and relegated to training duties only. Another class left over from the last days of the first war was the three "L" class submarines. They made patrols in 1940 before being turned over to the training command. Later they were transferred to Canada in a training role for ASW forces of the RCN.

HMS Porpoise was ordered in 1930 specifically as a minelayer. She carried 50 mines externally under her upper casing, and was equipped with a 4.7 inch deck gun. She displaced slightly over 2,000 tons. A further five mine-laying submarines of the Grampus class followed Porpoise into service. They were built to a modified-Porpoise design with slight modifications.

Shortly after WW I ended three classes of overseas patrol submarines were built (O, P and R classes). All carried eight torpedo tubes and a 4.7 inch deck gun. They were intended for long range operations in the Far East. However their designs were a problem. They suffered from leaks, including their fuel tanks. Nevertheless 18 were still in service in 1939.

The River class of submarine was intended as a true "fleet submarine", that is one that could match fleet speeds and maneuver with the fleet. They were intended as replacements for the K class, a steam powered monstrosity that had been built when it was not possible to achieve fleet speeds with the diesel engines available at the time. Three were built, HMS Thames (1932), and HMS Clyde and HMS Severn (1934). The diesel-powered River class boats were capable of making 22 kts, a remarkable achievement, but unfortunately fleet warship speeds had also increased – up towards 30 kts. They were well armed with six internal bow torpedo tubes and a 4 inch or 4.7 inch deck gun. However, the concept of the true "fleet submarine" died with them.[241] The goal was abandoned as unobtainable.

---

241   The U.S. Navy pursued the same goal, a submarine fast enough to conform to fleet movements. It too was unsuccessful but the designation "fleet submarine" stuck and was applied to the long range, high speed (20 kt.) submarines that later ravaged the Japanese merchant marine.

CHAPTER TWENTY-ONE –
ITALY

During WWI Italian submarines had been rather short ranged and operated principally in the Adriatic Sea, and made patrols of only a few days in length. German U-boats had greatly exceeded Italian submarine operating parameters, as had British submarines. Between 1925 and 1938, 22 different classes of Italian submarines were placed into service. Many of the classes were small, consisting of four boats. They fell into three different groupings, based upon displacement and range capability.

The three groups were: long range (1904 to 2190 tons submerged displacement), medium range (1010 to 1650 tons submerged displacement), and short range (810 to 870 tons submerged displacement). These distinctions are the author's rather than the Italian Submarine Service, in trying to present a coherent picture of that service. For comparison purposes the German Type VIIA U-boat was roughly 750 tons submerged displacement and it ranged fairly far across the Atlantic during WW II.

All the classes had two diesel engines and most carried eight 21" (533 mm) torpedo tubes, four forward and four aft. Their passive listening hydrophones were inferior to those carried later by German submarines. Their operating depths were roughly equivalent to those of Great Britain and France.

Rather than present information on each of the 22 different classes (which would be rather tiresome), a representative sample has been selected from the long, medium and short-range groups and their data is as follows:

- Long range (*Calvi* class): three laid down starting in 1932, 2060 tons submerged displacement, 276'6'" in length, 16.8 kts/7.4 kts, ranges 5600 nm @14 kts/120 nm @3 kts, 8 TT, 2 x 4.7" guns, 72 complement, operating depth 288' (90m), fuel 75 tons.

- Medium range (*Marcello* class): eleven laid down starting in 1937, 1315 tons submerged displacement, 239'6" in length, 17.4 kts/8 kts, ranges 2500 nm @ 17 kts/120 nm @ 3kts, 8 TT, 2 x 3.9" guns, 57-58 complement, operating depth 328' (100m), fuel 59 tons.

- Short range (*Adua* class): seventeen laid down starting in 1936, 860 tons submerged displacement, 197'6" in length, 14 kts/7.5 kts,,

ranges 2200 nm @14 kts/74nm @ 4kts, 6 TT
(4 fwd 2 aft), 1 x 3.9 in, 45-46 complement,
operating depth 256' (80m), fuel 47 tons.

The British and the Germans had taken the lessons of WW I submarine warfare and ASW to heart and set out to remedy their own defects. The Royal Navy developed Asdic (active sonar) to deal with submerged submarines. The Germans, sparked by Karl Doenitz's theories, developed a tactical system designed to solve the convoy problem that had baffled them in 1917 – 1918 and helped cost them the war. However, the Italian Submarine Service did not appear to learn anything significant from their own or others' WW I experiences.

Their submarine diving times were excessive, up to two minutes to become fully submerged. Operating in the Med where land-based aircraft with increasing speeds presented serious threats to surfaced submarines, their lengthy diving times made them vulnerable to sudden air attack. Their superstructures were quite large and thus more detectable visually at night. Their operating machinery was noisy and allowed surface ASW ships to track them with hydrophones.

Italian torpedoes were reliable but they did not develop a torpedo fire control mechanism capable of sending changing gyro angles to their torpedo tubes, similar to systems developed by the Germans and Americans. Training was apparently restricted to solitary patrol operations with simulated attacks on merchant ships under the Prize Rules. No training in anti-convoy operations was carried out. Neither was there any cooperation with the Royal Italian Air Force. The Italian Navy had no air arm and so air reconnaissance, if any, had to be provided by the Royal Italian Air Force. It was not.

The Italian Submarine Service had a marvelous opportunity to test itself and learn valuable lessons during the Spanish Civil War (1936 – 1939) when Italy supported Franco's rebel forces (see the appropriate section later), but it failed to do so. Italian submarines conducted a large number of patrols and sank or damaged some ships carrying war materials to the Spanish government ports. Her submarines were withdrawn after Great Britain and France established ASW patrols to deal with unidentified "pirate" submarines operating in the Med. However that experience did not seem to improve her submarine performance, which would be severely tested when Italy entered the war on May 10, 1940 against France and Great Britain.

Italian submarine operations during WW II will be covered in detail in a succeeding volume but one operation not directly connected is provided here. On 15 August 1940 the Greek cruiser *Helle* was anchored inside territorial waters at the Greek island of Tinos in the Aegean Sea. She was there carrying an official delegation to help celebrate the Feast of the Assumption in the port city. At 0830 torpedoes were fired from an unidentified submerged submarine. Two missed *Helle* and exploded ashore. A third struck her in the boiler room. About 75 minutes later Helle sank with the loss of nine lives and twenty-two wounded. The firing submarine was never officially identified. Italy declared its innocence and blamed the British for the cowardly act. Italy had joined the Axis attack on France on 10 June 1940 and was officially at war with Great Britain.

Greek divers recovered torpedo fragments from the shallow sea bottom. The markings were clearly Italian, pointing to the real culprit. The Metaxas government of Greece suppressed that information, knowing full well that Italy was intent on goading Greece into war. Officially the sinking was by an unknown submarine. Italian submarine *Delfino* was the firing submarine, operating on top secret orders from Mussolini. Greece refused to be drawn into conflict at the time. Two months later, on 28 October 1940, Italian forces invaded Greece from Albania and the two countries officially went to war.

CHAPTER TWENTY-TWO – JAPAN

Following the end of WW I, seven German U-boats were provided to Japan as war reparations. A large number of German submarine designers, engineers and former U-boat officers were brought to Japan under contract to assist the IJN in updating its submarine service technology and training. However by 1928 their services were no longer needed. Japan was ready to strike out on its own.

The Washington Naval Treaty of 1922 had set fleet battleship limits for Great Britain, the United States and Japan as 5:5:3 ratios in numbers authorized.[242] In 1930 at the London Conference the Japanese tried again to change the ratios but were unsuccessful in the face of British and American intransience. Both countries argued

---

242   The United States had stolen Japanese diplomatic ciphers in advance of the Washington Treaty Conference and was reading Japanese government instructions to its representatives as negotiations went forward. They knew that the Japanese fall-back position was 5:5:3 and held on until that point was reached.

that their naval obligations were worldwide rather than merely regional as Japan's were, and that being the case Japan would always have local superiority in the Far East because many of the British and American units would be tied down in the Atlantic.

The IJN, focused on the inevitability of a war between Japan and the United States sometime in the future, looked to long range submarines to offset American large warship superiority in numbers. They intended that submarines would conduct long range reconnaissance, and inflict attrition on the U.S. fleet as it proceeded westward to the relief of the Philippines.[243] This view strongly influenced Japanese submarine development during the 1920s and 1930s.

One other factor had a very strong influence on Japanese submarine theory, submarine development and submarine doctrine. It was a strong Japanese naval focus on a climatic naval battle, near Japan, in which Japanese surface forces would inflict a crushing defeat on the enemy fleet after having reduced some of its strength through submarine attacks as it proceeded westward from Pearl Harbor. Later in the mid 1930s Admiral Yamamoto would update that theory to add long range land-based IJN bombers and aircraft carrier battle forces to the equation, but the basic concept remained unchanged

The IJN focused on only one of the two major lessons of submarine warfare during WW I. That was

---

243   An interesting point of view held early in the 20th century and indicative of a long held Japanese intention to venture into South East Asia in search of conquests.

the demonstration of the capability of submarines to sink major warships. The other was the ability of submarines to sink merchant ships. The second role was seemingly ignored, to Japan's ultimate disaster. Great Britain had nearly succumbed to unrestricted submarine warfare upon merchant ships in 1917. Great Britain, like Japan, was an island nation heavily dependent upon its merchant marine to import foodstuffs and raw materials for industry. While it was a lesson unlearned for the IJN and the Japanese government, rather than for the Japanese Submarine Service, it was a crucial mistake.

The Japanese Submarine Service built submarines in three different categories, referred to by the first three letters in the Japanese Romanized syllabary: I, RO and HA. I – boats were long range, RO - boats were medium range and HA - boats were short range coastal submarines. We will concentrate on the development of I and RO boats in this discussion since they would carry out most of the submarine activity in which the Japanese engaged during the Pacific War, as the Japanese refer to their portion of WW II.

I-class

The development of I-class long range submarines followed two different functional roles that finally came together. The first role was that of a very long range scout (*Junsen*) that could conduct surveillance of an enemy's fleet and his ports, as well as long distance commerce raiding.

The second role was that of a "fleet submarine" (*Kaidai*) operating subordinate to a flotilla leader with and in support of the battle fleet, intended to aggressively attack major enemy warships and whittle down the numerical advantage. As time went on the differences between the two functional roles became less and the submarines designed for each role became closer in characteristics until they culminated in the I-class long range submarine, albeit with some armament or communications differences depending upon the primary function.

Both WW I British K-class fleet submarines and German U-139 "U-cruisers" served as starting points for development. The *Junsen* were to replace cruisers in a scouting role. Interestingly the U.S. Navy looked at dirigibles for similar purposes, calculating that for the cost of a single cruiser it could build three long range dirigibles. Scouting was a vital function in the vast distances of the Pacific Ocean. The *Junsen* emphasized very long range, high speed and good sea keeping qualities. Some *Junsen* would be equipped with small float planes and a hangar to improve their long range scouting capabilities. They suffered from limited submerged maneuverability and lengthy diving times imposed by their large dimensions. In combat they proved vulnerable to intensive ASW tactics using active sonar. Their large hulls proved good targets for sonar and their size reduced their submerged maneuverability.

In 1919-1920 the IJN laid down two submarines, I-51 and I-52, modeled respectively upon the British K-class and the German U-139 class. They would be compared for performance and would lead to the long range merged I-class.

I-51, based on the British K-class, was 300' in length; displaced 2430 tons submerged, was equipped with two diesel engines, and had a range of 20,000 nm at 10 kts. She had eight TT, 6 fwd and 2 aft, carried 24 torpedoes, one 4.7 inch gun, and a complement of 60.

I-52, based on the German U-139 class, was 330' in length; displaced 2500 tons submerged, was also equipped with two diesel engines but had a significantly lesser range of 10,000 nm at 10 kts.[244] I-52 also had eight TT (6 fwd and 2 aft but only carried 16 torpedoes, plus a 4.7 inch gun. She also had a complement of 60.

As developments proceeded the cruiser (*Junsen*) and fleet (*Kaidai*) type submarines approached each other in characteristics. In 1941 they essentially merged in the long-range I-class submarine.

RO-class

The IJN laid down four classes of RO type, medium range submarines between 1920 and 1941. The first was the L 4 type, modeled on the WW I British L-class submarine. Nine of these units were built between 1923 and 1927. They were 250' feet long, displaced 996/1322 tons, and

---

244   Both these submarine would be considered extremely long range by normal European standards but the Pacific theater was immense in comparison with European waters.

made 16/8 kts. They had a range of 5,000 nm at 10 kts/80 nm at 4 kts. Their operating depth was 200 feet and they had a crew of 60. They were armed with six bow TT, carried ten torpedoes and a 3 inch gun.

They were followed in 1933 by two K-5/K-6 type units, which were intended as prototypes for wartime series production. The K-5 characteristics were: 239 foot length, 790/940 tons displacement, making 19/8.5 kts. They had a range of 8,000 nm at 12 kts/90 nm at 3.5 kts. Their operating depth was increased to 245 feet, and they had a crew of 42 men. They had a reduced armament of four bow TT, and carried ten torpedoes and a 3 inch gun. The K-6 variant was longer and faster but had a lesser range. It carried a crew of 54 men with the same armament suite.

The KS (*Kaigun-Sho* (small)) type followed. Eighteen of these were laid down commencing in June 1941. Their requirements called for 21 day patrols to protect island bases in the Pacific. They were 199 feet in length: displaced 601/782 tons submerged, and made 14.25/8 kts. They had a range of 3,500 nm at 12 kts/60 nm at 3 kts. Their operating depth was 245 feet and they carried a crew of only 38. They had four bow TT and a reload torpedo for each tube. They also carried a 3 inch gun, although their original plans called for a twin 25 mm AA gun.

ST (*Sen Taka* –high speed experimental submarine)

Although many submariners are familiar with the WW II German Type-XXI high speed submarine, the *Elektroboot*, which led to post war development of the U.S. Tang class fast attack boats and the USSR's W-class submarines, few have probably heard anything about Japanese developments in the same field. During the period 1938 through 1940 an experimental and highly secret Japanese submarine, coded as vessel number 71, underwent trials. She was small, only displacing 213 tons, but could make just over 21 knots submerged using battery power. Great attention was paid to streamlining and all deck fittings were recessed. Her gun mount was retractable. She had high-capacity batteries. This development led to the wartime Sen-Taka type, with 24 units being ordered in the 1943-1944 programs. They were ordered too late to participate in WW II.

Japanese submarine training focused almost exclusively on attacking enemy naval units. They had no practice in attacking convoys. The IJN did focus on submerged attack by small submarines, which could be transported on deck of larger I-class boats. These submarines were not suicide weapons of the type that later evolved, called *kaiten*. The Japanese midget submarines each carried two torpedoes and were intended to penetrate enemy harbors, torpedo their targets and then withdraw for rendezvous and recovery by the "mother" submarine. The Japanese Submarine Service was unique in that aspect, as well as in carrying float planes aboard a large number of fleet submarines for reconnaissance.[245]

---

245   One French submarine, *Surcouf*, carried a floatplane. The Royal Navy and the U.S. Navy had experimented with the technique and then abandoned it.

CHAPTER TWENTY-THREE –
THE NETHERLANDS AND
OTHER NATIONS

S ubmarines were not limited to the major nations discussed earlier. In Europe the following nations operated the number of submarines shown in parentheses: Denmark (12), Estonia (2), Finland (8), Greece (6), Latvia (2), Norway (9), Poland (5), Portugal (3), Rumania (1), Spain (13) and Yugoslavia (4). Sweden had 20, and The Netherlands had 27 submarines commissioned or fitting out in May 1940, some involved in her colonial service in the Dutch East Indies (current day Indonesia). In the Middle East, Turkey had 4 submarines. In South America: Argentina had (3), Brazil (3), Chile (9) and Peru (4). In Asia, Siam (now Thailand) operated 4 submarines. There were a total of 112 submarines scattered among the "lesser nations" navies.

A useful rule of thumb well known to submarine operators is that you can keep one submarine at sea, on patrol, out of every three in your inventory. The second is either enroute the patrol area or returning from it, and the third is undergoing repairs and crew rest. A submarine operator can exceed the 1:3 ratio for a short time but not for very long. Both machinery and men need down time and repairs. The corollary to this rule is that unless a particular nation has a large number of submarines; their wartime effectiveness will be very limited. Submarines are an attrition weapon system under most circumstances. Operating a very few submarines may lend prestige to a small navy but usually means very little in real terms. A few submarines are necessary to provide realistic targets for ASW training of their own surface and air arms. To embark on a significant submarine attrition campaign against either enemy warships or merchant ships or both requires a large submarine inventory.

Because of the significant involvement of Netherlands' submarines in combat in the European theater and the Far East during WW II, additional material about the Netherlands Submarine Service is provided.

The Netherlands had remained neutral during WW I, but had a substantial colonial empire. With a long history of naval activity in European waters and South East Asia, the Netherlands maintained very capable although small naval forces. Among them were submarines.

The Royal Netherlands Navy (RNN) Submarine Service began in 1904 with submarine O-1. She was completed in 1906 and served until 1920. Four more boats followed from 1909 to 1914, the O-2 class. They were in commission from 1911 until 1935. The third class of submarine built in the Netherlands was the K I, with the "K" standing for *Kolonien*, or Colonial, referring to the fact that they were intended for Colonial Service in the Dutch East Indies. The "O" in O-1 and O-2 stood for *Onderzeeboot*, or under sea boat. K class submarines were larger and had greater endurance than their sister O-class submarines which operated in northern European waters. The classes would be separated by the different designator until 1937, when they would merge. After that the two slightly differing designs had become identical. All subsequent classes were designated as "O", whether intended for home or colonial service. K I was built between 1914 and 1918, and served in the Far East until 1928.

A fourth design, O-6, was built between 1914 and 1916 and served from 1916 to 1936. She was followed by K II, built from 1915 to 1920, and serving from 1922 to 1937 in the Far East. O-7 was built from 1914 to 1916 and served until 1939. Two K III class followed, being built from 1915 to 1920, and serving from 1920 to 1934.

O-8 was a war prize, so to speak. She started as HMS H-6, a Holland type submarine built by Canadian Vickers to an Electric Boat design for Great Britain. While on patrol in the North Sea she ran aground on the Dutch coast during WW I and was interned. Making the best of a bad deal, the British sold her to the Dutch and she entered their service as O-8. She displaced 343/443 tons, was 151' 6" in length and had a range of 1350 nm. The Germans captured her in 1940 when they invaded Holland, and placed her in their service as UD-1. She was used for training only by the Germans, and scuttled in 1945.

Three K V class submarines were built from 1916 to 1920. They served in the Far East from 1920 to 1942. They displaced 507/639 tons, were 188' long, and had a range of 3,500 nm and a crew of 31 men. Between 1922 and 1926 three O-9 class boats were built. They served from 1925 through 1945. They displaced 483/647 tons, were 180 feet in length, had a range of 3,000 nm, and a crew of 29. During that same building period, 1922 to 1926, three K XI class submarines were built for colonial service. They displaced 611/815 tons, were 218' 9" in length, and had a range of 3,500 nm and a crew of 31. They also served from 1925 through 1945.

From 1928 through 1932 four O-12 class boats were built. They began service in 1931 and ended it in 1946. They displaced 546/704 tons, were 198' 3" in length, with a range of 3,500 nm, and a crew of 31. They were a derivative of the K XI class. From 1930 through 1936 five K XIV submarines were built. They served from 1933 until 1946. They displaced 771/1000 tons, were 242'6" in length, had a crew of 38 and an operating depth of 264 feet. Their range was 3,500 miles

O-16 marked the merging of O and K classes. She was built 1933 – 1936, and served from 1937 until 1947. She was 896/1170 tons, 254'3" long, could do 18/9 kts, with a crew of 38. Two more O classes followed: Two O-19s and seven O-21s. The O-19s were minelayers, 998/1536 tons, 264'9" in length, could do 19.25/9 kts, had eight TT and a 330 foot operating depth.

The O-19s were built from 1936 – 1939 and served 1939 to 1945. The O-21s were very similar but slightly smaller and didn't have a mine laying capability. They displaced 881/1186 tons, were 255 ' long, had identical surfaced and submerged speeds, and also carried 8 TT. Four TT were forward and two were aft internally, with an additional two external amidships.

CHAPTER TWENTY-FOUR – UNION OF SOVIET SOCIALIST REPUBLICS (USSR)[246]

The events of 1917 and 1918 were tumultuous for the Russian Navy and its submarine service as well as for the Army and the nation. A Civil War between Red (Bolshevik) and White (Tsarist) forces engulfed the nation from 1917 to 1922. In March 1918 Allied powers (France, Great Britain, Japan and the United States) landed troops in Russia, ostensibly to secure war materials that had been shipped to the Tsarist forces and keep them out of the hands of the Germans. These troops entered Russia at Murmansk, Vladivostok and the Black Sea. They soon saw combat with Bolshevik forces who considered them as de facto allies of the White forces.

---

246   Much of the material concerning the Soviet Navy was derived from the excellent book *Submarines of the Russian and Soviet Navies* by Norman Polmar and Jurrien Noot (listed in the bibliography)

Great Britain sent a battle squadron into the Baltic in November 1918 to assist Estonia. Prior to that, Soviet submarine *Pantera* had conducted an unsuccessful attack on British submarine E-40 on 23 July. On 31 July *Pantera* was successful in another attack and sank 1,100 ton destroyer HMS Vittoria near Seskar in the Baltic. A year later Soviet submarine *Vepr'* unsuccessfully attacked British destroyers HMS Valorous and HMS Vancouver but escaped after a vigorous counterattack.

On 9 June 1919 British submarine L-55 attempted an attack on two Soviet destroyers in the Gulf of Finland. It was unsuccessful and their counterattacks forced her into a minefield area. She was then sunk by their gunfire in a surface engagement. She sank along with her entire crew.

The Tsarist (Russian) Navy was formally disestablished on 11 January 1918 and its successor – the Workers and Peasants Red Navy (RKKP) was established the same day. On 28 July 1918 all private shipyards were nationalized. The new Red Navy took over a number of submarines from the former Tsar's Navy. They totaled 52. Forty-one were in commission and seven were under construction, with four more in an inactive status. During the Intervention Period and the Civil War some 32 submarines were lost to different causes. There remained only fourteen submarines of the Bars (10) and AG (Holland) (4) classes, and they were considered obsolete.

During 1922, with the Civil War over, the future of the Soviet Navy was considered. There were two schools of thought. The first favored a traditional navy, based upon battleships and cruisers. The second, the "young school", favored a new approach, consistent with economic realities, and focused its attention on submarines, light surface craft and land-based aircraft. Neither school won the debate. Over succeeding years some money was appropriated for the repair of several battleships, cruisers and destroyers. By 1930 the USSR had three old battleships in commission, and 14 semi-obsolete submarines. The putative "enemy" for naval planning purposes was Great Britain, and the main theater of operations was the Baltic. The first new warships for the USSR would come from its first Five-Year Economic Plan (1928 – 1932)

Beginning in the early 1920s a *rapprochement* was established between the Soviet Union and Germany, both nations labeled as pariahs for different reasons. Discussions on various types of military cooperation took place. One of these involved a secret meeting in Berlin in March 1926. There a German – Soviet naval conference discussed possible joint training in submarines, similar to existing secret aviation training at Lipetsk and tank training at Kazan. However, unlike the other two arrangements, nothing concrete came of the proposal. However the Germans agreed to provide four of their advanced submarine designs to the Soviets.

Another source of submarine design information came from an unlikely find. In 1926 a fishing vessel discovered the wreck of British submarine L-55 in only

104 feet of water. During the period April through August 1928 she was salvaged by Soviet submarine rescue and salvage vessel *Kommuna*. Her dead crews' remains were transferred to England by a British merchant ship, where they were buried in a mass grave near Portsmouth.[247] L-55 was recommissioned in the Soviet Navy on 5 November 1931. She was studied by Soviet submarine designers and later served as a model for the Series III and IV of new construction Soviet submarines of 1931 and 1933.

The first Soviet Five Year Plan covered the period 1928 – 1932. Its naval aspects called for construction of 12 submarines, six Dekabrist class (Series I) and six Leninets class (Series II). The Dekabrist class boats were 924/1354 tons, 249 feet in length, could make 14/9 kts., had six 21-inch torpedo tubes forward and carried 14 torpedoes, had a double hull and seven water tight compartments. This last characteristic was a change from earlier (WW I) Russian-designed submarines that lacked water tight compartmentation and made them vulnerable to flooding accidents. The Leninets class boats were slightly larger.

In 1929 the Soviet Defense Minister approached the German government for assistance in submarine matters. This led to a visit to Wilhelmshaven, Germany in February 1930 by senior Soviet naval officers. One month later V. M. Orlov, commander of the Soviet Black Sea Fleet, met with German naval authorities in Berlin. Subsequently

---

247   The Soviet Union would not allow a British warship to enter her waters to take the L-55 crew remains home.

the Germans provided the USSR with submarine and torpedo designs. In 1933 Germany sold the plans for the S-class submarine to the USSR. A number of MAN diesel engines were also sold to the USSR.

The S-class or *Stalinets* class had its origin in a design by German firm *Deschimag* for a submarine to be built in Cadiz, Spain for the Spanish Navy.[248] The plans had been drawn up by the veiled German submarine design organization operating in Holland, *Ingenieurskantoor voor Scheepsbouw (IvS)*. The new submarine, E-1, started trials in January 1931 and German naval personnel were involved in her sea trials. One of them would later command a U-boat that conducted a covert war patrol off Spain in December 1936 during the Spanish Civil War. His operational experience in the Mediterranean Sea during E-1's sea trials was a distinct asset later. Several Soviet submarine designers also were embarked during E-1's sea trials in 1932.

The Soviets insisted on some design changes: larger diesel engines and a Soviet-designed deck gun, to the initial submarine design drawings for the S-class submitted by *Deschimag* in November 1933. Some Soviet designers were sent to the *IvS* office at *Deschimag* in Bremen to take part in the design work. The initial order was for three units, N-1 through N-3, later redesignated S-1 through S-3. The

---

248   Germany was forbidden by the Treaty of Versailles from having any submarines. The section on Germany discusses its successful efforts to evade the treaty well before Hitler's election to power.

class displaced 840/1070 tons, were 255' in length, and could make 19.5/9 kts using diesel-electric drive. They had four bow and two stern 21" torpedo tubes. They also carried a 100-mm deck gun and a 45-mm AA gun. A total of 50 S-class submarines were built, in two series. The first, designated Series IX, consisted of three units. The next series in order, Series IX-*bis*, included 47 units.

From 1927 to 1941 when Germany suddenly attacked its former ally - the Soviet Union, the Soviet Navy laid down nineteen classes of submarines. When the German attack caught Soviet leader Stalin by surprise on June 22, 1941 the USSR had the largest submarine fleet in the world – 218 submarines of all classes.[249] Many classes contained only a few in numbers, but others were quite large in quantity. By comparison Germany had only 57 submarines in commission in September 1939 when she began WW II by invading Poland.

At the small end in size were the *Malyutka* ("little one') class of only 202 tons submerged displacement with two torpedo tubes and no reloads and a crew of seventeen. However a total of 50 of these were built in the 1934 (Series VI) and 1935 (Series VI-*bis*) programs. Later, the 1937 and 1938 programs added another 51

---

249 Winston Churchill of Great Britain and Franklin Delano Roosevelt of the United States were among those who warned Stalin in advance of German plans and preparations for an attack. Soviet intelligence had also detected important information but Stalin refused to accept it and make timely preparations. As a result his Air Force was largely destroyed on its airfields during the first week.

M-class submarines of slightly greater displacements (five of 256 tons and 46 of 275 tons) and slightly increased crew size - 22 vice 17. Many of the M-class were assigned to the Soviet Far East Fleet. These small submarines were designed and built with rail transport in mind.

Russia, and the succeeding Soviet Union, had four distinct and widely separated fleets (Northern, Baltic, Black Sea, and Far East) because of its huge size. Transfer of large naval units, which could only sail from one fleet area to another, might be precluded by enemy action. In any case the distances were enormous. The easily transportable small submarines gave the USSR a capability to beef up its coastal defenses rapidly by moving them internally by rail between fleet areas as needed.

In the 1936 program were three Pravda class submarines (Series IV) , laid down in 1931 and commissioned in 1936. Four were planned but only three were completed. They were relatively large and were intended as *Kreyser* (cruiser) submarines to operate with the Soviet fleet, similar to Great Britain, Japan's and United States efforts to build fleet submarines. All were unsuccessful. The Soviet P class displaced 955/1671 tons, and was 287'5" in length. They were not good "sea boats" and their batteries took 20 hours to recharge. In that day before the introduction of the snorkel, submarines would patrol submerged during the day and only surface at night to recharge batteries while darkness hid them. Even so darkness rarely lasts longer than 8-10 hours so it is obvious that they were not an adequate design.

The *Shchuka* (Pike) Series III of 1933 were strongly influenced by the design lessons learned from former British submarine L-55. Series III included four units in 1933, and Series V in 1932 included 14 units with Series V-*bis*-2 adding 13 units. The 1936 Series X added 61 units for a total of 100 *Shchuka* class submarines in the fleet. They displaced 577/704 tons, were 187' in length, were powered by two diesel-electric power plants, could make 11.2kts/8kts, and had a range of 1350 nm @ 11.2 kts/110 nm @ 1.75 kts. They were armed with six 21" torpedo tubes (4 bow and 2 stern) and 12 torpedoes. In addition they had two stern mine tubes with a total of 20 mines. This last feature reflects the historical emphasis on mine warfare in Russia, which continued in the new USSR,. The final, 1936 Series X, units were slightly larger and had reduced machinery noise.[250]

In line with the emphasis on mine warfare capability the USSR built three series of L-class mine laying submarines. The first group of six was in the 1936 program. They displaced 1025/1321 tons and were 265'9" in length. In addition to six torpedo tubes forward, they had two stern mine laying shafts and carried 20 mines. The second group of L-class (Series XIII) was in the 1938 program. They were slightly larger at 1099/1399 tons and 273'4". They had six torpedo tubes forward and 2 aft, and a pair of mine laying shafts aft also. They carried 20 mines in addition to 18 torpedoes. The final group of 6 L-class

---

250 The final group displaced 587 tons vice 577 tons.

submarines was in the 1940 program. They were almost identical to the second group. The total for L-class mine layers was 19 submarines.

Another distinct class was the 18 boat series XIV K-class. They were designated as *Kreyser* (cruiser) submarines. They displaced 1480/2095 tons, were 320' long, could make 21/10kts, and had eight torpedo tubes: 4 in the bow, 2 in the stern and another 2 in a trainable stern casing arrangement. In addition they had two mine shafts under the control room and 20 mines. Initial plans called for a small float plane to be embarked, but none ever were carried.

CHAPTER TWENTY-FIVE –
UNITED STATES

At the end of WW I the United States Submarine Service had two recently designed classes of submarines in commission or building: the O class (8 boats), and the R class (27 boats).[251] Specifications for the O class are given here. The R class were slightly larger and had 21" torpedo tubes instead of the O class's 18" torpedo tubes: O class - 521/629 tons displacement, 172 feet in length, 2 diesel engines, speeds of 14/10.5 kts, a range of 5,000 nm at 11 kts, four TT forward (18") plus four reload torpedoes, a crew of 32 and 88 tons fuel oil. They were roughly the equivalent of the British E class submarines that had done well in WW I.

The next class was the S class, laid down in four groups, beginning in 1918 and ending in 1924. A total of 48 were built. A Lake-design prototype (S 2) was built,

---

251 The R class was divided by designer, R 1- R 20 (Holland), and R 21- R 27 (Lake). All the Lake-designed boats were scrapped in 1930.

considered inferior and not repeated. The other 47 were basically Holland design although a small number in Group 2 were built at Portsmouth Naval Shipyard to a Bureau of Construction and Repair (later BuShips, much later NavShips) design.

Twenty-five units were in Group 1, and their characteristics are presented here: 854/1062 tons displacement, 219'3" in length, two diesel engines, 14.5/11 kts, 5,000 nm at 10 kts, 4 TT fwd (21"), 12 torpedoes, a 4 inch gun, a crew of 42, and 168 tons of fuel. They had an operating depth of 200 feet and were of riveted construction. Displacement and length increased between groups and the largest was 1,230 tons submerged and 265 feet in length. Four of the S-class had an additional TT aft.

During the period of the late 1920s and the 1930s there was an ongoing controversy within submarine officer ranks over the most desirable design of future U.S. submarines. One group, essentially headed by a prominent submarine officer, Thomas Hart, who later became an admiral and was Commander-in-Chief U.S. Asiatic Fleet at the time WW II started, favored smaller, faster diving boats like the S-class.

Fortunately for the U. S. Submarine Service and all who served in it during WW II, that faction lost out to another group which favored larger, high speed, very long range submarines specifically designed to conduct oceanic warfare in the Pacific against the Japanese. They wanted high surface speed, ten torpedo tubes and a large number of torpedoes and got them, although it took a while and there was a minor deviation towards medium range boats. They also wanted improved habitability, including air conditioning which sharply reduced electrical grounds when operating in tropical waters.[252]

No U.S. submarine officer envisioned the unrestricted anti-merchant ship campaign that was directed immediately after the Pearl Harbor attack.[253] Pre-war training was basically focused upon attacks on naval ships and formations. Exercises tended to be formulaic, "canned" in the vernacular. The escorts "knew" where the submarines had to be to carry out their exercise functions and were alert to periscope sightings. Escort aircraft guarding naval formations became equally expert at visually detecting submerged submarines at periscope depth and dropping exercise marker bombs on them.[254]

Submarine commanding officers who were detected were marked down for the exercise, but more importantly in their fitness reports that controlled future promotions. Rigid exercise procedures thus tended to breed a generation of submarine commanding officers who were "risk-adverse". Passive sonar approaches from below periscope depth became the vogue with torpedo salvoes fired from

---

252 John D. Alden, The Fleet Submarine in the U.S. Navy, pp. 52-57.

253 In every submarine wardroom library was a copy of the Rules of Maritime Warfare outlining the dos and don'ts of anti-mercantile warfare. One of the main "don'ts" was "Don't sink merchant ships without warning".

254 Galantin, Op cit., pp. 13-18

100 feet depth, reducing the chance of a periscope sighting and adverse reports (and incidentally of hits since the sonar plots of the day were exceedingly primitive).[255] These ingrained habits would be replicated during a number of early WW II U.S. submarine attacks.

There was absolutely no training in unrestricted submarine warfare against an enemy merchant fleet. Any submarine commanding officer or Division Commander caught even suggesting that just perhaps some training along those lines might be appropriate would probably have been relieved of duty and sent back to General Service.

Following the S class a series of V class submarines were built. They originally were numbered V-1 through V-9, although they carried names and other class designators. The first were V-1, V-2 and V-3, Barracuda class. They were built from 1921 to 1926, overlapping S class production, displaced 2000/2620 tons, were 341 feet in length – a marked increase in size, made 18/8 kts, had a range of 12,000 nm at 11 kts, were equipped with six TT (4 fwd, 2 aft) and 12 torpedoes. They had a crew of 80, an operating depth of 200 feet and carried 364 tons of fuel.

A one-off derivative - Argonaut (V-4) followed in 1925 – 1928. She was laid down as the only purpose built submarine minelayer for the U.S. Navy. If the Barracudas were large, she was even larger at 2710/4164

---

255   Blair, Clay Jr., Silent Victory, p. 67

tons displacement, and 331 feet in length. She could make 15/8 kts, had a range of 18,000 nm at 8 kts, was equipped like the Barracudas with six TT tubes (4 fwd, 2 aft) and 16 torpedoes, but also carried 60 mines in two mine tubes aft under the casing. She had a crew of 89 and carried 696 tons of fuel. She also sported a pair of six inch guns, set before and aft of the conning tower, making her the most heavily armed submarine in the U.S.N. inventory.

Narwhal class (V-5 and V-6) followed in 1927 -1930. Also very large and equipped with six inch guns, they displaced 2915/4050 tons, were 371 feet long, could make 17/8 kts, had a range of 18,000 nm at 8 kts, and were equipped with six TT (4 fwd, 2 aft) but with an increased load of 20 torpedoes. Their operating depth was increased to 328 feet and they carried 732 tons of fuel.

The next V boat, Dolphin V-7, was a step down in size as the designers attempted to package the same range and power in a smaller unit. She was built in 1930 – 1932 and displaced 1500/2040 tons, had a length of 319 feet, could make 17/8 kts, with a range of 9,000 nm at 10 kts, carried six TT (4 fwd, 2 aft) and 18 torpedoes. She had a crew of 60 and a four inch gun and carried 412 tons of fuel. Her operating depth was 250 feet.

She was followed in 1931 – 1933 by the two Cachalot class (V-8 and V-9). They were somewhat smaller at 1170/1650 tons, 271 feet in length, They made 17/8 kts, and had a range of 9,000 nm at 8 kts. Their TT arrangement was identical to Dolphin but they carried

16 torpedoes, and had a crew of 50 men. They were the first class to incorporate welding in the hull, leading other nations in this feature. Their operating depth was 250 feet and they carried 333 tons of fuel oil.

The following class, "P", built in 1933 – 1937, became the progenitor "fleet submarine" in the U.S. Navy. The term fleet submarine no longer referred to a submarine with speed high enough to keep up with major fleet units, since modern battleships and cruisers could make 30 kts, but rather a relatively high speed (20 kts) submarine intended for long range operations (10,000 nm) in the vast reaches of the Pacific Ocean.

Ten P class were built. They displaced 1310/1960 tons, were 301 feet long, made 19/8 kts and had a range of 10,000 nm at 10 kts. They carried 6 TT (4 fwd and 2 aft) with 18 torpedoes, and a crew of 55. They had an operating depth of 250 feet and carried 347-373 tons of fuel oil. They were all welded construction. Five of the class had two external TT added, making a total of 8 TT.

All the submarines built subsequently, before the U.S. was dragged into WW II in December 1941, with the exception of two M class boats built in 1939 - 1941, would be "fleet type submarines". They would vary in minor dimensions but were very similar in all important characteristics.

Sixteen Salmon/Sargo boats followed in two groups during the period 1938 – 1939. They displaced 1449/2198 tons and were 308 feet in length. They made 20/9 kts and had a 10,000 nm range at 10 kts. Their internal TT armament was increased to 8 tubes (4 fwd, 4 aft) and they carried 24 torpedoes. They had a crew of 70, carried 318-428 tons of fuel, and had a three inch or four inch gun.

The final fleet class built before the start of the war was the Tambor class laid down in 1939 – 1941. Twelve were built. They displaced 1475/2370 tons, were 307 feet in length, and had a range of 10,000 nm at 10 kts. For the first time they had ten internal TT (6 fwd, 4 aft) that set the standard for U.S. WW II fleet boats, with 24 torpedoes. They had a crew of 80 - 85, an operating depth of 288 feet and 374 – 385 tons of fuel oil.

The 1938 program included two medium range, M class boats of 895/1190 tons, 239 foot submarines, built 1939 – 1941. They marked an end to construction of medium range submarines in the U.S. Navy. All subsequent submarines were "fleet" class long range boats.

PART SEVEN

SUBMARINES RETURN TO COMBAT IN THE SPANISH CIVIL WAR

(1936 – 1939)

Chapter Twenty-Six – Spanish Civil War (1936 – 1939)

The Spanish Civil War began on 17 July 1936 when ultra conservative military and political groups rebelled against the very liberal government of Spain. General Francisco Franco, a tough colonial soldier, rapidly rose to hold the main leadership position in the rebel camp. Atrocities and excesses by both government forces and supporters (Loyalists) and rebels (Nationalists) poisoned the political atmosphere.

A number of European nations gave assistance to the two sides. The Loyalists were supported by France and by the USSR. French support was not significant in the long run because the liberal-conservative quarrel in Spain was reflected in the French body-politic, rapidly paralyzing the French government's initial instincts to help another Socialist regime. The USSR dispatched large quantities of arms, ammunition and other supplies to the Loyalist side. In addition the USSR provided a large number of bomber and fighter aircraft and aircrews to Spain. The Comintern, an international Communist organization directed from Moscow, fostered the recruitment of the International Brigades to fight on the Loyalist side.

Nazi Germany and Fascist Italy stepped in to assist the rebels. Initially Germany sent transport aircraft to help Franco move North African troops by air across the straits to Spain in the face of a blockade by Loyalist warships. This action was extremely significant. Subsequently, after the USSR began sending massive amounts of material to the Loyalists, Germany sent the Condor Legion, a combined arms force to fight on the rebel side. Italy sent large ground and air units, all "volunteers", to Spain to assist Franco.

While the bulk of the bitter fighting from 1936 into 1939 took place on or over land, there were some naval engagements. Some of them involved submarines and will be the focus of attention in this book. Submarine activity not only included Loyalist submarines and Nationalist submarines involved in open warfare, but also covert German U-boat operations and the operations of "pirate submarines" (read Italian submarines) that sank merchant ships carrying material to the Government of Spain .

Loyalist Submarines (Spanish government)

Spanish government naval forces included twelve submarines at the start of hostilities. Many of the more senior officers in the Navy were conservative and opposed to the very liberal tack that the extremists of the Socialist government were taking. The Navy enlisted men were on the other end of the political spectrum. This situation led to mutinies and killing of many officers in Spanish surface warships at the outset of the Civil War. The Spanish government basically viewed the officer corps as conservative, monarchial in sentiment, and therefore untrustworthy.

In the Spanish Submarine Service the outcome did not descend to mutiny and murder of submarine officers but it did lead to their wholesale replacement. That led in turn to giving command to very junior officers. While reliable from a political point of view, they were ineffective operationally. As a result Spanish government submarines played a very small role in naval events. No Republican submarine sank or damaged any target during the Civil War.

On 19 September 1936 Republican submarine B 6 was sunk by Nationalist destroyer *Velasco* off Cape Penas near the port of Santander. On 12 October 1936 Republican submarine B 5 was sunk by Nationalist aircraft off Malaga. On 12 December 1936 Republican submarine C 3 was torpedoed and sunk off Malaga by a German U-boat, operating covertly. There were three survivors. On 20 October 1937 Republican submarine C 6 was scuttled after suffering heavy damage during a Nationalist air attack. On 9 October 1938 Republican submarine C 1 was sunk by Nationalist aircraft during an air attack on Barcelona.

Nationalist Submarines (Spanish rebels)

Nationalist naval forces did not include any submarines initially, all twelve of the Spanish Navy submarines having remained loyal to the legal government of Spain. Later Franco prevailed upon Benito Mussolini to provide a pair of Italian submarines. They were "sold" and transferred in March 1937 but were immediately put under repair and did not see action for well over a year.

In September 1937 Mussolini transferred four "Legionary" submarines to the Nationalist forces and they conducted war patrols with their own Italian officers and crew but with a Spanish Nationalist liaison officer embarked. They operated on behalf of the Nationalist forces from September 1937 through February 1938. They conducted 13 war patrols, made five attacks on ship targets and fired eight torpedoes – with no hits or sinking's, a miserable record.

German U-boats

In addition to sending transport aircraft to assist General Franco in moving his African troops across the strait to Spain, Adolph Hitler authorized the dispatch of the Condor Legion, a combined arms organization that fought on the Nationalist side and was quite effective. Although at the time Germany did not advertise its Condor Legion, everyone knew that German "volunteers" in Spain were there with the full support of the Nazi regime. However what very few people knew was that Germany secretly sent two U-boats, U-33 and U-34, to Spanish waters to conduct war patrols in late 1936.

The two U-boats sent on this top secret mission were among the most modern in the German U-boat Service. They were Type VIIA boats, the newest available. They displaced 626 tons surfaced and 745 tons submerged, with a surface speed of 16 knots and a submerged speed of 6 knots. They had four bow torpedo tubes and one external stern torpedo tube. With a crew of 44 men, they carried enough fuel oil to travel 4,300 nautical miles on the surface. Both were assigned to the 2nd Flotilla (*Saltzwedel*) under *Fregattenkapitan* Werner Scheer.

The operation was called "Ursula", reportedly named for *Kapitan zur See* Doenitz' daughter. Doenitz was FdU (*Fuehrer der U-boote)* at the time. Operational planning began under the direction of *Konteradmiral Herman Boehme, Flottenchef* (Fleet Commander).

Although Italy had already begun covert submarine operations in October 1936, the German authorities were intent upon their own submarine activity not becoming known. Italy's capability to maintain security about its submarine involvement was questionable since the only submarines in Spain belonged to the Spanish government, and they certainly would not be involved in sinking ships bringing war materials to their own side. German U-boat commanding officers were instructed to ensure that their submarines remained unidentified as German

U-boats. They were told to fly Italian colors if they had problems and had to stop off at the Italian naval base at La Magdalena in northern Sardinia. The two U-boats were assigned code names for the mission: U-33 - Triton, and U-34 - Poseidon.

Both boats had just been commissioned and their commanding officers were in their first commands and relatively inexperienced. Therefore more experienced officers were sent in to take command for Operation Ursula: U-33 – *Kapitanleutnant* Kurt Freiwald, who came from command of U -7; U-34 – *Kapitanleutnant* Harald Grosse, from command of U-8. Grosse also had operational experience in Spanish waters, having been secretly assigned to a German-designed submarine built in a Spanish shipyard in Cadiz.

The two boats departed Wilhelmshaven on the night of 20/21 November ostensibly for Training Exercise Ursula. At sea they removed all visible markings from their hulls and superstructures, and transited the Straits of Gibraltar surfaced on a moonless night of 27/28 November to avoid detection by British forces. They began their patrols on 30 November, the date having been chosen to allow Italian submarines to vacate those areas. No attacks on submarines were permitted prior to 30 November in order to avoid "friendly fire" casualties. The two boats' patrol areas were separated by a line at 0.44 degrees West; U-33 to the East including the port of Alicante. U-34 operated west of the line, and her sector included the naval port of Cartagena.

On 22 November an Italian submarine had attacked Loyalist light cruiser, *Miguel de Cervantes* off Cartagena and seriously damaged it with two torpedoes. [256] Because of proximity to the port, *Cervantes* was able to make port rather than being lost at sea. However, damage was so severe that she was out of commission for most of the war. But the element of surprise was lost. Thereafter Loyalist warships were on alert for submarine attacks.

On 1 December U-34 fired at a Loyalist destroyer but missed. The torpedo exploded against a shore side rock, although not alerting the target. On 3 December U-34 again attacked a Loyalist destroyer, *Almirante Antequera*, and missed again. On 8 December unlucky U-34 attacked a similar target with identical results.

U-33 fared no better. She found it difficult to achieve a firing position against high speed Loyalist destroyers, some of which were capable of making 38 knots at flank speed. One potential target had to be let go because of the presence of a British destroyer. Another time the Loyalist cruiser *Mendez Nunez*, with a destroyer screen, passed by in darkness. Very restrictive German rules of engagement (ROE) required absolute identification of targets as Loyalist ships, so U-33's commanding officer had to let them pass by without attempting an attack.

---

256   Salvage operations turned up torpedo fragments with what appeared to be Italian marking so it was clear to the Loyalists that Italian submarines were involved. However that discovery provided potential 'cover" for U-boat operations.

U-33 and U-34 reported each attempted attack back to U-boat headquarters at night when they were on the surface some twenty miles offshore to recharge their batteries. Not everyone in the German High Command thought that Operation Ursula was a good idea. Some were concerned over the lack of results and the possibility of German covert action being revealed to the world. Germany was embarked on a secretive major rearmament program and undue attention by Great Britain and France might impede its progress.

On 6 December 1936 Mussolini suggested to Admiral Wilhelm Canaris that Italy would assume responsibility for all submarine operations in the Mediterranean Sea, leaving any operations in the Atlantic to Germany. That suited Adolph Hitler very well. However he had no intention of sending German U-boats into the Bay of Biscay. On 10 December the German Minister of Defense von Blomberg advised the service chiefs that German submarine operations in support of Spain would be curtailed, and he halted plans to relieve U-33 and U-34 with other U-boats. [257]

On 10 December 1936 von Blomberg issued orders ending the two U-boats' war patrols effective the following day. They were ordered back to Germany. On and after 12 December Italian submarines would occupy the former German U-boats' patrol areas.

The early afternoon of 12 December found U-34 proceeding westward submerged off the southwestern

---

[257] Andrade, Op cit., p. 116

coast of Spain near Gibraltar enroute Germany. About 1400 she sighted Loyalist submarine C 3 on the surface heading towards Malaga, about four miles south of the lighthouse.[258] Technically C 3 was not a legitimate target for U-34. C 3 was too close to shore, there were fishing boats in the vicinity and a torpedo explosion might be noticed. Nevertheless, and understandably to this former submarine commanding officer, U-34's CO decided to attack. The target was clearly identified as a "C" class Loyalist submarine. He fired a single torpedo. It struck about eight meters aft of the bow of C 3 and she sank rapidly, leaving only three survivors in the water. They were rescued by fishing boats. That evening U-34 reported the successful attack to headquarters.

U-33 and U-34 returned to Wilhelmshaven on 21 December and turned their boats over to the original commanding officers. *Kapitanleutnant* Kurt Freiwald, CO U-33 with no sinking's, was awarded the Spanish Cross in bronze for his war patrol. *Kapitanleutnant* Harald Grosse, CO U-34, having sunk a Loyalist submarine, received the Spanish Cross in gold for his war patrol. However both former commanding officers had to wait until June 1939 for the official awards. The U-boat crews were sworn to secrecy under pain of death – about the patrols.[259]

---

258 Military, and European time, does not restart at noon. One pm is 1300, two pm 1400 etc., until 2400 being midnight.

259 The source of information about the patrols of U-33 and U-34 is an article titled "Operation Ursula and the sinking of submarine C 3" by Julio de la Vega, posted on Uboat.net.

In his book *The U-Boat Century: German Submarine Warfare 1906 – 2006*, Showell makes mention of U-26 and U-35 having been in Spanish waters during the Civil War. No other details are provided, and no sources are footnoted.[260] Uboat.net has a listing for each as it does for other U-boats, but neither listing includes anything about Spanish Civil War operations. For that matter neither do the listings for U-33 and U-34.

A uboat.net web page contains some more information about decorations awarded to German personnel for service in Spain. It states that there were a total of 26,117 awards of the Spanish Cross. It lists awards to personnel having served in U-25, U-26, U-27, U-28, U-31 and U-33, all having received the Spanish Cross in Bronze without Swords. Someone with ample spare time and a facility with the German language might provide a useful service by researching German records to determine whether any U-boats besides U-33 and U-34 actually made war patrols off Spain.

Pirate (Italian) Submarines

Early in the Spanish Civil War Italy began providing assistance to the Nationalist rebels. In late July 1936 Italian warships moved in to Tangier and various ports of Republican Spain. Ostensibly there to look out for Italian nationals and Italian interests, they assisted the Spanish Nationalists. In mid-November 1936 Italy

---

260   Showell, Op cit., p. 73 and p. 208.

formally recognized the Nationalist government at Burgos and consequently had to withdraw its warships from Republican ports.

Mussolini initially rejected requests for Italian submarines by the Nationalists, but did initiate a covert submarine campaign against Spanish Republican ships and other nations' ships in Spanish territorial waters from November 1936 through February 1937. Some records indicate that the number of Italian submarines were assigned to this duty were as follows: November – 1; December – 2; January – 10; and February – 2. However, Brian R. Sullivan, writing in the Journal of Military History, Vol. 39, No. 4, Oct. 1995, pp. 697-727, on *Fascist Italy's Military Involvement in the Spanish Civil War*, states that 36 Italian submarines were involved in this first set of covert operations. He reports that they tracked 161 potential targets, but could only maneuver to identify 15 as legitimate targets, and fired 28 torpedoes. They scored only four hits, damaging a Republican light cruiser and sinking two small merchant ships.

Franco Bargoni, who authored an official history of the Italian Navy, blamed the poor record on "bad training, deficient torpedoes, poor submarine design, and tactics unchanged since World War I operations in the Adriatic." Those criticisms are mirrored in another document available on the internet, "A Critical Examination of the Italian Submarine Fleet in 1941", which is attributed to Admiral Legnani and his staff. The later document examines the record of German, British and Italian submarines and submariners and attempts to identify deficiencies in the Italian Submarine Service.

Attacks on Italian and German warships in the coastal waters off Republican Spain had led to those nations removal from Non-Intervention Committee patrols, designed to limit outside assistance to the two combatants. In response Joseph Stalin of the USSR seized the opportunity to greatly increase the sea borne flow of Soviet material to the Republican side through the Mediterranean.

In a counter-response Mussolini unleashed a "Pirate Submarine campaign" from 6 August though 13 September 1937. Some fifty-nine submarine patrols were involved, as well as the use of Italian cruisers and destroyers to block the strait of Sicily. Italian torpedo boats sank a Soviet merchant ship off the Algerian coast.

Italian submarine *Iride* fired a torpedo at British destroyer HMS Havock on 30 August 1937, apparently through mistaken identification. Havock and sister ship HMS Hasty counterattacked with seven depth charges, but *Iride* managed to escape. Some oil was sighted on the surface at the scene so she might have suffered some damage.

Some of the publically reported "pirate submarine" activity during August and September 1937 was as follows:

- August 12 – Spanish tanker *Campeador* torpedoed and sunk off Tunis

- August 13 – French steamer *Peame* halted by a submarine off Tunis
- August 15 – Spanish motor vessel *Ciudad de Cadiz* sunk by a submarine near the western mouth of the Dardanelles
- August 18 – Spanish steamer *Armuru* torpedoed in the Aegean Sea
- August 28 - French ship *Theophile Gautier* chased by a submarine while entering the Dardanelles
- August 30 - Soviet steamer *Timiriasee* torpedoed and sunk off Algeria
- September 1 – Soviet steamer *Blagovje* sunk by submarine in the Aegean Sea[261]
- September 2 – British tramp steamer *Woodford* torpedoed by a surfaced submarine off Cape Benicarlo. Survivors reported that the submarine's identifying marks had been painted over
- September 2 – Soviet steamer *Molakieff* sunk by a submarine in the Aegean Sea

There were also air attacks, presumably by Italian aircraft, upon shipping in the western Mediterranean. During the campaign Italian submarines sighted 444

---

261   In a Diplomatic Note the USSR bluntly accused Italy of sinking *Timiriasee* and *Blagovje* and demanded compensation. Italy denied the accusation, refused payment and indicated that she would not attend a conference at which the USSR was present.

ships, but identified only 24 as legitimate targets. They fired 43 torpedoes and sank only four merchant ships and damaged a Republican destroyer.[262]

Great Britain was the driver in the Non-Intervention camp, anxious that the nasty conflict in Spain not escalate into another world war. She arranged with France to call an international conference, held at Nyon in Switzerland, to deal with the "pirate submarine" issue. Everyone in Europe knew that the "pirate submarines" were Italian, but the Italian government denied the charge, and so the charade progressed. British code breakers had focused attention on Italy as a result of Italy's aggressive operations in Ethiopia in 1935, so it is possible that they were reading the Italian Navy operational orders to its submarines. In any case, radio traffic analysis would have allowed the British to gain an insight into Italian submarine deployments in the Med.

On September 14, 1937 representatives of Great Britain, Bulgaria, Egypt, France, Greece, Rumania, Turkey, the USSR and Yugoslavia signed an accord to end attacks by submarines against merchant ships not belonging to either of the two warring Spanish sides. The Mediterranean Sea was divided into zones to be patrolled by participating powers. The Adriatic Sea and the Tyrrhenian Sea and the

---

262   Although the international uproar, and the British-French ASW threat, forced an end to the pirate submarine campaign, the USSR ended its effort to resupply the Spanish Republic by ship through the Mediterranean Sea. Further shipments went by ship from Soviet Baltic ports to French Atlantic ports and then overland to northern Spain, a lengthier journey.

waters along the coast of Libya were reserved for patrols by Italy in the event that she became a signatory.[263] The British and the French divided the rest of the international waters of the Mediterranean between them for ASW patrols by destroyers. Other countries patrolled their own territorial waters. The rules were fairly simple: **no submarines allowed submerged along traditional shipping routes**. If a submerged submarine was detected and refused to surface and identify itself, it would be attacked with depth charges. Great Britain increased its destroyer force in the Mediterranean. Subsequently the "pirate submarine" threat vanished as mysteriously as it had begun.[264]

Submarine warfare during the Spanish Civil War was strictly a sideshow. It offered a little unexpected excitement but had no lasting effect on the conflict. However the potential was certainly there. The Spanish government's main supporter was the Soviet Union. Lacking land connections with Spain, resupply of munitions and men basically had to be by sea. If Italy and Germany had openly taken on Soviet shipping in the Atlantic and Mediterranean early on during the war, very few supplies would have gotten through, and the Republic would have fallen even earlier.

---

263   Italy indignantly refused, claiming unequal treatment.
264   In its February 14, 1938 issue Time magazine noted that two British freighters had been sunk by pirate craft in the previous week. Other sources show the Italian submarine *Iride* as being on patrol in the Med at that time.

Great Britain was mainly concerned with the safety of her sea lanes through the Mediterranean Sea to India, as evidenced by her failure to impose sanctions on Italy over Ethiopia in 1935. She was also concerned over another world war so soon after the end of WW I. It is unlikely that she would have responded aggressively to an open German-Italian threat to the USSR. Her failure to back France in 1936 over German reoccupation of the Rhineland is another strong indicator of her probable actions in the case postulated. In any event the rebels won in Spain without an all out submarine campaign in support of their cause. The curious reader is referred to Antony Beevor's excellent book *The Battle for Spain* if interested in the international politics involved in that conflict.

Submarine combat operations resumed after Germany attacked Poland on 1 September 1939 marking the start of WW II. The number of submarines in commission in each fleet of the major submarine operators at that time were:

USSR	218
Italy	115
USA	99
France	77
Great Britain	69
Japan	62
Germany	57

Of course, the threat of unrestricted submarine warfare was over for good, or was it?

GLOSSARY

A-H	Austria-Hungary
AIP	Air-independent propulsion. The traditional submarine battery or a nuclear power plant both provide air-independent propulsion, but the term is normally used to refer to a diesel-electric submarine with another air-independent power source, e.g. a fuel cell, or a Stirling engine
ANZAC	Australian New Zealand Army Corps
ASDIC	Acronym for Antisubmarine Detection Investigation Committee, a World War I organization which lead to the development of active sonar, subsequently called "Asdic" in the Royal Navy.
ASW	Antisubmarine Warfare (sometimes explained as "awfully slow warfare" by naval aviators)

BEF	British Expeditionary Force
Broadside	Literally at 90 degrees left or right of the bow of a ship. Sometimes used to refer to firing the entire main (gun) battery of a ship at one time at a target
CO	Commanding Officer
COB	Chief of the Boat, responsible to the Executive Officer of a submarine for general crew evolutions (U.S.N. usage). Functionally, if not always technically, he is the senior enlisted man on board
Collier	A ship carrying coal, designed to replenish coal burning naval vessels at anchorages
Comint	Communications intelligence
Complement	The number of crew provided for wartime employment of a ship or submarine. In surface ships it is usually larger than the peacetime "allowance". In submarines allowance and complement are normally synonymous
Crash dive	More a Hollywood term than one used in submarines, a "crash dive" denotes a rapid dive to escape surface danger. In the old days when main

ballast tanks had Kingston flood valves at the bottom and vent valves on top, the Kingston valves were normally shut while the submarine was on the surface. The normal peacetime (slow) diving procedure was to open the Kingston valves and then the vent valves to allow sea water to displace the trapped air, enabling the submarine to submerge. If the Kingston valves were left open, the boat was said to be "riding the vents" requiring only rapid vent valve opening to submerge. A "crash dive" referred to the latter condition. U.S. fleet boats of WW II no longer had Kingston valves in their ballast tanks but rather open flood ports

Depth bomb — A depth charge in an aerodynamic bomb shape for delivery by aircraft

Depth charge — An underwater explosive charge in a cylinder shape with a hydrostatic (pressure) fuse set to explode when it reaches the desired firing depth

Flotilla — Literally a Spanish word meaning "little fleet". In the U.S. Navy, a Submarine Flotilla was the next organizational level above a Squadron. In 1973 the term was replaced by Group, e.g. Submarine Flotilla Seven became Submarine Group Seven. The commander of a squadron, flotilla or group is usually referred to as "Commodore" if he is not a flag officer

GIGO	Garbage In, Garbage Out
GPS	Global Positioning System. Artificial satellite system used to provide exact positioning information on earth.
Hydrophone	A listening device lowered into the water that receives sound waves from any transmitter, e.g., submerged machinery, fish, whales, submarine propellers
IJN	Imperial Japanese Navy
MTB	Motor Torpedo Boat
NM	Nautical mile. The nautical mile is 2,000 yards or 6,000 feet as opposed to the (land) statue mile of 5,280 feet. Speed at sea is designated in knots, with one knot equaling one nautical mile per hour
PCO	Prospective Commanding Officer
PRC	Peoples Republic of China

Operational Depth	The deepest depth authorized for normal operations, commonly referred to as "test depth" in the U.S. Submarine Service
Overhaul	An extended period in a shipyard where extensive repairs and modernization are accomplished
Q-ship	A naval auxiliary ship outfitted with a heavy gun armament concealed within collapsible deck houses, otherwise an innocent merchant ship in appearance waiting to lure a submarine into gun range
RAF	Royal Air Force
RCN	Royal Canadian Navy
Refit	A fairly short period assigned for repair of a submarine, usually alongside a submarine tender or depot ship or a submarine base equipped with repair shops, in the U.S. Navy often called an "upkeep" period
RN	Royal Navy (of Great Britain).
RNAS	Royal Naval Air Service (incorporated into the Royal Air Force in 1918 along with the Royal Flying Corps)
RNN	Royal Netherlands Navy

ROE	Rules of Engagement (specific restrictive rules established by a nation or service to govern specific military operations)
Sonar	An acronym for sound navigation and ranging, used in the U.S. Navy, usually referring to active sonar equipment which sends a sound wave into the ocean and can receive a reflected echo from a submerged target (Asdic in the Royal Navy)
SS	Steam ship (general usage)
SS	Diesel-electric submarine (naval usage)
SSG	Diesel-electric submarine carrying cruise missiles
SSBN	Nuclear powered submarine carrying ballistic missiles
SSGN	Nuclear powered submarine carrying cruise missiles[265]
SSN	Nuclear powered submarine
TDC	Torpedo Data Computer, an analogue computer that calculated gyro angle to hit a surface target

---

265 SSG and SSGN designations go back to the 1950s and 1960s when five U.S. submarines carried the Regulus I cruise missile. Modern SSNs carry Tomahawk cruise missiles that can be launched from dedicated vertical launch tubes or from torpedo tubes.

TT	Torpedo Tube
UK	United Kingdom
USAAF	United States Army Air Forces
USSR	Union of Soviet Socialist Republics (Soviet Union)
War shot	A torpedo with an explosive head instead of the exercise head used in practice firings
W/T	Wireless Telegraph or wireless transmitter (radio transmitter using CW (continuous wave Morse code))
Zeppelin	A WW I era rigid airship, or dirigible, named after the German airship company that manufactured and operated them in peacetime. The firm was founded by Count *von Zeppelin*.

INDEX

BIBLIOGRAPHY

Books

Abbot, Willis J., *Aircraft and Submarines* (G. P. Putnam's Sons, New York and London, 1918)

Bagnasco, Erminio, *Submarines of World War Two*, (Naval Institute Press, Annapolis, Maryland, 1973)

Barnett, Correlli, *Engage The Enemy More Closely* (W.W. Norton & Company, New York, 1991)

Beach, Edward L., *Submarine!* (Naval Institute Press, Annapolis, Maryland, 1946)

Beevor, Antony, *The Battle for Spain,* (Penguin Books, London, 2001)

Blair, Clay, *Silent Victory*, (Naval Institute Press, Annapolis, Maryland, 1975)

Blair, Clay, *Hitler's U-boat War: The Hunters, 1939-1942* (Modern Library, New York, 2000)

Blair, Clay, *Hitler's U-boat War, The Hunted, 1942-1945* (Random House, New York, 1998)

Boyd, Carl and Yoshida, Akihiko, *The Japanese Submarine Force and World War II* (Naval Institute Press, Annapolis, Maryland, 1995)

Calvert, Vice Admiral James F., *Silent Running* (John Wiley & Sons, Inc., New York, 1995)

Christensen, Clayton M., *The Innovator's Dilemma* (Harvard Business School Press, Boston, 1997)

Clancy, Tom, Submarine, *A Guided Tour Inside a Nuclear Warship* (Berkley Books, New York, 1993)

Compton-Hall, Richard, *Submarine Boats*, (Windward, Conway Maritime Press Ltd., London, 1983)

Doenitz, Karl Grand Admiral, *Memoirs*, (Da Capo Press, 1997)

Duncan, Francis, *Rickover, The Struggle For Excellence* (Naval Institute Press, Annapolis, Maryland, 2001)

Dull, Paul S., *A Battle History of The Imperial Japanese Navy* (United States Naval Institute, Annapolis, Maryland, 1978)

Evans, Dr. David C., Editor, *The Japanese Navy in World War II* (Naval Institute Press, Annapolis, Maryland, 1969)

Evans, David C. and Peattie, Mark R., *KAIGUN*, (Naval Institute Press, Annapolis, Maryland, 1997)

Fluckey, Admiral Eugene B. U.S.N. (Ret.), *Thunder Below!* (University of Illinois Press, Urbana and Chicago, 1992)

Frank, Richard B., *Guadalcanal* (Penguin Books, New York, 1990)

Galatin, Admiral I. J., U.S.N. (Ret.), *Take Her Deep!* (Algonquin Books, Chapel Hill, 1987)

Gannon, Michael, *Black May* (HarperCollins Publishers, New York, 1998)

Gannon, Michael, *Operation Drumbeat*, (Harper Perennial, New York, 1991)

Gannon, Robert, *Hellions of the Deep – The Development of American Torpedoes in World War II* (The Pennsylvania State University Press, University Park, Pennsylvania, 1996)

Giese, Otto and Wise, James E. Jr., *Shooting The War* (Bluejacket Books, Naval Institute Press, Annapolis, Maryland, 1994)

Gray, Edwyn, *British Submarines in the Great War* (Leo Cooper, South Yorkshire, 2001)

Gray, Edwyn, *The Devil's Device* (Seely, Service and Co. Ltd., London, 1975)

Harris, Brayton, *The Navy Times Book of Submarines* (Berkley Books, New York, 1997)

Hezlet, Vice Admiral Sir Arthur, *Electronics and Sea Power* (Stein And Day, New York, 1975)

Hezlet, Vice Admiral Sir Arthur, *The Submarine and Sea Power* (Stein And Day, New York, 1967)

Hoehling, A. A., *The Great War At Sea* (Barnes & Noble Books, New York, 1965)

Howarth, Stephen and Law, Derek, eds., *The Battle of the Atlantic 1939 – 1945, The 50th Anniversary International Naval Conference* (Naval Institute Press, Annapolis, MD, 1994)

Januszewski, Tadeusz , *Japanese Submarine Aircraft* (Stratus, UK, 2002)

Keegan, John, *Intelligence In War* (Vintage Books, New York, 2004)

Kemp, Paul, *Midget Submarines of the Second World War* (Chatham Publishing, London, 1999)

Knox, MacGregor, *Hitler's Italian Allies* (Cambridge University Press, Cambridge, England, 2000)

Layton, Rear Admiral Edwin T., *"And I Was There"* (William Morrow and Company, INC., New York, 1985)

Lyons, Michael J., *World War I* (Prentice Hall, Upper Saddle River, New Jersey, 2000)

Mahnken, Thomas G., *Uncovering Ways of War*, (Cornell University Press, Ithaca and London, 2002)

Marshall, George C., *War Reports* (J.B. Lippincott Company, Philadelphia and New York, 1947)

Massie, Robert K., *Castles of Steel* (Random House, New York, 2003)

Miller, Edward S., *War Plan Orange* (Naval Institute Press, Annapolis, Maryland, 1991)

Monsarrat, Nicholas, *The Cruel Sea* (Alfred A. Knopf, New York, 1988)

Morison, Samuel Elliot, *History of United States Naval Operations in World War II, Volume 1, The Battle of the Atlantic September 1939 – May 1943* (University of Illinois Press, Urbana and Chicago, 2001)

Morison, Samuel Elliot, *History of United States Naval Operations in World War II, Volume 4, Coral Sea, Midway and Submarine Actions May 1942 – August*

1942 (University of Illinois Press, Urbana and Chicago, 2001)

Neufeld, Michael J., *The Rocket and the Reich* (The Free Press: New York, 1995)

Parillo, Mark P., *The Japanese Merchant Marine in World War II* (Naval Institute Press, Annapolis, Maryland, 1993)

O'Neill, Richard, *Suicide Squads* (Lansdowne Press, London, 1981)

Payne, Stanley G., *Franco and Hitler: Spain, Germany and World War II* (Yale University Press, New Haven and London, 2008)

Polmar, Norman and Allen, Thomas B., *Rickover: Controversy and Genius* (Simon and Schuster, New York, 1982)

Polmar, Norman and Noot, Jurrien, *Submarines of the Russian and Soviet Navies 1718 – 1990* (Naval Institute Press, Annapolis, Maryland, 1991)

Roberts, William R. and Sweetman, Jack, (Ed) *New Interpretations in Naval History*, Ninth Naval History Symposium 18 – 20 October 1989, Naval Institute Press, Annapolis, Maryland, 1991.

Rohwer, Jurgen, *Allied Submarine Attacks of World War II European Theater of Operations 1939 – 1945* (Naval Institute Press, Annapolis, Maryland, 1997)

Rohwer, Jurgen, *Axis Submarine Successes of World War II* (Naval Institute Press, Annapolis, Maryland, 1999)

Sakaida, Henry, Nila, Gary and Takaki, Koji, *I-400* (Hikoki Publications Limited, East Sussex, England, 2006)

Shirer, William L., *Berlin Diary* (Alfred A. Knopf, New York, 1941)

Showell, Jak Mallmann, *The U-Boat Century* (Chatham publishing, London, 2006)

Sims, Rear Admiral William Sowden, *The Victory at Sea* (Naval Institute Press, Annapolis, Maryland, 1984)

Stille, Mark, *Imperial Japanese Navy Submarines 1941 – 1945* (Osprey Publishing, Oxford, England, 2007)

Strachan, Hew, *The First World War* (Penguin Group, New York, 2004)

Stumpf, David K., *Regulus The Forgotten Weapon* (Turner Publishing Company, Paducah, KY., 1996)

Tarrant, V. E., *The U-Boat Offensive 1914 – 1945* (Arms and Armour Press, London, 1989)

Tillman, Barrett, *Clash of the Carriers* (New American Library, New York, 2005)

Treadwell, Terry C., *Strike From Beneath the Sea* (Tempus Publishing Inc., Charleston, S.C., 1999)

Vause, Jordan, *WOLF, U-boat Commanders In World War II* (Naval Institute Press, Annapolis, Maryland, 1997)

von Trapp, Georg, *To The Last Salute* (University of Nebraska Press, Lincoln and Lincoln, 2007)

Williams, Kathleen Broome, *Secret Weapon* (Naval Institute Press, Annapolis, Md., 1996)

Williamson, Gordon, *Wolf Pack* (Osprey Publishing, Oxford, UK, 2006)

Winton, John, *Ultra At Sea* (William Morrow And Company, Inc., New York, 1988)

Magazines

Time, War in Spain, Submerged Pirates, September 13, 1937

Time, Nine to Nyon, September 20, 1937

Time, Peace and Pirates, September 27, 1937

Time, Submerged Submarines, February 14, 1838

Pamphlets

The U-boat Commander's Handbook (High Command of the Navy (German), 1943. (Thomas Publications, Gettysburg, PA., 1989)